My... Life Behind Bars

Jeff Echterling

Published by Jeff Echterling, 2024.

MY... LIFE BEHIND BARS

First edition. April 19, 2024.

ISBN: 979-8223667629

Written by Jeff Echterling.

Table of Contents

Acknowledgments

2015 editing by: Urzula Urzua / Andrew Nummy.

Cover Art by: Connie Bacon.

Dedicated in loving memory of:

Mary Ellen (Cornwell) Echterling 12/11/37 – 7/17/93

I would like to attempt to thank everyone that has seen me through or played any part in the events that make up this story. Obviously, I'm sure to leave a few out. None are intentional, I swear.

First and foremost, I must thank my mother to whom I dedicate this book. She not only gave me life, but also inspired the little good I've done; the crappy stuff is all my own. I've now lived longer without her than I did with her, but she still influences me. With everything, I stop and think, 'what would she say, what would she do, what would she think.' I'm still trying to make her proud.

Also, thanks to my family: Donna, Greg, Jennifer, John, Adeena, Grant, Tyran, Chris, Laurie, Dave, Ron, Wendy, Tyler, Justin, Lucas, Tim, Holly, Kurah, Adalyn, Steven, Tammy, Jasmine, Sue, Jim, Nick, Elizabeth, Eric, Karen, Tom, James, Michelle, Rosemary, Richard, Andrew, Matthew, Brad, Heidi, Amanda, Dwayne, Levi, Mackenzie, Savannah, Amber, Ashley. Dad, Richard, Peggy, Charlie, Edna, and Stan.

My friends: Jon, Stan, Drew, Brian, Frank, Coco, Dave, Erin, Adam, Raul, Derrick, Cody, Nichole, Rachael, Greg, Lorenzo, JP, Louise, Nina, Robin, Urzula, Guy, Larry, Patti, Cheryl, Amy, Alison and Connie.

Shannon, Anais, Brenda, Julissa, Armando, Vero, Stephanie, Mike, JB, Joe and everybody at Fullerton Restaurant.

The Club Deluxe: Jon, Cheri, Kevin, Kate and Beth.

And all the girls I've loved before: Caryn, Becky, Beth, Dorothy, Ami, Donna, Amie, Amy, Kerry, Bridget, Brooke, Barbara, Anamarie, Kristen, Angelica, Kirstin, Destiny and any other ex's; the ones that got away or should have.

The years of self-destruction and madness have left only these memorable few, but these I will never forget.

Thank you all.

Preface

Not unlike anyone else that has worked in a restaurant, nightclub, or bar, I've seen and experienced some really crazy shit. This business can drop you into a lifestyle like no other. Add obvious, but untreated and undiagnosed bipolar disorder, and the lifestyle is amplified.

Those in the medical field can probably relate to the long hours, lack of sleep, and just plain bizarre events, but at the end of the day, they can always say they were trying to help. I've seen people at their worst and helped them get there. Then, all too often, go there myself.

Frequently, I would be sitting around with friends, trading stories of the day, the past week, or reminiscing about things that happened years ago that we still talk about. Every time we would do this, I couldn't help but think that if all these stories were put together, it would make a great book.

So, I started to put this together, but the original idea was lost as the pages progressed. It took seven years to complete this book, and things changed. The end result ultimately became a collection of my own personal experiences. How it was, how it is and how it will probably be.

The majority of this book is directly based on actual events. The names have been changed to protect the innocent and, in most cases, the not-so-innocent. Situations, places, times, and names have been blended and combined, so not to directly imply, expose, or offend any real people that may have been involved. I have no problem airing my own dirty laundry but have no intention of airing anyone else's.

So many of the things that have happened to or around me, I don't even believe. Anytime we would tell the stories, and someone would ask, "Did that really happen?"

Our only reaction was to laugh and say, "You can't make this shit up."

This is in no way an exact account of anything. I didn't keep a journal or any record of these events. This is just how I remember it.

I hold no ill feelings towards anyone that may have been portrayed in a bad light. I don't hold grudges and fully admit my own part in it all. No one is more to blame than me.

Looking back over my life, I have plenty of regrets, but when we get together and tell these stories, it's almost always a good time.

At the worst points of your life, someone might say, "One day you'll look back at all this and laugh."

At the time you will probably think to yourself, as I did, 'Bullshit!' But true enough... I'm laughing now... about some of it.

Chapter One: Waking Up

My eyes are still shut, but I can feel myself coming to. So many mornings, (at least it feels like morning to me... more often than not, it's late afternoon) I dread opening my eyes. I'm often surprised by my surroundings.

I remember one time opening my eyes after a long, good sleep; sitting at a desk in the front row, my head held up by my left hand, only to see the whole classroom staring back at me and trying not to laugh. I jerked upright and turned towards the front of the room to see the Mother Superior glaring at me, but never saying a word about it. It was CCD, the Catholic version of Sunday school on Saturday. I was about 12. This wasn't the first time and would not be the last. Luckily this was just embarrassing and in no way dangerous.

Actually, I've opened my eyes to find myself in any number of embarrassing or frightening scenarios. I might have been behind the wheel doing sixty in the middle of traffic (God only knows how I survived that one). Other times I might have been slumped over the steering wheel along the side of the road (How I got through those times without ending up in jail, killing myself or someone else, I'll never know). Like a lot of people, I feared waking up in a stranger's bed, hoping she's of age, it was safe, and I didn't have to go coyote. Too many times I found myself on the floor of some bathroom, hopefully not lying in puke, but if I did wake up in puke or blood, I prayed that it was my own.

It could have been anything. The most surprising times were when I woke up in my own bed safe and sound. I don't think this is one of those times.

With my eyes still shut, I start to hear voices... conversation... activity. I can tell it's not the TV. I know I'm not alone and might be out in public somewhere. It's not cold and doesn't feel like the ground, so I'm not out on the street. I feel a mattress and a pillow under me with a blanket over me. I'm in bed, but not a normal bed. I start to hear beeping and machinery. I notice that the head of the bed is propped up a bit.

I'm in a hospital.

Given the angle of the bed, when I open my eyes, the first thing I see are my feet pushing up under the blanket. There's a defibrillator lying between my legs. This must have been a bad one. A nurse, sitting in a far corner of the small room, stands up when she sees that I'm awake. She's talking, but I can't quite make out what she is saying yet. She checks some machinery over my left shoulder, which I can't see.

I'm moving slowly and trying to shake my head clear. Weak and lightheaded, I quietly struggle to mutter, "What happened... Where am I?" I cough a little... my throat hurts like hell... and I start to remember why.

I remembered that I was working all night, opening a new location. As a regional manager and still in training, I had been doing regular checks on all my locations for a few months now. I had thirty-five locations in five states: Michigan, Indiana, Illinois, Ohio, and Kentucky. Opening new locations meant more money, so after an additional month of training, this was the first new location that I was taking on by myself. For the last three or four days I had been working almost twenty-four hours a day, trying to impress my supervisor who was coming to check my progress.

It was already 6 in the morning. I had a doctor's appointment at 9 which was about sixty miles away, and I was supposed to meet my boss at noon. It wasn't really a doctor's appointment. It was my psychiatrist, but I always wrote 'doctor's appointment' in my planner in case anyone saw it.

I had gotten into some trouble about a year ago and got probation which requires AA meetings, random drug testing, and monthly meetings with a psychiatrist. This was supposed to be the last meeting.

Less than three hours of sleep is useless, so I knew I had to stay up and decided to get a little help. Mass amounts of caffeine and energy drinks weren't cutting it.

I remember fondly the day I was first introduced to Red Bull, the first of many energy drinks to hit the market in the late nineties.

I was waiting tables at a sports bar in Austin, Texas, where I live with my brother. It was '97 or '98. This place wasn't just the oldest bar in Austin, but the oldest in the whole state, and it looked it. It was the first public place in Texas to get air-conditioning. Still to this day, it has the flashing neon 'air conditioning' sign out front.

People in Texas are crazy about air-conditioning. It might be a hundred and twenty degrees outside, and they've got the AC set at about forty. This extreme difference in temperature is why everyone is always sick. In the summer, about sixty percent of the population has a cold. People bring sweaters to work when it's a hundred degrees outside... sweaters in the summertime never made sense to me.

Anyway, these guys came in and sat down in my section on a particularly busy afternoon. Towards the end of their meal, one of them reached into his bag and pulled out this silver and blue can that was only about half the size of a regular soda or beer can. He handed two of them to me and asked me to try them. I remember thinking that it might be a beer or some kind of malt liquor. Even though I was frequently stoned out of my mind at this job, I didn't want to get busted drinking. So, I quickly hid them behind the bar, which just made it look even more suspicious. They assured me that it was non-alcoholic, but more than anything else, I was just too busy to bother with it.

After finishing the first half of a double shift, I tried one. It was great. It offered twice the jolt of coffee with no caffeine crash. The second shift was a breeze.

I was hooked.

This particular morning, I needed something stronger.

The location I was working on was in a really small town, and good drugs were hard to find. Also... being a small town, even if I managed to find some, it was sure to get back to the owners or employees. I wanted to keep this job.

So, I wrapped up my work, jumped in my car, and drove about forty miles closer to my doctor's office. At one of my stops for gas, well out of town, I picked up a bottle of pills that truckers sometimes use. They are supposed to be diet pills, but in actuality they are more or less over-the-counter speed. Not all truckers are on a diet. I washed down about half a bottle with a Dr. Pepper. Needless to say, I was wide awake for the ride to my doctor's appointment.

I arrived at my doctor's office about fifteen minutes early and after checking in, started flipping through a magazine. As part of the check in, they make me piss in a cup. It didn't occur to me that the speed might show up.

My mind was racing, but I felt I had my composure well in check. Just as my watch beeped 9:00, Dr. Beamen came into the waiting room and invited me back. I sensed she noticed right away that something was wrong. However, she didn't let on about her suspicions, and we started with the usual small talk. At $50 an hour, fitted to my income, we were talking about the weather.

Finally, she came out with it and asked, "Are you on something right now?"

Quickly, but calmly I responded, "No." I paused for just a second to fish in my pocket for my 'one year' gold coin to show her. "You know... I've been clean for over a year now." Continuing, but with a little more attitude this time, "And you got my urine sample that we still do eevverrry visit." (I hear they sometimes take a strand of your hair for DNA testing now.)

Being direct, she pointed out something I didn't think she knew. "You know that is part of the deal... and even though you've never come up dirty, you also know what drugs don't show up in the urine sample." Now she was just glaring at me, waiting for my half-assed explanation. With the results of today's test still not in, it was foolish of me to reminder her. The speed would probably show up.

I jumped right into it like it was nothing. "Ok... I've been working a lot of hours lately, and I may have over done it with the coffee." Seeing that this didn't satisfy her, I continued, "I did take a few energy pills." Real quickly, but sounding more and more guilty, I added, "They're over-the-counter diet pills... They're perfectly legal." Given the fact that I was about a buck twenty soaking wet, she knew as well as I did that, I had no interest in dieting.

"How much did you take?" she asked, now just writing in her notebook.

"The whole bottle." I answered... very matter-of-factly. I had taken the other half of the bottle just before coming into the office.

Although trying to hide her surprise, her head jetted up from her notebook, and a look of terror was apparent on her face. Still sounding calm and noticing that I'm not really showing any side effects, she asked, "How many pills come in a bottle?"

"About thirty." I said, still very nonchalantly.

With increasing concern on her face, but maintaining her monotone questioning, she asked, "Do you know how many milligrams per pill?" again, face down and writing in her notebook.

This whole part of the conversation was like playing tennis. So, I volleyed back, "I have no idea. Just guessing... maybe five." This time a little concern of my own came through in my voice.

It didn't take her long to do the math. Then more calmly than ever, she said, "Will you excuse me for just a few moments?" and casually proceeded to leave the room.

Although she had never left the room in the middle of a session before, her leaving had no effect on me. Somewhere between five and ten minutes later, she returned. After picking up her notebook from her chair, she sat back down.

This time the conversation was much more like normal. We continued to talk casually about work, my family, and my social life. Work took up the majority of the conversation and there wasn't much social life to speak of. I threw in some stuff about meetings, so that she knew that I was going (another part of the deal).

Although I was trying to hide it, I was shaking like a leaf, and it felt like my heart was going to jump out of my chest throughout the entire meeting, but at about a quarter to ten, I was feeling pretty relaxed. To be honest, I always did at the end of our meetings. It really did help, and this time was supposed to be the last time I'd have to do this, so I was more relaxed than ever. Just as I felt myself start to slip into this euphoric state, there was a sharp knock on the door.

Without even acknowledging me or getting up from her chair, she called out, "Come in," as if she were expecting the interruption. She knew who it was. It was the paramedics, coming to take me away .

As she slipped into the background, she attempted to explain to me that she had to call them. One of the paramedics began to check my vitals while another was writing stuff on a clipboard. It later occurred to me that the euphoric state I was slipping into was not just relief from these meetings, but possibly something more.

Talking to Dr. Beamen and basically ignoring me, the clipboard guy, shocked and with a 'you dumb kid' attitude, said to her, "I can't believe how calm he appears. When did he take the pills?"

I answered, "About an hour ago."

Then he asked the other paramedic, who was kneeling beside me, "What's his pressure?"

She responded with a list of numbers and medical jargon that, as far as I was concerned, was all Greek to me. (Actually, I think it was Greek, or maybe Latin). Then, she asked me in plain English and in a pleasant tone, "How are you feeling, Jeff?"

"I feel fine." I responded very calmly, as if to say, 'what's all the fuss about?'

They put me on a gurney. Then, in a little more than an accusatory tone, she asked, "Why did you take so many pills?"

I realized then that they were under the impression that I was trying to commit suicide... again. (That's part of how this all started.) So, I responded, trying to hold back my disbelief of the situation and hopeless disappointment in Dr. Beamen's opinion of me, "I was only trying to stay awake. I can't really afford the luxury of a full night's sleep this week. I feel fine, and all of this is totally unnecessary."

Evidently, I didn't convince them, and they carted me off to the hospital.

I do remember getting to the hospital and having anywhere from four to seven doctors and nurses working on me. They were all moving very quickly and wearing these clear plastic face-shields and what looked like full-length paper smocks. They were twisting and pulling me in every direction as they put in all these wires and tubes. No one asked any questions, and I remained fully alert, calm, and cooperative. That is... until they started talking about pumping my stomach and putting in a catheter.

I was catheterized once before. I remember waking up years ago to see some guy with my dick in one hand and a tube in the other. I was disoriented and didn't know where I was. There were four guys wearing blue, two on either side of the bed holding me down, and I thought they were cops. I thought I was in trouble and for some reason tried to get up and run. Just as these four guys dropped down on me like the defensive line sacking the quarterback, dude with the tube said, "This might hurt a bit," as he jammed the catheter into me.

Although not as memorable as my past experience with the catheter, I had had my stomach pumped before. That time I was completely unconscious. This time was pretty much the polar opposite. The stuff they were working on getting out of me had me more than wide awake.

I was able to bypass the catheter by voluntarily pissing in a cup... again. This also slightly postponed the stomach pumping, but not long enough.

They started by trying to cram a tube, which was as big as my middle finger, up my nose. It hurt like hell, and I began to groan and scream in agony. It didn't fit, so they gave up on that route. I breathed a sigh of relief, but it was short lived, as they decided to force it down my throat instead.

I was choking... and gagging... and begging them to stop. It felt like it was tearing my throat. Then, I started vomiting and spewing up this black sludge that they were pumping into me. It burned like hell. Every once in a while, it sprayed them in the face, which explained the plastic shields. This was by far the most excruciating experience of my life.

Then... I suppose I eventually passed out from the pain or the experience as a whole. Which brings me back to the nurse checking machinery, the defibrillator between my legs, and the hospital bed in which I'm now lying. However, it doesn't quite clarify everything.

The nurse might have been talking the whole time, but I'm just now starting to hear her. She's totally dumbing it down and possibly exaggerating a bit. She claims that I was fighting them, but it seemed a natural defense, given the circumstances. I remember trying very hard to be as cooperative as possible, so it would be over with quickly.

She goes on to explain that, considering the amount that I took, they were afraid my heart would just explode. This is her exaggerating, I'm sure, but it explains the defibrillator. That is why they were in such a hurry to get it out of my system or at least neutralize what already made its way into my bloodstream. That's what the black sludge, or what I found out was activated charcoal, was for.

The doctor comes in shortly after I wake up and starts asking the standard questions.

"Do you know where you are?"

"Hospital."

"What year is it?"

"1998."

"Who's the president?"

"Clinton." I must have passed. He starts to explain everything.

From what the doctor tells me, also dumbing it down, my heart did stop. Apparently, they had to shock me back to life. I later discovered bruises on my chest and back, so I guess that part is true.

Then, I just kind of slept for what turned out to be a little less than two days. By then, everything was out of my system and, outside of being a little weak from not really moving for two days, I was healthy. They are quick to remind me just how lucky I was that there was no permanent damage to my heart, brain, or anything else.

During their explanations of the whole thing, I'm able to find out just exactly where I am. As it turns out, it's the same hospital I ended up in a few years ago, after an actual suicide attempt. It's a pretty good hospital in a small town in Northwest Indiana, not far from where I grew up. It also happens to be only a few towns over from my psychiatrist's office and the town where two of my five sisters live with their families.

Back when I first started with Dr. Beamen, I listed my second oldest sister, Annie, as my emergency contact on the forms. Well, considering this is an emergency... they contact her... and she shows up.

She shows up with her husband, who, only about three or four months ago, was in the hospital himself. He had just had emergency surgery to repair five vessels around his heart. The whole family had been there for that, and it had been a serious touch and go situation. Everyone had been really scared.

Anyway, I feel terrible for putting them into similar surroundings so soon after what they had just gone through. I don't want them to have to relive it. Besides, they didn't have to come by at all... I'm fine.

Then, possibly as kind of a karma thing, my mind starts to play tricks on me. While they are standing alongside of the bed, my sister Annie holding my hand, an old reoccurring nightmare of mine comes back to me.

You see, about five years ago my mother died, and the whole experience messed me up in a bunch of ways. I remember vividly, the whole family packed into this small ICU room. There were about ten of us just helplessly standing there watching her die.

After about three months of various surgeries and procedures, there was nothing more anyone could do. My mother had been sick for years. The nurse informed us that it wouldn't be much longer. Then, one by one, each individual family member walked up to the side of her bed... held her hand... and said their goodbyes. Everyone except for me, that is.

I just couldn't pry myself away from the wall I was clinging to. It seemed to be the only thing holding me up. I stood there and watched everyone else say their goodbyes. I just stood there and watched her die. I couldn't move at all, not even for my last chance to say goodbye to my mother... (I've actually never forgiven myself for that).

Anyway, for months after this, I would have the same dream every night. In the dream, it was me lying there... and the family was one by one saying their goodbyes to me. One by one walking up to the side of my bed... holding my hand... and saying their goodbyes to me.

That's how it was supposed to be... that was the plan. I was supposed to die first.

When the dreams first started happening, I would wake up right away, short of breath, sweating like mad, panicked, and crying my eyes out. Eventually I would stay sleeping, afraid to open my eyes and see it wasn't real. Either way, I would eventually wake to find the pillow soaked with tears.

It stopped for a while.

Then about six months later, I went in for a routine doctor's visit. At this particular time in my life, I had a regular doctor, and I only lived a few blocks from my sister Annie. There was something wrong with my car, so I asked her to take me. At one point during the exam, they were drawing blood. I've had my blood drawn about a million times, but this time I felt a bit woozy. I remember actually saying, 'I think I'm going to pass out.' ... and then I did.

When I woke up, I was lying there in the hospital bed, and my sister was holding my hand. I immediately started crying, shaking, and hyperventilating... basically, freaking the fuck out. It was just too real... my dream come to life.

And now five years later... here we go again.

Here I am lying in a hospital bed, ICU no less, my brother-in-law standing there and Annie holding my hand. I don't freak out this time, but the junk I'm hooked up to does. I'm trying to maintain my composure, trying not to upset my sister and her husband. However, the machines that I am hooked up to make it more difficult to hide.

The crap starts beeping like mad, and despite my attempts to calm down, my sister's and brother-in-law's faces go a bit white. The nurse jumps up from her chair, and the doctor comes running in. I'm sure they all think I'm having a heart attack.

After checking all of the machines, they shoot something into the IV and in a few minutes everything is fine.

It's just a mild panic attack.

The sedative they hit me with makes me tired. I assure my sister that I'm going to be fine. We make arrangements for them to move my car from the psychiatrist's office to the hospital parking lot. Then, after a few more pleasantries, they leave. I probably could fall asleep right after all this, but my mind is all over the place.

“No more!” I think to myself. No more. Dear God... no more. This can never happen again, and I will do everything in my power to make sure it doesn't. I can't keep finding myself in these situations. Out of work, broke, alone, lost, moving from one place to another every year or so, changing jobs after only a few months, popping in and out of hospitals, scaring and worrying my family and friends... it all has to stop. Right here... right now, it has to stop.

Finally, I am determined to do whatever it takes, and I want to jump out of this bed and leave right here and now. I feel reborn and want to start my new life... as a new man... on a new path... as soon as humanly possible. The doctors, on the other hand, have other plans and my body isn't strong enough to take me anywhere just yet.

I could stay and rest a little longer. Take my time and make some solid plans, then go do whatever I set my heart to. Besides, I don't have much choice at this point.

After one more day, they move me to a regular room. As I get my strength back, I become more and more antsy and ready to leave. The fact that I am seriously jonesing for a cigarette isn't helping either.

At one point, I ask if they could take me outside for a minute, so I could smoke. Obviously, they say no. They do however, put me on 'the patch'. I'm not trying to quit, but they tell me that it will help with the cravings.

While reading the package, I notice that one patch was the time-release equivalent of about fifteen cigarettes a day. I tell them about what I read, then begin my attempt to explain that I smoke about thirty cigarettes a day. So, in my sweetest voice I ask, "How about two patches?"

Apparently, it doesn't work like that.

The following day, I get a visit from Dr. Beamen. We exchange the usual small talk, and then she starts in, "I would like to admit you here for a week or so. Just to make sure you're alright."

"No fuckin' way!" I immediately respond. Then, continuing very slowly and emphasizing every word, "I was not trying to kill myself. I was only trying to stay awake for what was, from my calculations, our last meeting. Not to mention, a highly stressful day ahead. All of which I talked about openly in our meeting." Then, calming down a little, "If I missed our meeting, we would have to keep doing this. I'm over it... I'm fine. I've met every little ridiculous requirement they held me to. I'm done." The psych ward took its toll on me the last time. I wasn't going to go through it again.

As pissed off as I am, it's not easy, but I do my best to put as much sincerity as I can muster in saying, "This job has been great, and it has kept me so busy I haven't even had time to even think about all that shit. That was a messed-up time... and I didn't take it very well, but I'm fine now."

Being quite dismissive, she decides to end our little conversation by saying, "We don't want to aggravate your condition, so why don't we discuss this later when you have calmed down."

"There's nothing to discuss. I'm done," I reply as she leaves the room.

This less than pleasant conversation reminds me of two things: my job for one, and also how all this got started... but mostly my job.

Considering the fact that I haven't been to work in days, and I missed the meeting with my supervisor, plus the fact that my supervisor more than likely had to finish the opening himself, I'm betting there's not much I can do to save my job. My only hope is to play on their sympathies. They knew I had a doctor's appointment (at least they thought it was a doctor's appointment), and I could use that.

So, I call my boss. After apologizing for my absence, I try to explain that the doctor thought he noticed something and had me admitted. I add that they have me on a bunch of painkillers, which causes me to be a little out of it. That is why I didn't call sooner. I wanted to be coherent. Then I tell him that it turned out to be nothing, and I would be back to work on Monday.

He attempted to fake some genuine concern... wished me well... and then asked me to call him on Monday before coming in. His tone of voice and the very fact that he stressed calling before coming in, made it perfectly clear.

My only thought at this time is, 'Damn. They're gonna take the company car.' Being out of work didn't bother me.

The thing is, my car was repo-ed a little more than a year ago, round about the same time a whole bunch of other shit went down. After that, I moved from Waukegan, Illinois, to Austin, Texas. Getting around in Austin without a car wasn't easy. Finding the right job and being able to work good shifts without wheels was a regular issue.

So, when I was offered the job as the Regional Manager of a pizza joint, which came with a corporate credit card, expense account, and a company car, the deal couldn't have been better. They let me pick from a list of zones I could cover. I picked the Midwest, so I could work with Dr. Beamen. She had closer contact with the courts, and it just made things easier. I told my new bosses that I was a diabetic, which I hoped would explain my regular doctor's visits. The job was easy, it paid well, and the set up was perfect.

Now, with everything that has happened, the thought of being unemployed again didn't bother me. However, the idea of going back to Texas broke and without wheels sucked. I knew I had to get out of here and get things sorted out in a hurry.

As I'm planning my next move, the phone next to my bed rings.

More than a little confused, I answer it, "Uhh... Hello?"

"Mr. Etch... ree... ling?" the voice on the other end asks.

Wondering who knows I'm here and knowing that anyone that is butchering my name that badly is probably not delivering good news, I respond, "Who is this?"

"Jeff. My name is Roger Livingston. I'm a public defender; I got this number from a Dr. Beamen. I was given your file, and I need to bring you up to date." I can hear papers shuffling as he pauses a second. Then he continues, "Yesterday, Dr. Beamen reported your alleged relapse and/or overdose to me. Now, I know that your probation period ended last week." (At this point I'm assuming the worst). He continues, "I'm not sure what you did to piss her off, but our records show that you have met all of the requirements. Despite the difficulty we had getting a hold of you at times, you managed to stay in complete compliance.

"Taking all of this into consideration, the judge is not pursuing her claim and you are free and clear. This matter will now be taken off your record." He pauses again... more papers shuffling... then continues, "We need to send you your copies of the final paperwork for your records. The most recent address we have for you is in Austin, Texas, on Guadalupe. Is that correct?" (He pronounced it, 'Guada-loo-pay', which in Spanish is correct, but in Austin, they pronounce it, 'Guada-loop'. You would think that they say it like that because the street loops... but it doesn't.)

Anyway... stunned, I reply, "Uhh... Yeah. 2842 Guadalupe." I go ahead and pronounce it the same way he does.

"Ok. Then, I guess that's it. Stay out of trouble now."

Then, in the middle of saying, 'Thank you,' he hangs up.

At this point, I'm lying there thinking, 'Did that really just happen?' It was like a free gift with the purchase of a small problem.

They said that it was 'limited probation' and as long as I followed the requirements to the letter, it would not stay on my record, and I would be free and clear after a year. I didn't really expect it to work out that way, but I was due some good news. That's one thing I no longer have to worry about... but I still gotta get out of here. Even though Dr. Beamen can no longer hold the court stuff over my head, she might still be able to keep me here.

It's almost 1 AM, and I can't sleep. The guy in the bed next to me has the TV on, and there is an old episode of M*A*S*H playing. I'm more or less lost in thought, but I'm also sort of watching the show. M*A*S*H is one of my favorites. While listening to one of Hawkeye's monologs, the perfect plan comes to me. As I think of it, I let out kind of a sinister laugh, which happens to be during a pretty serious part of the show. The guy in the next bed gives me a look, as if to say, 'Dude, you're sick. There's nothing funny about this.' His reaction only makes me laugh more.

Now, I can sleep.

As soon as I wake up the following morning, I insist on seeing the doctor. I've waited long enough. I'm going home today.

He starts by trying to tell me that Dr. Beamen has asked him to wait for her to decide whether to release me or to move me to the fourth floor - the psych ward.

Really quickly, and kind of smart-assed I ask, "Does Dr. Beamen have privileges at this hospital? Is there anything medically wrong with me?"

"No... But Dr. Beamen is a friend of mine, and I respect her judgment. She feels there is reason to believe this was a suicide attempt."

Smugly, I say, "It doesn't seem smart to give sleeping pills to someone you think is suicidal." He's not amused.

I continue with a more easygoing tone, "If you really thought I might be suicidal or unstable in any way, why then haven't I seen a representative from the psych department here?" Not waiting for an answer, I continue, "Have you or anyone working here noticed any erratic or unusual behavior since I've been here?" From the look on his face, I can see that he's sympathetic, and I go on. "No... you haven't... and you gave me sleeping pills because I've been having trouble sleeping. I've always had trouble sleeping... and before all this happened, I had gone about four days without any sleep at all.

I've heard that over exertion of the adrenal glands, brought on by extended periods of sleeplessness, can cause one to exhibit irrational behavior." Now, I'm just paraphrasing exactly what Hawkeye said. The medical jargon, coupled with the fact that he didn't see that episode of M*A*S*H has gotten his attention. "I'm not suicidal. Taking that many pills was irrational, but I'm not suicidal. I might be an insomniac, but I've gotten rest while I've been here, and I'm not a threat to myself or anyone else." Finishing with the utmost sincerity, "I've been here for almost a week now, and I would like to go home."

He continues to just stand there with a blank stare, showing no emotion or reaction at all. After taking a second to collect his thoughts, he says, "Will you excuse me for just a few moments?" then turns and walks out of the room. I feel like this has happened before... and I'm pretty convinced that I'm screwed.

Less than five minutes later, a nurse comes in the room with a clipboard. "Sign here," she says blankly, handing me the clipboard and a pen. I sign, not really knowing what I'm signing (not smart). After taking back the clipboard and looking over the papers, she points at a cabinet in the corner of the room and says, "Your clothes are in there. You can get dressed and then come out to the desk for the rest of your things." As she turns to leave, she adds, "The desk is right outside." She says all of this without showing any emotion at all. I can't tell if she feels defeated or if she just doesn't care, probably the latter.

'They bought it,' I thought. (I didn't realize it at the time, but my self-diagnosis was actually pretty close to dead on).

I get dressed and head towards the desk, as instructed... head held high and a little cocky. They hand me a bag that has my keys, wallet, and other random stuff I had in my pockets. Smiling ear to ear, I examine the contents of the bag. Almost everything is in there.

“Uhh... wasn’t there a pack of cigarettes with all of this?” I ask, trying not to sound too desperate.

“Oh, yeah. Hang on,” one of the nurses says, as she turns back towards a locking cabinet behind the desk.

Then one of the other nurses reminds me, “You know you’ve been wearing ‘the patch’ for the last few days and you can’t smoke for twenty-four hours after you take it off.” She can tell I don’t care and continues, “If you do you could have another heart attack.”

I’m pretty sure she was just trying to scare me... but what did she mean by ‘another’ heart attack?

Then the first nurse hands me a different smaller bag. This one has my smokes and lighter in it. I guess they always keep this type of stuff separate.

There are three nurses behind the desk, and they all have these silly grins on their faces, as if to say, ‘He’ll never make it.’

I gather up all of my stuff, put everything in the right pockets, throw the nurses a quick wave and a, “Thanks.” Then I start walking towards the elevator, as if I know where it is. On my second lap past the desk, all three of them just point down the one hall I haven’t tried yet.

In the elevator, I reach into my shirt to remove the patch. Thinking of their warning, I’m more concerned with the use of the word ‘another’ than what might happen if I don’t wait twenty-four hours. Regardless, I light up as soon as I get into my car. It takes me about ten minutes to find my way out of the hospital and about twenty minutes more to find my car. That’s around a half an hour... that should be enough.

It's a long drive back to Austin. I know I've lost my job, and they're gonna come for the car soon. At least I'll get home.

At my first stop for gas, I see that this place has the same pills. I don't need them. Not after everything I've just been through. I don't think I'll have any trouble keeping my eyes open this time.

As I go to pay, I discover that my company credit card has been canceled.

Chapter Two:
Going Home

I got back to Austin in record time. As I open the door, it hits me that I haven't been here in almost three months. With this job, staying in hotels for months at a time was common. The place is impeccably clean. Knowing that they are coming to get the car soon, I make a point of getting everything out of it. I'm kind of glad my brother isn't home. I'm not really in the mood to field a bunch of questions. I just dump my stuff next to the futon and flop down on it.

The living room has basically been my room. It's only a one bedroom, which is another reason why I liked this job. I love my brother, but we haven't had much luck sharing small spaces. The fact that I would be on the road at least nine months out of a year only made the job more appealing.

There are only about a million loose ends that I need to tie together before I make my next move. However, as I look at my watch, the only thought that comes to mind is that there is an AA meeting in about a half an hour. Struggling with what to do first and weighing out what I have the energy for, I decide to put the plan on hold for an hour and go to the meeting. I could use it. I haven't been to one in almost two weeks.

Not bothering with the car, I jump on the bus to get to the meeting, and the theme song to 'Cheers' comes to mind. 'Sometimes you want to go where everybody knows your name... and they're always glad you came.' The 'always glad you came' part is one of those things that I like about the meetings. It isn't always true at the bars.

Sometimes the only difference between AA and the bars is the lighting. I would include that at the meetings, there usually isn't an endless supply of drugs and alcohol, but that's not always true either. There is usually someone who knows that people at these meetings are often at their weakest... and they are ready to take full advantage of that.

There are also those that compare the meetings to church. I don't know how many churches you can go to that are one giant cloud of smoke and everyone is swearing like truckers. I never heard a story in church that included getting a blowjob from a hooker while a needle was hanging from your arm. Most of the details about Mary Magdalene are usually left out.

I guess I find that comparison a little sacrilegious, but everyone finds God in their own way. Then you go back to where you found Him, when you lose Him. That makes sense to me, but I didn't find God in AA. I always had Him... I just choose to forget He's there at times.

Anyway, I'm not going to this meeting to get reconnected, I'm looking for some peace of mind. It's usually soothing to hear that other people have it a whole lot worse than you do. That may sound callous, but that's a big part of it... and not just for me.

It's also kind of cool when you hear that your story of pain has helped someone else. I never thought talking about my problems or struggles could help other people. In therapy I was only trying to help myself. On the other hand, I didn't want anyone thinking that the way I got through those times was the right way. In almost all cases, I just got lucky. This time is no exception, but now I have to put it behind me and figure out what to do next.

The last meeting that I went to was somewhere in central Indiana. The meeting before that was just outside of Fort Wayne. I haven't been to this one in months. Generally, if you haven't been around in a while everyone automatically assumes that you've been drinking or using again. It makes no difference though. As soon as I get off the bus, I can see the front of the building. There are about fifteen people hanging out, not ready to go in yet, and I recognize a few faces.

I kind of sidle my way into the mix and light up a cigarette. No one has acknowledged me yet and I haven't acknowledged them either. I'm just listening to the conversations. Some are actually talking about steps and things they are doing within the program. Most are talking about work, relationships and bullshit from daily life, but that's OK. Parts of the program are designed to make the day-to-day stuff easier.

We still have about five minutes before the meeting starts, and if you get in too early, you are bound to get stuck reading something. There are always a few formal readings at the beginning of every meeting. This is AA, (Alcoholics Anonymous) and not NA, (Narcotics Anonymous) so there aren't nearly as many readings, but still. Sometimes, I just don't feel like being involved. I'd rather just stay in the back like a fly on the wall and take it all in.

As it gets closer and closer to start time, I notice that no one else is making any attempt to go in. Then, their van pulls up to take them back to the halfway house. They must have been here for an earlier meeting. Addiction is a great equalizer; sometimes you can't tell the lawyers from the thieves. I slide inside so they don't take me with them. As soon as the door closes behind me, Jack sees me and crosses the room to greet me with a big hug.

Jack had been my sponsor at one point, and I've been seeing him in meetings since my first meeting in Texas. He's really a good guy, but a little too religious and huggy for my comfort level. Growing up, it had to be a pretty serious situation to get a hug. Even within my family, displays of affection were rare. Outside the family you could forget about it. A good handshake was more than enough.

Jack also talked about God and Jesus way too much. Don't get me wrong. I respect anyone with a solid belief system, but sometimes it can be a little extreme. Mine was a simple catholic upbringing. There was church every Sunday and the holidays, but no more than necessary. Plus, if we were in a hurry, we would go to a church in Highland. That place didn't have a choir, so there wasn't as much singing which really cuts down the time. We could get in and out in about twenty to thirty minutes.

I have my beliefs, but I don't feel the need to talk about them. I took the stuff my mother taught me and the good stuff I heard at church, (the little that I agreed with), plus other things that I just simply feel strongly about and developed my own catholic-tainted Christian belief system. Jack, on the other hand, was Baptist. Texas Baptist at that.

I went with him once to his church. It was huge. There were cameras everywhere and it was being televised. Behind the altar was an Olympic sized pool for baptisms. It had glass on one side so you could see in. To me, it was like a scene from an old James Bond movie... they would be at some bar that had what looked like a big fish tank behind the bar with girls dressed like mermaids swimming in it. The whole thing was very theatrical and intense. The music was fantastic, and everyone was really into it.

My church was led by a very soft-spoken, monotone, young priest. The music was still the high point, but most of the time what you heard was restless coughs and some snoring.

Anyway, his beliefs and mine were worlds apart. In the rooms of AA, you could get a taste of every belief system and religion known to man. Anyone taking religious studies in college should attend a few meetings.

I remember getting into a conversational debate with some guys after a meeting about whether or not an alcoholic could drink the sacramental wine. I mentioned that if your faith is strong enough... you could, because it isn't wine... it's the blood of Christ. Few agreed.

There are some guys that are so hardcore they won't even take certain medications or even use certain hygiene products, because they have alcohol in them. If I have just had surgery, I'm taking the painkillers. I never drank aftershave or mouthwash to get drunk, and I never tried to get high off of an antihistamine. That's not to say that no one has. Plenty have. That's why so many are so careful. It doesn't take much to send someone back to their addictions when their addictions are strong enough.

I always felt that 'intent' played a big part, but there were many times that I sat down to have a few with no 'intention' of getting drunk. So, I could be wrong. That's why it was always so scary talking with some of these guys. You might say something that someone else takes to heart... it doesn't work for them... and they wind up dead.

It sounds extreme, but you never know whether or not your next drink or drug could lead to something that ends your days. For most, even one more is just not an option, so you pay close attention to every tip you can get about staying clear of the next one.

My timing is good enough that I don't have to talk with Jack for too long. The meeting starts right away. I don't have to read anything, and we run out of time before it's my turn to share. It's perfect. I don't remember anything specific that was said, and I didn't talk to anyone afterwards. I get back on the bus and go back to the apartment, but for some reason I feel a lot better, as I usually do.

When I get back, my brother is making dinner. Without even looking up he says, "You got a bunch of messages." Then, nothing for a while. Then, "How long you in town for?"

"I don't know yet." I respond while heading to the answering machine. I'm assuming that he knows I was fired if he listened to the messages. I go ahead and play them in front of him.

There aren't any messages from work, but five from a friend of mine back in Chicago. Most of them are the usual, "Hey, it's Nate. Call me back." In the last one, he mentions that his fiancée left. He doesn't sound too broken up about it, but it was a nine-year relationship, and she was paying most of the bills, so I know he's hurting. He just never shows it, ever.

Nate is my best friend, and we've known each other since '93 - the same year my mother died. He was going through a lot that year as well. That's a big part of our friendship - getting each other through the tough times.

We met while working at the same restaurant in South Holland, Illinois. I've done a lot of moving around and have worked at a lot of different places, but despite often living pretty far apart, we have always stayed in touch.

Nathaniel Williams, II is his full name, and his mother's name is Vanessa. Yeah, Vanessa Williams is his mother... different one of course. In most circles, especially professional circles, he went by Nathaniel. It just sounds more sophisticated. I got away with calling him Nate.

We are a lot alike, but still pretty different. He's about my height, but a little heavier than me. He spends a lot of time and money on his hair. He's always impeccably dressed. He wants to look good, but given his attitude, I would never call him vain. To look at us separately, you'd think we'd have little to nothing in common. He talks about big plans for the future; I have none. He grew up in Chicago; I grew up in a small town. He's definitely a ladies' man and confident as hell; I'm generally single and pathetically shy. He plays and knows sports and cars; I'm an idiot when it comes to that stuff. He's five years older and black, but we were still able to convince some people that we were twins. Both of us being Geminis, we technically are twins, but that's not how we mean it, and they still believe it.

He always cracks me up. We bounce jokes off of each other like Abbot and Costello. He makes me seem funnier than I actually am. We've almost never had a disagreement in almost six years of knowing each other. Six years may not seem like much to some, but for me, it's my longest running friendship, by far.

"You hungry?" my brother asks.

"You got enough?" I reply, trying to sound considerate. I'm starving, but my brother and I both have gotten good at just cooking for one.

"Plenty. Help yourself," he says as he finishes making up his plate and then heads to the futon to sit and watch TV. So, a nap isn't happening.

The last time I saw my brother was about a month ago at Christmas. Everything was great then. I bragged to everyone about my new job, my expense account, my company car, the company credit card, and all of the heavy responsibility. I felt like I had finally made it and things were just about to get a whole lot better. I wanted to prove to them that I was over all the madness and had a hold on my life again. I rarely had much good to talk about at family parties. I was usually broke and unemployed and even if I had a job, it was a crappy one, and I'd lose it in less than six weeks. This one had lasted about three months, but here I go again. I didn't want to tell him the truth yet.

I eat pretty quickly and go into the other room to call Nate. He answers in a pretty depressing tone... so I try to keep my tone upbeat. "What's up, man? Sorry, I've been out of touch lately. Things have been crazy." He knows me well enough by now that he realizes that 'things have been crazy' means 'I've fucked it all up again', but he doesn't comment on it.

"She's gone man. I'm gonna get kicked out of here and have to live with my mother again. This sucks." He tells me in a way I've never heard him talk. He's usually weirdly happy all of the time, no matter how bad things are.

"What happened to the hotel you were working at? I thought things were going pretty well there, and you should be able to handle the bills on your own." I'm not asking about her. I know why she left, and I always wondered why she'd stuck around that long. I love Nate, but he cheated every chance he got and never made any effort to keep her.

"Evidently, the hotel was owned by Hyatt, and they claimed that I lied on my application when I said I never worked for the company before. I worked for the Hyatt like four years ago for about a month. I forgot about it, and I didn't really know this one was also a Hyatt. Anyway, they dropped me like a hot rock about a month ago, and I wasn't making that much money there anyway."

"Dude, that blows, but stay up, man. You'll get through this. This ain't shit compared to stuff you've easily got through before. And hey, I might be able to help out. I just got to wrap some stuff up first." I tell him in hopes that he'll break out of this. We both struggle the same way with keeping work and paying rent, but there is usually one of us that is in a position to help out. When we're both down it gets crazy.

"How you gonna help? You got it like that right now?" he asks.

"No. Actually, I just lost my job, too, but I'm about to make a move. And with everything you're going through, I think I might move up there with you and we'll build it all back up together. Texas ain't got shit for me, and I miss Chicago. Just hold on to the place for another week or so and keep your head up. I gotta go right now and take care of some shit, but I'll see you soon." Sometimes I gotta cut our conversations short and jump out when I can, or we'll talk for hours... (usually about nothing).

I was wanting to move back to Chicago anyway, and Nate's problem just makes the decision easier.

After hanging up the phone, I take a deep breath and prepare to tell my brother what's happened and what my plan is. I've bailed on him twice before, and he's bailed on me once in Indianapolis... we go through this. He can handle the bills on his own, and I think he'd prefer to have the place to himself. Regardless, it's still hard to tell him. With every time I have to tell a family member that I've lost my job or that I'm moving, I feel I lose more credibility. I've had hundreds of jobs and usually only hold them for about three to six months. I've also had about thirty different addresses. My info is always written in pencil in everyone's address books. I doubt if any of them have any faith in me whatsoever.

Very much to my surprise, my brother takes the news incredibly well. He doesn't seem shocked or concerned at all. He almost seems to understand. If anyone did understand, it would be him. He has a lot more drive and motivation than I have ever had, but he too tends to move around and change jobs a lot. He just does it under significantly less drastic or desperate circumstances. When he moves or changes jobs, it's simply because he wants to, never because he has no other choice.

I have one other option. I could stay, but that would mean my brother would have to carry me until I get back on my feet. He would, but I just don't want him to have to. I did think he would be a little more concerned about my moving back to Chicago, considering the circumstances surrounding my move to Texas.

The plan is set. I would move back to Chicago and while helping Nate, I would get back on my feet as well. After talking it over with my brother, I go to sleep early. When I get up in the morning, one of my coworkers is knocking on the door. He is here to take the car.

I buy a bus ticket and let Nate know when I will be getting into Chicago. I meet up with a friend of mine from the meetings, (not Jack), and we talk about the move. He convinces me that the speed overdose was a relapse, and I would have to start over with my clean time and my steps. I eventually agree. It is hard to give up a year of clean time, but we start on the steps right away. We spend the night working through the first four steps, and I do five through eight on my own in the park. I would never recommend going through them so quickly, but this is my third or fourth time through, and it has gotten easier for me. I feel better about everything and am looking forward to starting over in Chicago.

My brother sees me off at the bus station, and the twenty-four-hour trip ahead doesn't seem to be part of my thoughts. I feel like I am finally heading home.

Although I only actually lived in Chicago for the brief time when I stayed with Nate and Pritina (Nate's fiancée) just before moving to Texas, I always considered the Chicago area my home. It was near everyone in my family, except my brother and I had several friends that lived around there. I grew up near Chicago and I spent the majority of my life in or close to the city. Even throughout my moving around, I was never more than four hours away. Chicago has always felt like home.

The bus trip is just that - a trip. I have three huge bags stored under the bus and three smaller ones on my lap and set under my seat. Comfort is less an issue then having things available. I have easy access to all my music, my 'Big Book' (AA's bible), and some snacks, but I don't need them that much. Throughout the ride, I am pretty entertained by the people sitting next to me.

The first leg of the trip, Austin to Dallas, I sit next to an elderly man that is actually touring the country on the bus. He paid a flat rate of around two hundred dollars and was free to get on and get off wherever he chose. He is traveling the whole country, visiting family and seeing the sights. The way he describes it, it seems like a hell of a way to spend the next two months, but he is thrilled. Talking to him makes the beginning of the trip kind of calm and peaceful.

The second leg of the trip, Dallas to St. Louis, I sit next to a man that seems out of sorts in a way. It is the end of January and even though it is Texas, he has no coat. In fact, he has nothing. No bags, nothing. All he has are the clothes on his back and a single manila envelope that he is clutching tightly the whole ride. We talk about music, and he is impressed with my tastes. He is about twenty years older and thinks it is cool that a young kid like me likes the same stuff he grew up with. I can talk for days about music.

Just before St. Louis, he confesses that he has just gotten out of jail. He dances well around the subject, but I can gather from the little he does share that he killed his neighbor back in high school and has been locked up for the last twenty-five years. The tail end of our time together is... well, interesting. His plan is to get off the bus in St. Louis and reenter the world, live with his cousin for a while, rebuilding his life and never looking back.

The last leg of the trip, St. Louis to Chicago, no one sits next to me, and I have time to listen to music and read, but my head has different plans. I am pretty much spent by now and my mind starts to reflect on how this all started...

Ok, almost two years ago, I was living with my sister Shannon. I was living with her because I couldn't keep my life together and pay my own bills. Things had always been bad in that respect, but at this particular time in my life, it was really bad. I couldn't hold a job for more than a few weeks, and it took me months in between to find another job. I was also drinking a hell of a lot at the time. The fact that I was in a pretty major depression wasn't making things any easier.

Before that, for about four months I'd lived with Brenda, another one of my sisters (I have five sisters). I was accustomed to staying up late and sleeping late. Not because I was lazy, (well, not entirely) but because I worked as a bartender most of the time. I was used to going to work at 3 or 4 p.m., which meant I could sleep till about 2. I usually didn't get done with work until 3 a.m., and it took me a while to wind down after work. So, I didn't go to bed until about 5.

Needless to say, this lifestyle clashed with the 9 to 5 lives of my sister and her family. Because I lived in the basement, I didn't think they heard me watching TV or listening to music. I thought I was quiet. What I didn't realize was that she was a parent, and parents are tuned into the slightest little sound and can sense the slightest movement. Even though they're not my parents, I was in their house, and they knew when I was up.

It's kind of like when you realized that Santa Claus was actually your parents. The whole, 'he knows when you've been sleeping', starts to make more sense when you realize the true power of parenthood. It's kind of scary, but true. Whatever you do, they seem to know.

Not being a parent myself, and the fact that I lived an admittedly selfish lifestyle, I didn't realize how much I was upsetting their routine. Also at this point, I've lived with Brenda three separate times because I'd screwed up my life.

I didn't know then, but later found out that the main reason she's been willing to help me in the first place was because of a promise Brenda had made to our mother before she died. Brenda couldn't stand our father. After finding out that our mother asked him to make sure I was all right after she died, (me being the baby of the family) ... well... my sister was pretty sure that he would not make good on his promise, as it wasn't in his nature. So right after he left, she then made a promise of her own to take care of me. Evidently, the fear that I wouldn't make it was a big reason my mother wouldn't let go. When comforted that I would be taken care of, (I guess) a few days later she did let go.

Anyway, the clash of lifestyles and my ignorant indifference towards my sister's expectations caused her to ask my sister Shannon to take me in. 'Please, get him out of my house' might have been said. I don't know how it went down. They didn't really fill me in. I got the gist of the story, though, from Shannon when she found herself ready to kick me out of her house.

I just couldn't relate to the lifestyle of parents, spouses and the whole family life. Despite not being very good at it, I had been on my own for about four years at that point. While living with them I tried to be considerate, but looking back, I guess I was just being selfish and pretty much oblivious. I took my loving and giving family for granted.

When I was on my own, I was defiant and bound to prove to them all that I didn't need anyone, but my defiance only made me need them more.

Anyway, for the second time in only six months, I got kicked out of another sister's house. I'm not saying that I didn't deserve it, but it was the beginning of a pretty bad year.

While still living with Shannon, I'd got a job a few blocks away. It was good that I was working, but I wasn't really making enough to live on my own.

I started dating a co-worker, Dana Mansfield. This girl was a few years older, but we got along pretty well and had a lot of fun together. The apartment above a friend of hers in Waukegan was vacant, and I was able to take it. It was a nice place: one bedroom and big for $325 a month. I was finally on my own again, and I was sure my sisters were grateful to have me out of their homes.

I took a second job in Gurnee, which soon became my only job. I was making decent money there, and the long commute to Evanston from Waukegan just sucked.

Even though Dana and I no longer worked together, our relationship progressed. We spent every day together. She stayed at my place so often she probably could have just moved in. We even talked about getting married. She was the first one to mention it and often talked of going to Vegas for a quickie private wedding. It really felt like we were meant to be together. Everyday together we seemed to get closer and closer. I knew I had the tendency to fall in love a little too easily, but this really felt like the real thing.

Then suddenly, all hell broke loose. My job started cutting back my hours and dicking me around. I found out that Dana was cheating on me after not seeing her for a little more than two weeks, and finally having to pretty much beg her to tell me the truth.

Despite the fact that us breaking up tore me in two, we decided to attempt to remain friends. I only agreed to this because she was the only person I knew in the area and the only reason I moved out there in the first place.

I went to work, and they threatened to take me off the bar schedule because of some bullshit that they had made up. They said it was something about customer complaints. The truth was they hated the fact that I didn't want to work in the kitchen anymore. Ticket times went way up after I moved to bartending.

They were messing with my livelihood. It pissed me off so much that I couldn't think straight. In the middle of the dinner rush, I went back to the kitchen to check on some food that was taking close to an hour, which would never have happened if I were still working back there. It still wasn't ready, and I had to continue to try and keep these people happy and drunk while explaining how it could possibly take an hour to prepare a burger and a salad.

On my way out of the kitchen, while shaking my head in disbelief, my eyes got stuck on the wall that had our corporate training certificates on it. I was trained in every job in the building and good at them all. Seeing mine up there and realizing that it meant nothing at this point, my frustration got the best of me, and I punched the certificate with everything I had. As my fist hit the glass in the frame, it seemed to happen in slow motion. All of the white noise of the busy restaurant was gone and the only thing I heard was the glass shattering and a deeply echoed thud as my fist went through the certificate to the wall. The certificates were hung at a point in the restaurant that was in plain view of both the kitchen and the whole dining room. The sound was louder than anything, and the entire restaurant seemed suspended in time as everyone's eyes were fixed on me with blank stares.

I showed no emotion and without missing a beat, I went back behind the bar, wrapped my bleeding knuckles in a towel, and continued to make drinks in the service bar using only my left hand, as if nothing happened. I managed to make about fifteen drinks before I was surrounded by the entire management team.

The general manager, also showing no emotion, looked me dead in the eyes and said calmly, "Jeff, I need to see you in the office."

I knew what was next, and as I marched passed her and everyone else, I was taking my uniform shirt off on the way. I had a feeling that I wouldn't need it anymore. After she caught up to me in the office, I held it out to hand it to her and said that I'd turn in the rest of my uniforms when I came back for my last check. She didn't take it and said nothing while she stared at the shirt. Then without looking at me, she simply said, "Go home," but not in an angry tone, more concerned than anything else.

I kept the shirt, fighting the urge to throw it, wrapped my hand with it and headed for home. When I got to the house, I went straight for the bottle of Jack Daniel's that I always had on hand, took a huge swig, then noticed my shirt on the table. It was covered in blood, as were my pants.

The next afternoon, I woke with a hangover and the realization that I moved out here to be with a girl that ended up tearing my heart out. After taking less than a month to become the most valuable employee and going above and beyond my job title every day, they dumped some shit on me that pissed me off enough for me to snap and lose my job altogether. I was out here in the middle of nowhere with no one and no job. I'd be broke in two weeks. I'd be evicted in three.

I couldn't go home; there was no home. To most people, home is either their parents' house or their own. If you lose yours, most can go back to their parents'. My dad had left when I was eight and his house was never home. My mother was dead, and I had just gotten kicked out of two different sisters' houses. There was no 'home'.

Frustrated and needing to talk to someone, I called my now ex-girlfriend, Dana. We had hung out and had talked several times since we'd broken up. So, this wasn't anything unusual. My phone had been cut off because I hadn't paid any bills in about two months. Since my job had started messing with my schedule, I was making less and less money. So, I had to go to the corner and call from a pay phone.

Some guy answered.

It was her new boyfriend who was apparently living with her now. We'd only broken up two weeks before. "Is Dana there?" I asked, calmly and politely.

"Yeah," he says flatly. I still hear his breathing and know he hasn't even turned from the phone.

"Can I talk to her?"

"She's in the shower."

"Ok. Can you have her call Jeff when she gets out?" I asked, trying hard to hold back my disdain for his attitude.

"Sure," he answers, then immediately hangs up.

Realizing that she can't call me, I figure I'd just call back in half an hour. She never took longer than that in the past.

As planned, I went back to the pay phone to call again. He answered this time, too.

"Is Dana there?" I asked again, this time not masking my frustration very well.

"Uhh, she's busy."

"Dude, I really need to talk to her. It's important." This will be the last time I make the effort to be nice.

"Sorry 'bout your luck man, but she's busy." This time he's getting a little too cocky and way past pissing me off.

"Look, man, if you don't make some kind of effort to put her on the phone right fucking now, I'm gonna come over there and stab you in the fuckin' eye!" I couldn't believe I said it, but I meant it.

"Bring it on, asshole." Now he's opened the door.

"Look, man. You don't know me, and you better think twice before you try to get all tough." I offered my only warning.

"I'm scared." His sarcasm was far from subtle.

I had to laugh a bit then replied, "Congratulations, dickhead. You just won a beat-down. I'll be there in ten minutes." Click. I slammed the phone down hard and headed towards my car.

A little less than a block away I saw an empty parking space where my car should have been. I was ten degrees past the boiling point. I headed back to the pay phone and called the cops to report my car stolen. After sitting on hold for what seemed like twenty minutes, the woman on the phone told me that it wasn't stolen, it was repossessed. I wasn't that surprised. Like I said, I hadn't paid any bills in about two months, but I hadn't made a car payment in close to six.

More determined than ever and feeling I had nothing to lose, I called a cab. While waiting for the cab to arrive, I charged back into my place and began to go through all of the knives in the house. I picked out the biggest and sharpest carving knife and tested it on my forearm. As my own blood ran down my arm, I was struck with the thought of prison. A car horn went off out front. My cab was here. If I brought a knife, I was sure to do time, but if I killed him with my own hands...? I was screwed either way, but nevertheless, I left the knives at home.

I had the cab drop me off about a block from Dana's house in Grayslake. I wasn't even thinking of how I'd get home. I marched right up to the door and rang the bell. I heard voices inside, but no one answered. I rang again. I held the button down on the third attempt, ringing constantly for like five minutes. Not hearing it outside, I thought maybe the doorbell was broken. I knocked hard. No response. I wanted them to hear me. I backed away from the door to the middle of the yard and started yelling, "KENT! GET YOUR ASS OUT HERE! YOU CALLED ME OUT. YOU SAID BRING IT. NOW ANSWER THE CALL." No response, but I no longer heard anything going on inside. After a few minutes, I screamed again, "KENT!" Dana mentioned his name once while we were hanging out as friends.

The door opened.

It's some other dude. "Calm down and shut the fuck up. You're pissing everyone off. Just leave."

A little calmer, but with a look of cold steel on my face, I said, "He called me out. He needs to face me, and I'm not leaving until he does."

"Look, man, there's about eight guys here. He's not coming out, but we will happily beat the crap out of you if you want." He was smaller and probably bluffing, but I did hear a lot of voices inside.

"He needs to face me." Calmly at first, I leaned my head back and shouted, "KENT!" I can get pretty scary when I'm pissed, but truth be told, I've never been in a fight in my life. I was only 5'7" and around 125 pounds, out of shape, and a chain smoker. Kent was a tattooed punk from the east coast, 5'10", worked out, and was four years younger. Without this level of anger, he probably would have killed me, but I wasn't backing down.

"Jeff, if you don't leave right now, we are going to call the cops," Maria, Dana's roommate, called out from a window on the second floor. I hadn't even seen Dana or Kent this whole time.

"Call the cops. He called me out. I'm not leaving till he faces me." I'd even convinced myself that I'd lost my mind.

At this point I was leaning against a car in the driveway, smoking a cigarette and waiting for him to come out. I heard cars coming down the street behind me. I turned and saw twelve, I kid you not, twelve squad cars with around 20 cops. I was still leaning against the car and taking another drag from my cigarette when four cops surrounded me.

Possibly because they noticed that I was perfectly calm and not really an immediate threat, five of the squad cars left, but only five. Two cops went up to the door. The door opened, but I didn't see who opened it. The cops went in, and the door closed behind them.

One more cop came up directly in front of me. Looking me in the eye, he said, "Wha'ch'ya doin' here, boss?"

"Nothing." Still, just leaning and smoking calmly.

"You're aggravating these folks, and they want you to leave," he said sternly, but in his 'good cop' voice.

"This guy called me out. He said, 'bring it on'. So, I'm here and I'm not leaving till he faces me." I told him in an even tone as if I really expected him to just say, 'Ok... carry on.'

"What happened to your arm and hand?" he said instead.

I had forgotten about that. My hand was still cut up and covered in dried blood from when I hit the wall, and my arm was cut from when I tested the knife. "That was an accident that happened yesterday," I explained, simply, hoping it would suffice.

"Put your cigarette out."

"I'm almost done." I was pushing my luck.

"My partner is going to put your cuffs on now, and I don't want you to burn him." The cop was still calm and giving me plenty of chances to cooperate.

"Are you arresting me?" I asked arrogantly. Cops love that... right.

He Mirandized me as another cop grabbed my wrist and shook the cigarette out of my hand, then cuffed me. They put me in the back of the squad car. A few minutes later, the cops inside came out and all the squads left. They took me to the station, all along never saying anything. They put me in a room, un-cuffed me, took my fingerprints, and then asked me to sit on a bench. I sat there for about fifteen minutes, and no one said anything. Only one guy was left in the room with me. It wasn't a cell, just an empty room. It was all gray cinder-block walls. There was the bench I was sitting on, a desk with only a few papers on it, and nothing else. Then, there was this guy sitting behind the desk, his back to me, writing.

"So, what's the deal here? Do I pay a fine or something?" They never said what the charge was. Hell, they never said anything.

"You could face up to ninety days in jail or a $10,000 fine, but for right now we're just holding you 'till you calm down."

"I'm calm. Can I go home now?" I asked in my most serene voice.

"What happened to your arm and hand?"

"Yesterday, I got mad at work and hit a wall," I confessed calmly.

"Where do you work?"

"The Cork and Tap, up by the mall," I told him honestly.

He didn't respond. He sat there, filling out his paperwork.

Fifteen minutes later, another cop came back into the room with some papers. "Come here and sign this," he told me. Then asked, "Where do you live?"

"Waukegan."

"How did you get out here?"

"You drove me." Seeing that he's not amused, I answered quickly, "I took a cab."

I signed the paperwork, they gave me the instructions to arrive in court in a week, then they set me up with a phone, and I called a cab. I smoked half a pack in the forty-five minutes it took for the cab to arrive. They weren't in a hurry to pick up someone from the police station.

When I got home, there was still the bottle of Jack, and all of my knives were still laid out on the table. My choices seemed very clear. I couldn't go to jail. I couldn't stay here. I'd nowhere to go and nothing to do and no reason to do it. I took a big swig of the Jack, all along staring at the knives. I picked up my favorite knife and the bottle and headed for bed.

I sat there for hours. No music, no TV, no talking to myself, no sounds or motion at all. Just staring blankly straight ahead, clutching the bottle in one hand and the knife in the other. At this point, I believed if I got drunk enough, then killing myself would be easier.

At about three in the morning, I kind of shook my head clear and got up. I set down the bottle and knife and put my shoes on. The plan wasn't very clear to me, but nevertheless I headed out the door and down the street. I ended up back at the pay phone. I picked up the phone and dialed 911. I told them I thought I might kill myself. Then they put me on hold, no joke! They put me on hold. 'Fuck it then,' I thought to myself, hung up and headed back home.

I sat back down on the bed and tried to drink myself to sleep. I couldn't fall asleep. I couldn't get drunk. I couldn't pass out. I just laid there numb and staring at the ceiling.

I just started to doze off when the doorbell rang. It was almost four in the morning, and I couldn't think of who it might be, so I ignored it. Then there was a knock on the back door, and a voice called out, "Jeff? This is the police. Let us in." I still just laid there. Then I heard the doorbell downstairs, again. They were going to wake up my neighbor, Dana's friend, that had gotten me the apartment. They were waking her up. Then, there was knocking on the front door and at the back door. "Jeff? We just want to make sure you're OK," another police officer at the front door called out.

For some reason, I thought they might just go away. However, the fact that they were at both doors worried me a lot. They must have woken my neighbor, and she let them up the stairs. My doors were locked, but did that matter?

My bed was actually an air mattress on top of a very thin futon cushion, and I was still gripping the knife in one of my hands. If they were to burst in, I could have just jammed the knife into the mattress. They would think it was a gun, then come around the corner and fill me full of lead... saving me the effort. It got really quiet for a while. There were no voices, no footsteps and no more knocking. Maybe they would go away.

Just as I started to think it might all be over; I heard the front door open. I turned the knife towards the bed. They were only a few feet away, just around the corner. They were talking as sweetly as they could, and I sensed they were starting to come around the corner. Then, I noticed them out of the corner of my eye. They were coming, guns drawn. "Put the knife down, Jeff." They knew it was a knife, so my plan was blown. I loosened my grip, and the knife fell from my hand onto the floor. I started bawling uncontrollably, and the next thing I knew, I was waking up in a hospital.

I think the police coming had something to do with the Kent and Dana thing. When I called 911, I don't remember giving an address and I called from a pay phone. How did they find me? The 911 operator must have sent them somehow. When I woke up, I had bandages on my hand and forearms, both forearms. Although I don't remember doing it, I apparently put quite a few cuts up and down each arm.

Anyway, although it's way too late to make a long story short, I'll at least save you most of the details of the hospital. At one point towards the end of my stay, I had to call my landlord, who might have been evicting me at that moment. Surprisingly he was very understanding. He said he was the one that let the cops in and was there that night. So, he was sympathetic. I asked him if he could go up to my place and get rid of the bottle of Jack I had. The nurses behind the counter all smiled as if they convinced me to do it. He agreed and gave me time to move out.

I made arrangements to move my stuff into Nate and Pritina's apartment in Chicago. The day after my arraignment, I moved in with them. The judge set a court date in three months. At the time, no one said anything about not leaving town, and I wanted to get as far from Waukegan as possible. Not to mention Nate and Pritina's place was just too small for three. My brother was already living in Texas, and he was the last person that was still willing to take me in. I rode back with my brother just after Christmas. Texas was pretty damn far away, so to me it was perfect.

Three months later, when I came back for the trial, things were very different. Despite extreme efforts to change my mind on everyone's part, I defended myself. The charges were actually disturbing the peace and disorderly conduct. Notwithstanding the damning evidence against me (the worst being Kent's testimony describing how I threatened to stab him in the eye) and six witnesses for the prosecution, when my turn came, I spoke very calmly and explained my side of the story.

I explained all of the circumstances that led up to my snapping: the job, Dana, my family, my living arrangements, and my car. Then I presented evidence of my subsequent hospitalization, the anti-depressants I'd been taking ever since, my apartment and job in

Texas, my sponsor's name and proof of my attendance of twelve step meetings, as well as the therapist I'd been seeing in Texas. I put most of this together on my own. It was ample evidence that I was sick and was now getting help and doing a whole lot better. Plus, my thorough explanation of how I don't care to ever have any contact with the plaintiff and her friends ever again, compounded with the fact that I lived about fifteen hundred miles away now, all seemed to help.

I was found guilty, but the evidence of my recovery efforts plus the fact that it was my first offense convinced the judge to give me a pretty mild probation. He later contacted my psychiatrist in Texas to oversee my therapy and to make sure I continued with my medication as well as continued to attend meetings. She would report back directly to him. (Dr. Beamen took over after I started the Regional Manager job.) I could not go anywhere near Grayslake or Waukegan. I would also be randomly drug tested and had to stay out of trouble for a year.

Grayslake and Waukegan were still far enough from Chicago, and the year had passed with no real incident. Returning to Chicago was no longer an issue.

After going over all of it again in my head, I found myself still on the bus and was starting to enjoy the calm. Then at one of the stops between St. Louis and Chicago, these teenagers got on and sat at the back of the bus just across from the bathroom. Evidently, they thought that a cross-country bus trip was a good time to take acid for the first time. They were loud and obnoxious, and it didn't take long before each of them was taking turns throwing up in the bathroom. The smell was ungodly.

I thought about the distinct differences in the characters along the ride. It made it seem as if I were actually going back in time. Watching a man grow down from the elderly man at peace with life, the middle-aged man starting life anew, and then the kids playing with life. I couldn't have paid for a better lesson, but I swear I'll never travel on a bus again.

When I got off the bus in Chicago, Nate wasn't there yet; he's rarely on time. It was freezing cold, and I was completely exhausted. I thought of the movie, 'Back to the Future', and how whenever the car finished a trip in time, it was covered in frost; Marty couldn't get it started and no one was around... Yea, I need some sleep.

Chapter Three: Caffeinated

I sleep hard on the couch as soon as Nate and I get back to his place. Later, I would set up my futon mattress on the floor in the corner and put some of my things out in the living room. After the move from Waukegan, I had a lot of my stuff stored here that I didn't take to Austin. Nate has his room, and I take the living room. It would be basically the same set up my brother and I had in Texas. Even though the futon mattress was pretty thin, it was still better than the couch. I'd slept on plenty of couches, but the futon is more like a real bed. I was going to be here for a while.

When I wake up, it's time to start looking for work. Nate drives me all around the city to some places that were hiring, and I drop off applications and resumes. My resume is reasonably strong, and I interview well. At my first interview at a restaurant in '91, the guy asked me, "Why do you want to do this for a living?" I don't remember how I answered, I didn't know then. Today, I love the rush of the busy times and the camaraderie with the rest of the staff. Today, I don't know how to do anything else, and I'm good at this.

Nate had been looking for work for months. On my third day in town, I find a job. I feel a little guilty but only a little. I'm ready to dive right in and start making things better. And that is exactly what I do.

The job is waiting tables at a fine-dining restaurant in The Loop. I can't count on Nate for a ride to and from work all the time, so I have to learn the bus system. They had buses in Texas, but they didn't run very frequently or cover that much of the city. Chicago has one of the best public transportation systems in the country. From the South

Side, I would have to take either a Metra train that didn't run very frequently, three buses that took two hours or one bus and the Red Line on which I never felt completely safe. The actual time difference between the three options isn't that different. The three buses are the most effective, but it means getting up really early to make it to work with the two-hour commute. I also have to stand most of the time because the bus is always packed. After several weeks, I notice by looking over people's shoulders that most people were reading books either about faith or losing weight. Are these the two biggest concerns in life?

Two hours standing on the bus or not, I do what I have to do.

Luckily, work has a cappuccino machine, and even though I'm exhausted after the commute, a few double or even triple espressos get me moving.

I hadn't done any real fine-dining service, and I'm not very good at it. During dinner service, there were maitre'd's, sommeliers, front waiters, back waiters and bussers. I don't really know which is which, but we work as a team. During lunch, I'm just a waiter.

Not being the best at a job is new to me. In the past, I could usually work my way into the mix and found my way to the top in a hurry. I had gotten used to trying to be and eventually become the best. Other employees would come to me with questions and looked to me for leadership. The management was always giving me projects and adding responsibilities. I liked it. I liked it a lot.

This place makes me feel like I've just started in the business instead of having almost eight years of experience. I feel like an idiot kid. I'm given mostly lunch shifts. The dinner shifts are reserved for those servers that have more fine dining experience and could sell wines. Most places I'd worked in the past only had about a half a dozen wines, and they were all basic and simple. This place has over two hundred different kinds, and it required a hell of a lot of wine knowledge. They have daily tastings and classes, but as an alcoholic, I don't do any tasting and am left to the notes of others. I either have to study or settle for lunch shifts. I settle.

Being downtown and in the heart of the loop, lunch shifts are pretty busy and profitable. Most people have to go back to work, so they don't drink much wine. However, there are still plenty of folks that don't have any problems with a seven-martini lunch.

Lunch guests are in a hurry, and the turnover is quick. We have live jazz during dinner and people would hang out for the show. You might have the same three tables for the entire four-hour dinner shift, but you'd make about a hundred dollars a table. Whereas at lunch, you would make anywhere from five to fifty bucks per table, and I could serve around twenty tables. I don't mind working lunches at all. I'm clearing four to six hundred a week, which isn't bad considering the fact that I'm not the best at the job and don't get that many shifts.

Some of the managers felt my service style was much too relaxed for their taste, but none of my guests ever complained. I waited on the mayor's wife, and she seemed to love me. I also waited on James Ward, one of the city's biggest food critics, twice. He was a nice guy and seemed to enjoy the fact that I didn't appear intimidated by him. Most people treated him with kid gloves and were hyper-concerned with doing everything just perfectly. I just didn't know any better. I never really served a celebrity or public figure before, but quickly came to realize that this would be the biggest difference between working in Chicago and working anywhere else.

Up until now, most of the people I'd served were just your average ordinary Joes. In Chicago, your odds of serving a celebrity or a millionaire were pretty good, no matter where you worked. It didn't have to be a high-end place. John Cusack was often seen in this dive bar on Damen. The place reeked of stale beer and smoke. It was the last place you would expect to see anyone that made more than forty thousand a year. High end, fine-dining, jazz clubs in The Loop expected celebrities and got them. I was never one to gush. I just thought it was cool to see that these people actually existed in real life.

I work a pretty steady schedule, and the cash flow is good, and I'm able to help Nate get caught up on bills. He still hasn't found work. Despite making plenty of money, I'm still a little nervous about losing this job. I'm not a fine dining kind of guy. So, I'm still sending out resumes and looking for something else. Meanwhile, the job continues to more than pay the bills.

Feeling pretty proud of myself, I invite my dad to join me for dinner at the restaurant. I thought it would be a pretty good opportunity to act like a big shot. Considering the fact that I was almost always broke and kind of a loser, whenever I was doing well, I tried to do something to prove myself to my family.

He comes to the city with his wife, two of his business partners, and their wives. I am dressed to the nines and ready to make a good impression. Our server is a friend of mine and treats us like kings. My plan is going off without a hitch. They are impressed.

Then, as everyone is finishing their meals, the music starts. Not having worked too many dinner shifts, I'm not very familiar with how it works. Apparently, you are supposed to stay quiet and not move around while the band plays. Maybe my dad and his friends didn't get out much or, like me, are just not used to jazz clubs, but they don't exactly go along with this. The whole table is getting frustrated with the fact that drink service has slowed down during the music. I guess the servers are expected to stay quiet and still during the performance as well.

The maitre'd comes over to my dad to ask everyone to quiet down... three times. We decide to move into the lounge, away from the stage. Even in the backroom, we are still apparently making too much noise and are asked to leave. So much for trying to make a good impression, but at least it seems that everyone has had a good time.

I don't really care that we didn't fit in with the pretentious upper crust. All the more reason I don't mind working lunches, but my concerns about losing my job got a little more serious.

Jerry's is a new blues club that's opening in River North, and I just got hired as part of their opening team. To get to this new place, I'm told to take the number 66 bus after getting off the Red Line. I'm taken aback when the bus announces its route, "Chicago to Austin". Austin is a street at the edge of the city, but to me, it's like something calling me back to Texas. I have no idea why. I'm really enjoying Chicago. I am excited that this is a brand-new place. I've done a lot of openings, and I love them because everyone starts at the same level and jumping ahead of everyone is somehow easier.

I work out my two weeks' notice and manage to juggle the two jobs until my notice is up. I would normally just stop showing up or just walk away. I'd been in this business long enough to know when I was about to be fired, and I rarely gave them the satisfaction. Plus, I kind of enjoyed the drama of just disappearing.

Jerry's is huge. It is two stories and seats about 500 people. It's by far the biggest place I've ever worked. It's kind of like a Hard Rock Café for the blues, complete with all the memorabilia on the walls. It also features a full menu of interesting barbecue items. The blues and barbecue are not exactly a new thing for Chicago. In fact, one of the city's best blues clubs is right across the street. That club only seats about 150 people and doesn't serve food. Despite a lot of direct competition, this company is confident, and they pour millions into making it work.

We have three weeks of training before we open, and they throw this party for the staff a week before opening. We have a chance to taste all of the food that will be on the menu. Now, I'd had real South Side Chicago barbecue before and am skeptical that this big place will not measure up, but it does. The food is fantastic. It's always easier to sell a product that you actually believe in. I also happen to love the blues and even bought this book that listed a bunch of the greats. I would later collect autographs from each of the performers right next to their segment in the book. Almost everyone that played there was in the book.

They have a band for this party, too. It's ridiculously loud. Eating in a nightclub was never something I would do. The deafening music is not exactly conducive to an enjoyable meal. However, it ends up being a blast, and here no one has to stay quite or worry about disrupting the band.

Despite my concerns about the concept working in the long run, I am loving this place more and more. I'm also able to forge several quality friendships with my coworkers.

The first guy I get to know is Jerry Clayton, and no, it's not his place; just the same name. He acts sometimes like it's his place, and some people would go along with it just for laughs. He's only about 5'3", with long dreadlocks and some crazy ideas. Some people call him Rasta-Smurf. We sit together at the party, and he has a lot to say. I can't hear half of it, but I smile along.

Then there's Raymond Evans, or Ray, a slightly intimidating black guy at almost seven feet tall and ultra-confident. His confidence occasionally comes across as arrogance, but overall, it works for him. He is brilliant, a real intellectual, and that serves him well as a bartender - being able to talk about anything with anyone.

Victor Palma, a proud mix of Italian and Latino from the West Side, is one of the funniest guys I've ever met. He's probably not someone you would want to mess with, but you can tell that he would be a shirt-off-his-back kind of friend.

Kimberly Culver is one of the corporate trainers from Michigan and just kind of crazy cute. She's about 5'5", with medium length dark hair, a button nose, and a beautiful smile.

Rebecca Simpson is also one of the corporate trainers from Michigan. She's tall, skinny, long dark hair, with a face that fakes innocence.

Stacy Lavergne. What can you say about Stacy? I'd not met many guys named Stacy, and I'm still not sure that I have. He is about 6'5" and only about a buck ten, flamingly gay, loud, and outspoken. He takes five minutes to say hello. It's more like HEEEELLOOOOO. He's quite the stereotypical homosexual but loves it. His flamboyance makes him free and open, and highly entertaining as a bartender.

Then there's Billy Kilpatrick, a straight guy in his mid-twenties that insists on being called Billy and not Bill. He's strange but funny and kind of cool... at times.

Billy and Victor were friends before working here. Other than the fact that they had worked together at other places before, their friendship always seemed odd to me. Billy is from Bridgeport, a predominately white, kind of conservative neighborhood on the

South Side. He's careful about how he shows it and who he shows it to, but he's a bit of a racist. Nevertheless, most of the time he's a pretty good guy; otherwise, we wouldn't be friends.

Victor is totally different.

Victor is from the West Side and a former gang banger. He's tough, but very serious about putting that life behind him. He lives in Logan Square and takes care of his mother and sister. He's really open-minded and just a plain riot to be around.

They just don't seem to fit as friends. Billy, the poser wannabe, and Victor, the hard as nails real deal. The only thing that made sense to me was that Billy was kind of a sidekick to Victor. Billy would unknowingly set up a joke by saying something stupid, and Victor would hammer it home with the punchline, a kind of Martin and Lewis team. The only thing is Billy's never funny on his own.

West Side, South Side, North Side, Lincoln Park, Bridgeport, Bucktown, Logan Square, Wicker Park... the list goes on. It all means something that I haven't quite figured out yet, but I understand it means something. Chicago is very diverse but divided in many ways. Your neighborhood says a lot about who you are... most of the time.

We have a blast at work, but I'm starting to catch hell for not hanging out with them after work. Nate and I live on the South Side, and it takes a while to get home. Buses stop running after certain hours, and I can't imagine how much a cab would be. I'm also still going to meetings and don't feel very comfortable hanging out at bars. At this point, considering the speed thing a relapse and starting over, I have about four months sober.

It's getting to the point that everyone else's friendships are growing at the bar after work, and I'm getting pushed out of the mix. So that night, instead of heading straight to the train after clocking out, I go across the street.

The sign out front just says, "The House". It's a small bar; at best, maybe 100 people could be crammed in there. There's no pool table, no dart board, no dance floor, no DJ... just booze and lots of it. It's no dive-bar... the staff is wearing ties and it's clean. There's a tall guy with a ponytail at the door. He's flirting with a few girls that are hanging out front and doesn't bother to card me. I'm twenty-five, but I look like I'm seventeen... I get carded all the time.

I'm barely in the door when I see half our staff gathered in the front section. I head up to the bar and order a Coke. Non-alcoholic drinks are sometimes just as much as real drinks, but they seem to notice that I'm with the work crew, and they don't charge me anything. I leave a five to show my appreciation. Five dollars per Coke adds up. Then, Victor notices me and calls me over.

"You finally made it over. I know it's kind of out of the way being across the street and all, but it's open till four, and the staff is cool. Whachya drinkin'?" he asks with that giant grin he always has.

"It's a Coke." I answer, with nothing to hide. Then I add, "I don't drink."

"That's cool. Come on over." Most people gave me a hard time about not drinking or at least asked why. He does neither.

At the table, there are actually people from several different restaurants, not just ours. Joe Harms, the manager, is even hanging out with us. It's usually taboo for management to hang out with staff. Jerry's drinking some cheap beer and smoking other people's cigarettes. Raymond is sipping some high-end scotch and is surrounded by three or four girls at all times. Victor is drinking Long Islands and standing the whole time: so, he could act out his stories.

Rebecca, Kimberly, and Stacy are drinking martinis in what Stacy refers to as 'the Big Girl Glass', a ten-ounce martini glass. Billy has some dark draft beer and is feeding Victor straight lines. Billy is the only one that is visibly drunk already.

The conversation doesn't slow down much when I arrive, so I'm quickly included in the mix. Somebody's always telling some story that we can all relate to, because we all work in the business. There'd be some twist to it that most of us didn't see coming, and we'd laugh like mad. People would stand up at the table to illustrate part of a story. Someone would knock over a glass or a bottle and it would spill or break on the floor. There's never a lapse in the conversation, and we don't go more than five minutes without cracking up. I never notice the server, but the drinks never stop coming. Even my Coke stays full.

The lights go up, and it's a quarter to four in the morning. I can't believe I stayed so late, but the conversation never let up enough to make an exit. The buses aren't running anymore, and after drinking about twenty Cokes, I'm wide awake. Everyone else is wasted and starting to make their ways home. I have to be back at work at eleven, and it takes me two hours to get home. Maybe I'll get tired and be able to get to sleep when I get home instead of having to stay up all night to make sure I don't run late the next day.

Walking to the train, I notice a sign in the window of a high rise only three blocks from the bar. They are renting rooms for four and a quarter. I can't help but think of the convenience, but I also can't help thinking of Nate. When I get home, the cat has pissed on my bed again.

After a few months, things are going along fine. Nate's found work at another hotel and is pulling his own weight, not that it ever bothered me that he wasn't before. Despite paying for most everything, it's still his place and I still feel like a guest. Now, I know he would do the same for me, so like I say, it never bothered me.

We never argued in all the time we'd known each other and that didn't change while living together. I did have to say something after a while about the TV. I could only stand so much wrestling, and I was never entertained by watching someone play video games. I never played video games. I didn't understand the fascination especially amongst adults. Most TV shows we both liked, and after agreeing on a limit to the wrestling and video games, while I was around, we got along perfectly.

I'm getting used to the buses and trains, and work is awesome. At this place, I could be the best again. I am picked pretty early to head up the training staff after the corporate trainers leave. They stayed for three weeks after we opened, and then went back to their respective locations. All new hires will be trained by me and my team. I love the responsibility and added work. To me, it's a tangible reward for doing my job well.

I would miss Kimberly, Rebecca, and the rest of the corporate training staff. Everything I knew about this place and almost everything that made me good at this job I learned from them. We all had tons of fun working together and hanging out at The House, and like I said before, Kimberly was crazy cute.

As it turns out though, I don't miss Kimberly and Rebecca for long. They both move to Chicago permanently a few months later and became a regular part of the staff. They must really like it here. The eight of us - Jerry, Raymond, Victor, Stacy, Billy, Kimberly, Rebecca and myself - become fast friends and hang out all the time. Working with these guys makes the job easier. They all know their jobs and do their work, and it's all like second nature to us, which allows us time to goof around and have fun. After work, it's the bar or hanging out at someone's place.

We never hang out at Nate's and my place, which is fine because it's kind of a mess and all the way on the South Side. Plus, Nate's schedule is different, and he rarely gets the chance to hang out with the rest of us.

Life is pretty nice for about six months which was my usual cut off point for any job. The after-hours hanging out catches up with me, and I start oversleeping and coming in late. Andre, Nate's brother, moves in with us and brings his girlfriend. This place was too small for two people, and it's definitely too small for four. Andre doesn't abide by the wrestling and video game rules, and it's hard to get a decent night's sleep with him and his girlfriend up all night in the living room. Nate and I both work a lot and are hardly around, so it's not that much of a big deal, but after a while, I notice that money is coming up missing.

I have to move out.

Nate's working and doing OK, Andre and his girlfriend could contribute, and Nate would be fine. I tell him about the money and mostly explain that I need to be closer to work. He has a car and gets around without any trouble, but for me, it's a little more of a hassle. It's not personal, but that doesn't stop him from being hurt.

Nate reluctantly helps me move my stuff into the high rise that advertised rooms for four and a quarter. It's a small room with a bed, a dresser, a mini-fridge, and a microwave, like you would find in a dorm. The apartment doesn't fit much, so I leave a lot of stuff at Nate's. It's not great, but I can walk to work and stop running late. No buses and no worries about the late-night train rides. It makes sense, and it quickly makes a difference in holding my job. I stop being late and get more sleep... at least for a little while.

The nights get later and later until the days begin to bleed together. I go days without sleep, and when I do get to sleep, I almost always oversleep. People at work always say, 'How can you be late? You live three blocks away.'

We would hang out at the bar until four AM, then go to a coffee shop for breakfast, then to someone's place to hang out some more, then it was off to work again. I can't understand how the rest of them managed it, but I can't keep up, and I'm the sober one.

We go out to Raymond's place one night after the bar closes. His apartment is huge, and he has this couch that takes up more than half the front room. It's a semicircular couch with giant ottomans that fill in the circle, making a half-moon. It sleeps four comfortably and five of us sleep there ... uncomfortably. Everyone else is on the floor. After only a few minutes of trying to sleep, I give up, and Raymond and I stay up talking. We smoke everyone's cigarettes after we run out of our own and just talk. I tell him all about the Dana thing, my upbringing, my family and my mom, and he tells me about his upbringing and some of his exploits. His exploits are pretty hard to believe, but the way he tells it, it's perfectly true in every way; I'm sure of it. He's somehow wealthy, and his apartment, clothes, and lifestyle show it. He talks about several investments and business ventures he's involved in, but I can't help wondering how he finds the time for anything else. We hung out all the time for months, but never really knew each other that well, just that we had the business in common. Raymond and I are on a different page after that night. We actually know each other.

Victor wakes up to find his smokes gone, so we go to the store, then off to work again. I was never late when I stayed up all night.

One day after being out all night, we go by work to check the schedule. Joe is breaking open this huge plastic tub. There's a pig suit inside that was dressed like a chef. It's for some upcoming parade that the company is going to put some of us in. I'm jacked up on mochaccinos and volunteer to put the suit on and dance in the street to drum up business. Mostly, I just feel like acting the fool and burning off some useless energy. Other than the people that saw me put the suit on, no one knows it's me. I'm jumping around and making everyone laugh, but I assume that most people are wondering just how drunk I am.

There's another night when it's just Raymond, Victor, Kimberly, Rebecca, and myself. We hang out at Kim's and Rebecca's place and have a barbecue. The smaller group does more talking about real stuff, real life, and gets closer. I feel like I actually know these guys. It also becomes apparent that Raymond and Rebecca are hooking up. Over the last few months, we'd all found out that Raymond was a bit of a player, and a real relationship with him seems impossible. Rebecca must not have been convinced.

Nate and I haven't hung out in weeks.

The barbecue turns out to be the beginning of a four-day run of parties, work, the bar, the coffee shop, and no sleep. At one point, we sneak a bottle of rum into the movies. None of us have heard anything about this movie and don't really care. Everybody is comfortably drunk, and I am, as usual, lit up on caffeine. The movie is 'American Pie', and I didn't think anyone was even paying attention to the movie until the one character says she stuck a flute in her pussy, then we all laughed so loud I thought we would get kicked out. Most of the time, all we did was laugh, so I don't really know if the movie was that great or not. It's towards the end of the four-day run, and I seem to be floating through it all. No rational thought is possible at this point.

When I finally get home, I crash out for about eighteen hours, sleeping through an entire shift. It's the third time I've done that, and I know I'm fired. I don't leave the house or answer the phone for about three days. Then one morning, I just go to the restaurant, turn in my uniforms, and collect my last check. I go home and isolate myself for about four more days.

Now after a week of not going to the bar or hanging out with anyone, I show up at the bar one night around two AM. Everyone's there and wondering what has happened. It's simple: I'd missed too many shifts. Victor says to me, "Don't sweat it. You'll find something else. We all pretty much fell out after those four days. It was crazy. I think Joe would have understood, and I'm not sure you would have been fired, but after not coming in for three days, what choice did they have?"

"I know. I was just cashed."

"Are you hangin' tonight?"

"Yep. Up for anything. Don't have to worry about work for now."

Raymond and Rebecca are off to the side, but the rest of us sit around and are back at it without missing a beat. I'm comforted that no matter where life takes me, these guys would always be my friends.

After the bar closes, some of us go to the beach. I'm not really sure who all goes with; I'm focused mostly on Kim. At the bar we started talking, just the two of us, and we keep on talking as we leave. She tells me that she's been working for the company for four years, and the training team has taken her all over the country. The Chicago opening was the most fun she had had, and Rebecca felt the same.

So, they decided they would get off the training team for a while and just stay in one place. I'm glad they chose Chicago.

I don't know how we got on the subject, but I find myself telling her about my mom. I usually have to be pretty comfortable with someone before saying much about my family, but to talk about my mom, I had to be very comfortable. I must have rambled for hours, but she's listening contentedly and seems quite interested in the story, so I keep going.

I tell her all about how I was a bit of a sickly kid and was in and out of the hospital for asthma problems and a few surgeries on my ears, but at some point, my mom started ending up in the hospital even more than me. I grew up in and out of the hospital, so anyone being in the hospital never seemed like that big of a deal to me.

I was about eleven when my mom was in the hospital yet again. My aunt and uncle were taking care of us kids; nothing new there. At dinner my uncle started to tell us that our mom had actually died for six minutes, and she wasn't doing too well now. All I heard was that she had died, and I lost it. I locked myself in the bathroom and was crying like crazy, so much that I eventually passed out on the floor. When I came to, I just went to bed.

A week later, mom was home.

She took me aside and told me that there was a reason that she didn't die, that her job wasn't done yet. She had raised six of her seven children, but I still needed her around. I wasn't grown up yet. Her job wasn't done.

So, I decided never to grow up. I would spend the next few years destroying myself with alcohol, drugs, cigarettes, and dangerous behavior. I was determined to show her that I wasn't growing up and that I would always need her around. If that didn't work, at least I would die before she did. It kind of worked. I stayed a mess, and she stayed reasonably healthy. That is until I graduated high school.

After high school, I was supposed to be a grown up and less dependent on her, but I drank my way out of college and had to move back home. When I came home after quitting school, she was in the hospital again. When she got out, she told me that she wasn't upset that I quit school, but I would have to get a job.

I'd worked summers with my dad's construction crew for the last five years, but I didn't really want to do that for a living. My sister got me a job at the restaurant where she was working. I ended up loving the job and I was good at it. That's where I met Nate and four other great friends. After about six months, I was doing pretty well and decided to look for a place of my own.

I moved out the day before Easter at the age of nineteen. I was on my own and taking care of myself. Three months later, it was like a self-fulfilling prophecy. My mother died. I was grown up and her job was done, so she died. At least, that's the way it appeared to me. The same eleven-year-old logic.

Three years later, I would find myself in a hospital after a suicide attempt. This time I wasn't really sure what had led to it, but it was the first time I was introduced to the psych ward. I was there for two weeks. They felt my drinking and drug use was the main cause of my depression and suggested that maybe now that my mother was gone there was no sense in trying to take myself out. They sent me to a rehab for another two weeks, and I was introduced to AA and NA. I'd been on and off for years now, but now at this point, I had a little over nine months clean and sober.

The true story of why I don't drink is a long one. The short one is that I already had had my share, which is true.

I shake my head clear and notice that Kim is still listening intently, now with a look of concern, but I don't think I'm boring her. I feel like I've maybe opened up too much and would maybe scare her away, but it only seems to draw us closer.

She kisses me, and we hold each other for what seems like ten minutes or at least until the rest of the crew decides to leave the beach.

A few days later, I start working at this bar up by Division. It's still walking distance from where I live, and the timing couldn't be better. Money is fast running out. I split my time between working the door and occasionally working the bar. The bar is better money, but I'm the new guy and have to do the door shifts on the weekends, the busiest times.

One weekend, this girl I'm carding asks, "Is your name Jeff? Jeff Echterling?"

Now, some of my close friends don't know my last name. So, I'm thrown by who she could be. It turns out she knew me from high school. I haven't seen or heard from anyone from high school pretty much since graduation. I'm mostly surprised that I apparently still look similar, eight years later. I don't recognize her at all, but high school was pretty much a blur, and I was busy destroying myself. We don't say much; she just seems to want to point out that she knew me, and I don't have time to talk because the line is about thirty deep.

My head is down looking at IDs for hours, but at one point, I hear a bunch of people yelling out, "Lieutenant Dan! Lieutenant Dan!" as Gary Sinise walks by. It's pretty cool. 'Forrest Gump' was one of my favorite movies, and I guess he's a Chicago guy. Now being a Chicago guy and running into old friends and celebrities in the same night is just more reason to love this city. I'm so glad I moved back here.

The bar is a karaoke bar. People seem to get pretty serious about their karaoke, and some people are actually pretty good. I can't stand karaoke, but it doesn't take long before it's just background noise and I don't even notice it anymore. The place is a shit hole, but it's always packed. Division draws a lot of people. It's the hot spot for college kids, but I never really understood why. Most of the bars are shit holes, but regardless, they stay packed. This is great for making good money, and the few regulars that we have are cool, which makes it easier to tolerate the college kids.

This guy in his sixties works the day shifts and plays classic jazz on a radio that he brought in himself. He plays old tapes of sessions that I guess he was a part of back in the day. Very cool. Whenever I have the chance, I love talking to the guy and hearing his stories about Louis Armstrong and Charlie Parker.

At night, there's this bartender that I call Kahlua Carlos. If he didn't know how to make a certain drink, he would just put Kahlua and something else in it and that was that. Kahlua goes into a lot of drinks but has no business in a lemon drop. This place has its characters.

We watch baseball every afternoon and then around nine or ten, the music, if you could call it that, starts. We'd close at two AM, and it took about an hour to clean up and cash out. I'd barely make it over to The House in time for last call, but always did to see the crew.

I had only been in the city now for around nine months, but I'm on my third job and my second address. That's just how it goes sometimes. This time, I'm not out of work long and things get back to normal pretty quickly. Normal is, however, a relative term.

Chapter Four: Baseball, Beers & Bullshit

"So, what's up with you and Kim?"

"Yeah, that Dana girl was like two years ago, and you haven't been laid since."

"Two years! You gotta hit that."

Victor and Raymond are running me over the coals at The House tonight. They are relentless. I have to say something, I guess. "We're just not there yet."

Raymond cuts me off, "It's been almost a year for her, too, and there's just no sense in putting it off."

Victor jumps in with a different approach, "We're gonna set this up, and if it ain't you, it'll be one of us. Let's draw straws right now."

"Wait a minute. You're still with Rebecca and you're... well you're just not gonna walk in and take her like that," I say, while drawing my straw after Raymond. Victor got last pick. I got the short one, but I don't know what that really means yet.

"You're it. Let's go talk to her."

"What are we gonna say? We drew straws, and now you have to have sex with me?"

We've been at the bar for an hour now, and they haven't talked about anything else. They walk over to Rebecca and Kim as I pay the bill... another part of drawing the short straw. The four of them grab me, and we start heading back to Kim's and Rebecca's place. I don't know what has been said, but I am hoping for nothing.

When we get to Kim's and Rebecca's, it's like any other night. They are drinking margaritas, and we're all just talking and joking around. Nothing is said about any straws. Thank God.

It's about 6:30 in the morning, and Kim gets up and says, "I'm going to bed." She grabs me by the hand and walks me to her room. I see behind me that Raymond and Rebecca are going to Rebecca's room and Victor is setting himself up on the couch.

As soon as Kim closes the door behind us, we start making out like our ship is going down. I pull away and ask, "Is this because of the straws?"

"What straws?"

Nothing more is said.

It's a few weeks later, and Y2K is just around the corner. Some people are freaking out, but most just don't give a damn. Apparently, all computers are supposed to fuck up and the world is gonna go haywire. I am hoping that my credit history will get wiped out, but other than that, I guess I just don't know enough about it to be worried. I'm looking forward to DJing at the bar on New Year's Eve. Every DJ in the city is going to be playing '1999' by Prince, and I won't be left out. Any excuse to play Prince.

The regular guy has been working at a lot of other places, and now I get to DJ instead of working the door on the weekends. However, it's 11:30, and everyone has gone downstairs where the karaoke is going on. Right at midnight, all the power goes out. It was just the owner messing around, but a few faces in the crowd look genuinely concerned. What a big fucking joke.

Did I sidestep the Kim thing enough?

Well, we hang out as usual and have sex one more time that first week, but decide we were better off as friends. It's actually mutual, and no one is hurt. I'd rather have a girlfriend than be alone, but she's just not the one.

In February, Kim and Rebecca move back to Michigan.

DJing doesn't bring in much money; in fact, it costs money to keep up. I have to keep buying new music and playing what everyone wants to hear. I spent a lot of money on music I hate just to keep the party going on the weekends. I would much rather bartend.

After a while, I am working five to six nights a week bartending and making pretty good money. No more DJing and no more door shifts. I am faster than any other bartender they have, which means I can easily out-ring them. Plus, the customers seem to like my speed and consistency.

Like I said before, the bar was kind of a shit hole, and the owner was pretty lackadaisical about running the place. At one point, some guys came and took the ice machine because he had missed a few payments. Hard to run a bar without ice. We were actually running with bags of ice from the grocery store for a while. At another point he was gone for three weeks and didn't order any booze. Just before he returned, we were down to a few bottles of cheap bourbon and about half a dozen cases of Budweiser... nothing else. The other bartenders and I still showed up to work and served what we had. During the winter, there were times that the heat wasn't on. It was an old building and wasn't insulated very well, but people still showed up and drank their beers every day.

Around March, he gets ambitious and decides it's time to clean up the place and fix some things. This is great, but he's using the bar staff to do all the cleanup. This means basically working double shifts, cleaning during the day and working the bar at night. It takes a few weeks. This is a big job, and the place is a huge mess. Starting into the third week, I have had it. That's enough for me.

One night at The House, Billy is acting really strange. Not 'drunk strange', but really strange. He has his mom's car and is about to leave. I take his keys and offer to drive him home. I'll take the train back.

He passes out in the car on the ride to his place. I had only been there one other time and can't find it with him asleep. I get within memory and shake him for about five minutes to wake him up. There's puke all down the front of him, but he bounces up as if he's just had twelve cups of coffee.

"We're there. Just turn here, this alley, this garage and I'm home."

My memory is better than I thought.

I see him inside just to make sure he's OK. At this point, he's wide awake and jumpy as hell, but seems sober. Somehow, he had passed out for a little while, had thrown up and is now fine.

"I'm gonna go home. You seem fine."

"How are you getting home?"

"Train."

"Let me drive you to the train. It would be about a twelve block walk otherwise. Come on." He grabs his keys and heads off to the garage.

Other than being a little jumpy he seems OK, and I really don't want to take the twelve-block walk. A short drive he can handle, but the long walk I don't have in me.

We get in the car, and he floors it out of the garage and is hauling ass down a blind alley. I am plastered to my seat and can't even speak; I am so scared.

He continues to blaze through the alleys and is now out on Halsted, blowing stop lights and cutting people off left and right. At one point, he crosses into oncoming traffic to pass someone. I don't know what to do. I keep thinking, 'We're gonna die.'

Just as I'm about to jump over and slam my foot on the break, a squad car pulls up behind us. Now Billy's in fight or flight mode, and I'm screaming, "Just pull over! Just. Pull. Over! Stop this fucking car!"

He turns off onto a gravel driveway leading to some factory. He's blowing up dust so much that we can't see out the windows. I can't see anything. Then, he pulls up past some fences and parks the car.

"Let's go!"

"You're out of your fucking mind."

Cops are on both sides of the car with guns drawn. My hands are on the ceiling.

"Put your keys on the roof of your car, then keep your hands up."

One cop eases his way closer to Billy, still with the gun drawn.

I kid you not, Billy actually says, "What's the problem?"

"Get out of the car." Then, talking to me, "You stay right there and don't move."

A second squad car pulls in, and it takes three cops to wrestle Billy to the ground to cuff him. They cuff his ankles together, too. He's flipping the fuck out. Now they're coming for me.

The one cop that's been on my side of the car this whole time asks me to get out and put my hands on the car. He searches me, and I'm not moving or saying a word. He seems to notice that I am calm and sober.

"Were you drinking?"

"No, Sir."

"What is your friend on?"

"He's been drinking, and I think he takes Prozac. Other than that, I have no idea what's wrong with him." Billy had told me a few weeks ago about the Prozac, but didn't really get into it, and I didn't ask. The cops thought he was on PCP.

Billy's locked safely away in the back of one of the squad cars and after about a half an hour, they just let me go.

"Which way is the orange line?" It turns out we were only a half block away. I can't sleep at all when I get home.

Three days later, Billy is back at the bar.

"Sorry about all that."

I take him outside. "What the hell! I thought you'd be going away for a while."

"They took me to Read. It's a psych hospital, and then they let me go after seventy-two hours. My court date is in a month. Will you go to tell your side of what happened?"

"Do I have to? I think I was lucky to not get locked up with you. I would like to stay out of this."

"No, you don't have to." Then he turns to leave.

"Dude, wait. Just let me know when and where. I don't know what I could say to help. You're fucked."

He never says anything else about it ever again. The court date came and went, but he never told me when or where. Nothing happens. He never talks about it, and I really don't want to know, but nothing happens.

I find another job in early April. This is in another part of town, and it takes a few stops on the Red Line to get there. No big deal. The owner is this nice old lady in her early sixties, I think. The place has been in her family since like 1900. After a quick and simple interview, I'm hired. She asks me to come in at 4:30 on Wednesday afternoon.

I show up about thirty minutes early. The daytime bartender takes me on a quick tour to see where everything is kept, runs me through the price list and is gone by a quarter after five. The bar is mine. It's the fastest training I've ever had.

At closing time, I'm told to call upstairs where the owner lives, and she would come down and cash me out and lock up behind me.

At about twenty to two, I call last call, get everybody out and lock up by 2:00. I finish cleaning up and am ready to go by 2:30. I call upstairs as instructed, and she comes down as promised.

"How did it go?"

"Fine. The prices are pretty easy to learn, and everything is set up to where I could find stuff fast."

"It looks like you did all right. This is the highest ring for a Wednesday in a while." That's not really reassuring. I thought it was pretty slow, but Wednesdays are not known for being big nights out.

“Everything is clean, and you’re done at least a half an hour earlier than anyone else. You’re a keeper.”

She gives me a few shifts and sends me on my way with a quick, ‘thank you’.

It's the easiest first day I ever had and ever hope to have in the future. I like this place; I like it a lot.

They have live music on the weekends with a big stage on the main floor and a smaller one in the basement. However, the basement is the main show. It's musty and poorly lit with pipes, beams and ducts running everywhere, but they pack ‘em in.

The bar upstairs is huge at about forty feet long. It has around twenty-five bar stools and more than thirty people would belly up when it was busy. The basement bar only sits about four people and is the tiniest bar I’ve ever worked. It's set up more like a beer stand than a bar. I can reach everything without hardly having to move my feet. Behind me are two reach-in coolers that hold the more popular beers, and then I have two igloo coolers with ice down by my feet with random stuff. As far as booze goes, they have fourteen basics: one row of the seven well bottles and then a few mid-grade brands. Nothing top shelf, but down here, I don’t need it. It's all about speed.

I love the rush of non-stop service. The tiny bar would get about six or seven deep and turn around fast. The 100 to 120 people down there drank a lot, and for one person, it stayed busy.

They have two bartenders working the upstairs bar and the whole floor packs in about 200 people. At this place, I prefer the basement bar because of the rush, even though the money is better upstairs. The basement bar is only open for the show, about two and a half hours with breaks. Sometimes they have two bands, and it would go anywhere between four hours or all the way till closing time.

It is only about 10:30 tonight, and the owner's son who is running the soundboard right around the corner from the bar starts yelling at me. He's trying to get me to throw this guy out that's up by the stage acting a fool. I'd thrown people out several times, so this is nothing new. I jump the bar and run through the crowd to the front of the stage. This huge guy at about 6'6" and around 300 pounds of pure muscle is stripped to the socks holding a beer and wasted out of his mind. This isn't going to be easy.

The naked part is no big deal because I won't be grabbing or pushing this guy anyway. Looking him in the eye, I just softly say, "You gotta go. Put your clothes on and get out. You gotta go," shaking my head in disbelief the whole time.

He knows he's in the wrong and was probably just waiting for me or someone or anyone to ask him to leave. I walk him all the way upstairs until I get within earshot of the doorman, and he takes him the rest of the way out. Apparently, the local rugby team gets together here every year, and every year someone does this. Next year, someone else will be throwing out the naked guy.

A few weeks later, they hire this new girl to work the bar. The basement is to be her main spot. Owners prefer pretty girls as bartenders, but let's see them jumping the bar to throw someone out. I'm sure there are plenty of girls that can and most girls in the business are far from timid or shy. They don't hesitate to cut someone off or tell 'em to leave, but it's usually the doorman or one of the guy bartenders that actually does the throwing out.

This girl is about 5'4" and probably only a few ounces over a hundred pounds. She is also not some little timid or shy chick. She's tattooed up and has a shaved head, not bald, but only about a quarter inch of hair. Her face is absolutely beautiful and makes up for the crew cut. I generally prefer long hair on girls, but this fit her personality perfectly somehow. She has energy that's unstoppable and would work out just fine in the little bar. I feel for her, being all alone down there, but the owner's son usually works the soundboard, and I'm sure he'll help out if need be. I hope. Drinkers tend to behave themselves a little better around girl bartenders, too. A little. Mostly, I'm gonna miss the rush, speed, and intensity of the smaller bar.

They ask me to train her. It takes four nights, or two weekends, to get her up to speed, but she's ready. There isn't room for two behind the bar, so I kind of have to show her everything from the side. The first weekend she watches, and the second weekend she does everything while I just stand on hand. In that time, we talk a lot. Jessica Lamon. Her name, her face, even her hair cut fits her perfectly. She's a riot and seems to make me funnier than I actually am. I walk her to the train every night. Even if she gets off way before I do, she always waits around. It's not a bad neighborhood, but I like to think she wants the company. I'm hooked after only a few weeks of knowing her.

We start dating right away.

There aren't many actual dates, mostly just working together and hanging out, but that's true of most of my girlfriends. For me, I guess, the difference between just a friend and a girlfriend is simply the sex. The sex with her is amazing.

The first night I was at her place, she made some pasta with a ton of garlic and later that night... I'll just say everything tasted like garlic... everything. I'll never have anything with a lot of garlic without think of her and I'll have a big stupid smile on my face that no one will understand.

I rarely date anyone that I don't either work with or at least meet at work. We did go to a Cubs game once and out to dinner a few times, but mostly we hung out at her place or at The House. I introduce her to Nate, now that he's coming into the bar here and there to see me. Plus, due to a lighter schedule, he's hanging out with us at The House, too. Things were usually serious when the girl got to meet my best friend. If they met the family, it was really, really serious. Only about three girlfriends over the years had actually met the family. Come to think of it, I myself had only met the families of eight different girls in all the time I'd been dating.

Nate did end up having to move out of his place and is now living with his mom. His job is going fine, but his brother had moved out, and he and his girlfriend were not helping out anyway. It kind of sucked for him having to move home, but it's nice to have that option.

He likes Jessica and is happy for me and thankfully doesn't hold a grudge about me moving out on him.

Somewhere in June, at around 2:30 in the afternoon, I get a call at work from Billy. I haven't heard from him in a while, and I didn't think anyone had this number. He's in jail, but this has nothing to do with that one night. He's wasted in the middle of the day and wants me to bail him out. How am I on his call list?

Somehow his bail is only $200, and he promises to pay me back, but I can't leave work. He says that he's not going anywhere, but to please come that night. As soon as I get off work at around four, I take the trains and buses necessary to get to 26th and California (Cook County Jail).

Even though I've done nothing wrong, I'm treated like a criminal going through the process of getting any information on Billy. I sit in this room for two hours before someone tells me that he's not there anymore. His father had come to get him. I was pissed, but I get over it. Billy is still a friend, and it hasn't cost me anything but time.

Hanging out at The House is the same as ever except now, with Jessica, I am somehow more comfortable. It's also nice to have Nate around again. With Rebecca gone, everyone else in the group is single, but Victor is hooking up with Britney. She is crazy about Victor and just stares at him with bright eyes and shares his giant smile. Britney Wallenberg was one of the hostesses at Jerry's, and I later found out that she was only twenty. A few months later, they would throw her a twenty-first birthday party in The House. You can't hang out underage at some place for a few months then have your twenty-first birthday party in the same place. It's not for me to say anything about it though.

At the end of July, the owner at my job asks me if I know anyone that knows anything about kitchens and would be willing to open up the spot they have in the back. It's a small kitchen that they aren't using, and they want to offer some kind of food. Hotdogs, hamburgers and wings... bar food... simple stuff. Without really thinking it over and based only on how she asked the question, I say, "I've worked in a few kitchens." As part of being the best at some places, I would work in the kitchen as well as the bar and the floor. It made me more valuable, but at a few places they preferred me in the kitchen. Remember what happened at The Cork and Tap?

I talk about it at The House with some of the guys from Jerry's. Billy and Jerry are interested. I am obviously hesitant to include Billy in anything, but he hasn't had a drink in over a month. He would hang out, but it was Cokes, just like me.

They would be investors and would work the kitchen once in a while to give me a break. None of us have any savings, and we are planning to just go day by day at first. We put together a simple menu and call it 'The Pickle Grill'. We are all twenty-six and have no idea what we are getting into.

'The Pickle' was this on-going joke that Victor started up. He would talk about giving some girl 'the pickle'. No degree needed to follow what he was suggesting, but what really made it was that he would make a loose fist as if he were holding... 'the pickle' and then rub his fist on your face and make a gross sexual moan while doing it. Even though he didn't have anything actually in his hand, you would just cringe with the suggestion. It was sick, but always made us crack up.

At first, we're only open for lunches and weekdays, so I can still work the bar at night to make money. There isn't much of a crowd during lunch, but it's a way to get started and lets people know that the place is starting to serve food. Our needs aren't big enough to use a major distributor, so we get everything once a week from a grocery store. Our profit margin is a joke.

After working seven days a week and doubles four days a week because Billy and Jerry aren't working any shifts, I have to start giving up some of my bar shifts to keep the kitchen going. I get Jason Ardmore a job there working lunches while the regular lunch guy starts covering my shifts at night. Jason is the doorman at The House, and we have become pretty good friends. Sometimes the heavy drinking and stupidity of hanging out at The House would get to me, and I would go hang out in front with Jason just to get some air and quiet for a minute. It kept me sane and made it easier to stay sober. This had been going on since the first night I went across the street. Spending that much time out there I got to know him pretty well.

Jason works the bar during the day while I run the kitchen, but business is slow going there for a while, and we spend most of our time watching baseball with the couple of regulars that come in during lunch. Occasionally, they would eat, and it was enough to get the place smelling like food which would sometimes attract more customers. Whenever there were a few customers, I would always go fry up some onions and bacon to fill the place with the smell of food just to stir up some business. It worked most of the time, and lunch slowly started to pick up, but we are far from making a profit.

The owner wants the kitchen open all week, but I can't seem to pull in Billy or Jerry. I am determined and stupid, so I start working seven days a week with two doubles when I bartend. I no longer have the time nor the energy to hang out with anyone, and my relationship with Jessica is reduced to the two nights a week that we work together. The kitchen picks up quite a bit, but it's barely covering its cost, and I'm not making much money only working two nights. Bills aren't getting paid, and it's looking bad. After only about three weeks of this, I crash and crash hard.

Billy actually comes in and works on Monday, the one day I oversleep. I go in when I wake up, and we talk about having to let it go. It's not a hard decision and doesn't take but a few minutes to tell the owner and wrap it all up. The owner understands and is happy to keep me on as a bartender, but the two shifts are all that are available now.

It's not enough.

With the free time I have just acquired, I set out to save my relationship with Jessica. She had gone too long without seeing me other than crashing at her place two nights a week. I try to explain that I have the time now, but that's not enough.

Friday night, I oversleep and am three hours late for work. I don't have it in me anymore. In this venture, Jerry's lost a hundred dollars from helping to buy food and supplies but no time. Billy lost a hundred and fifty dollars and one afternoon of his life. In less than a week, I've lost my business, my girlfriend, and now my job.

Two months later, I'm still out of work and now three months behind in rent. I get a five-day notice, and they feel the need to post a new one on my door every day. I've barely left the apartment in all this time. I just don't have it in me to look for work every day, and the few days a week that I do get out, I'm physically and mentally exhausted by the time I get home. This is the most I've seen of my place since I'd moved in. I have no idea what kind of toll spending this much time in such a small room has on somebody. When it came time to evict someone, this was the kind of place that didn't wait to put your shit out on the street. I'd seen them do it to other residents. I don't have much, but I don't feel like losing everything.

I show up to court on the fifth day, the day of the hearing. The landlord won't budge but is willing to give me two more days to get my things out. I can't move back with Nate; there was no room with his mom. Family was out, and there seems to be no hope.

Then...

Billy, of all people, comes through. He sees it as kind of a way of returning the favor for trying to bail him out of jail and the whole messed up night. He lives with his mom and sister in Bridgeport, but I could have the basement. He's neglected to tell me when I moved my stuff over there that the basement is only half finished, and the other half is literally just dirt. There is a room down there, but I can't sleep there. The mold, smell, and dust would kill me with my asthma. They offer me the couch, and I am glad to have it.

I go to The House that night. Billy stays home. Not everyone is there yet, and it's just me, Ray, and Victor.

"I need a drink," was the first thing out of my mouth. I've lost everything... my apartment, my business, my girlfriend, my job, and now my mind. It's been close to three years since I'd had anything to drink, and almost two since the speed thing. Maybe I'm just feeling sorry for myself, but this is rock bottom. I know a drink isn't going to change anything, but at this point it can't hurt.

Raymond says, "I'm not stopping you."

Victor looks a bit disappointed but says nothing.

I walk up to the bar and before I get there, they put a Coke in front of me. "Can I get a CC and seven?"

Dell is working the bar tonight and gives me a funny look but doesn't say anything. His name is Alexander Dell, but he goes by 'Dell' because there's a waitress named Alexandria Long and goes by Alex. Alex looks like she's sixteen, but she's twenty-two and has waited on us almost every time we've been here. Both had been working there from the beginning and had never seen me with a drink in my hand.

It's only about one AM, and there's lots of drinking time, but it doesn't help me. I have about eight drinks but can't get drunk. I really want to just get drunk and shut some things out for a while, but nothing. Nothing. I can't get drunk. It's been almost three years, and I should have been just plowed by now, but nothing.

Victor is sitting in the back with Britney and doesn't say anything to me all night, but he hasn't really talked to anyone. Tonight, he is the only one visibly drunk. I envy his stupor.

Maybe the next night I'll be able to try again, but for now, it's back to Bridgeport and the couch.

Chapter Five: Modern Day Vampires

The booze is the blood, the night is the power, the weak are all around us. There is strength in the night.

We are, in ways, vampires. We are weak during the daylight, but strong at night. We need a certain fluid to survive and at times when we share this fluid with others, they become one of us. We prey on the weak to get what we need, be it sex, money, sustenance, and of course, more of the fluids that we love.

We wind down and grow tired when the sun rises, and when we wake up, we are still weak and struggle until the sun sets again. Then, our power emerges. The booze gives us strength and confidence to bend others to our will. When a drink is bought for you or by you for someone else, there is a bond; a bond that usually doesn't last longer than the night, but a bond, nonetheless. The already drunk, the timid or shy, the secretly afraid, or those that are out of place... they feed us.

The booze is the blood, the night is the power, the weak are all around us.

I haven't been sleeping much.

Although Billy, his mom and sister are very considerate and wonderful for sharing their home with me, I try to spend as much time as possible out of their house.

With my lifestyle, this isn't hard.

Victor, Raymond and I are on a rampage. We go out every night as usual, but now we're going to a lot of different bars. Everywhere we go, we're treated like local celebrities. We walk right up to the front of the line at places and get right in. No cover charges are ever paid. Half our tab is comped, and the staff always pays us the utmost attention. We want for nothing.

Women come to us. People we don't know buy us drinks. I always wondered why. Maybe Victor and Raymond had already laid the groundwork and set up this celebrity. They seem to know everyone in the city, but I'm treated like a king as well. I'm told that some people think Raymond and I look familiar or like they should know us. A 5'7" white guy and a 6'9" black guy just looked odd as a pair. Odd enough that people think there's something to it. Every doorman and every bartender know us, and the more we go out, the more people shake our hands and welcome us. We are kings.

People in the business all seem to know each other. There's an internal bond due to having had the same experiences. At some places, there is something called 'street prices', which means discounts just for being in the business. Not every place does street prices and if they do, it's always an inside deal. No one ever talks about it. There is just a common bond we all share. You come to our place, and we do our best so that you'll have a good time, and your bill will be cut down as much as we can get away with, and when we go to your place, the favors returned. The kicker is the 50-100% tips on every tab. We all know what it's like and we take care of each other.

Tipping huge is a big part of it. Servers, bartenders, and cab drivers all get a piece. Whenever tipping is expected, we set out to be the biggest. We throw money around like it's nothing to us. Raymond called bartenders and servers 'the richest poor people on earth'. We would work hard and make good cash, and we would play hard and spread that cash around.

That's the tough part about holding so much cash; it seems to spill all over the place. It's not wasted though; we spend it well and always handle ourselves like professionals. Playing hard makes the working hard easier. It rarely feels like work. Our coworkers are our friends, and the customers are our friends. It's just a big party, but everyone pays their way. It's like our own system of taxes, (which we never pay). Everyone gets their proper percent, and everyone is taken care of.

Being a cash business, not all tips are claimed as income. This is no secret, and the government does its best to keep up with it. The credit card tips are claimed automatically; the cash is up to you. The more you claim, the smaller your pay checks are, but the larger your tax refund would be. We always got a tax refund. It wasn't always very much, but I never owed anything and every year I would get at least something back. The only problem is that on paper, it looks like we make nothing. This makes getting loans or even finding an apartment harder, but for me, I'm not looking for any loans. Thankfully, there seems to always be some place to stay. A place of my own at this point seems a pipe dream.

Out of work and crashing on Billy's couch you might think, 'How do you afford this lifestyle?' I'd had a few short-term jobs here and there, but they were just that... short term. A week or two was all they'd last.

There was this pizza place that had just opened, but because there were so many places for pizza in the city, it took too long for business to develop, and I made no money.

Then, there was this Italian restaurant on the near west side that I was asked to leave. It wasn't the owners or management that asked. It was one of the regulars. I bumped into him coming around a corner and felt a gun on his hip. He asked, "How long have you worked here?"

“This is my second day.”

“Make it your last.”

I never went back.

Billy and his mom aren’t charging me rent, so the little money I'm making just goes to food and hanging out. If it wasn’t for so much stuff being discounted or completely comped, I don’t know how I would be getting by. I am good though, and if I can’t afford to go out, I don’t.

One night hanging out at The House, Joe Harms asks me how things are going, and I tell him how hard it is to find a decent job. He shocks the hell out of me and offers me my job back at Jerry’s. I jump at the chance.

He notices that I'm drinking and knows that I never did before but doesn’t say anything about it. What he doesn’t realize is that I've never slept better and over sleeping would not be a problem anymore. In only a few days, I'm back in the mix, stronger than ever. This time, though, I'm not taking it too seriously, and being the best again isn’t in my mind.

In the time I've been gone, Victor has worked his way onto the bar schedule and is working most shifts side by side with Raymond. On the weekends, though, Victor is stuck in the service bar where you don’t deal with customers at all, and you just churn out the drinks for the servers. Stacy works the weekends with Raymond and seems to cover their off days while also filling in wherever necessary. He seems to work all the time. Stacy starts hanging out with us more and more too, but actually we are just hanging out with him more. Going to the gay bars with him becomes part of the routine. I join the dart team that Stacy is on before I realize that every place, we would be playing would be a gay bar. Hanging out with the crew is one thing, but adding on the dart tournaments is a little too much.

I believe in 'live and let live', so I have always respected people's differences and accepted them for who they are. However, there is one stereotype that I've experienced to be true. Gay guys seem to be relentlessly looking for sex. They hit on anyone and seem to believe that if you are on their turf, you are free game. Saying that I'm straight had no effect. Saying that I was with friends didn't slow things down either. Making me feel uncomfortable seemed to be a sport.

The lifestyle I respect completely, but being relentlessly hit on is just something that doesn't sit right. I don't think of myself as all those attractive and straight girls rarely hit on me, so being hit on is just something that I've never been comfortable with. Stacy, Raymond, and Victor don't help either. Raymond and Victor are dealing with their own predators, and Stacy thinks it's all hilarious.

I'd never been the type of guy to hit on random girls. Conversations started on their own, and if it went in that direction, then that was fine, but I didn't push it.

Any guy that is the type that pushes it and hits on every girl in the place and doesn't seem to understand 'no' should be required to go to a few gay bars and see what it feels like. That would be just desserts, but for me, it was just plain uncomfortable, and I didn't feel like I deserved it. I never minded the free drinks, but the leering across the bar was too much and there didn't seem to be any look that you could give back that would deter them. It wasn't all the time, and it wasn't every time, but it was enough.

I felt that when I was hanging out with friends or playing on the dart team that I had reason to be there just as everyone else did.

I respected the situation. Why, then, was the favor not returned? Anyway, this was one stereotype that seemed to hold true.

I don't subscribe to the stereotype that homosexuals want to turn everyone gay. I just think that there are gay men who really, really hope you are. The reality behind every stereotype is that they are true often enough to keep them alive.

Homosexuals are a given in the restaurant business for some reason. I believe it's due to the fact that the nature of the business not only allows but encourages people to be themselves. I've never questioned the lifestyle or disapproved for any narrow-minded reason. Respect and acceptance should go both ways... (no pun intended).

Like I said, I wasn't hit on all the time, but it was enough to take me off the dart team. Hanging out with the crew was always different and didn't slow down. There was maybe safety in numbers. Stacy would always be a good friend. His personality and individuality, coupled with the fact that he himself never made me uncomfortable, sealed our friendship. He had no jurisdiction over his other friends or any strangers in the bars. My comfort level was always up to me.

Britney and one of the servers from Jerry's had gotten a great apartment that was only a few blocks from the job. This neighborhood was pretty expensive, so we all wondered how they managed it. I still don't know. It wasn't like my old building. This was a full-on two-bedroom apartment, and it was nice.

They had a housewarming party, and the whole crew showed up.

Victor and Britney were still going strong, and she became a regular part of the crew. Nowadays, the crew seemed to either be all of us or just Ray, Victor and myself. This time it was all of us, and this party was packed with people from work as well as staff from The House. Alex, Jason, and Dell all had had the day off, so they came by around ten and stayed till it broke up at five in the morning. Victor had to work, so he was just there in the beginning, helping set everything up. He would come back after work. I had the day off, so I was there for the whole thing.

Before the party started to jump off and after Victor had gone to work, it's only eight o'clock, and Britney is already wasted. We are sitting around with her roommate waiting for people to show up. Britney decides that she wants to dance and turns up the music. Her roommate, who is gay, starts dancing with her. They are kind of grinding on each other, but it's no big deal. Then, she starts doing like a strip tease and gets down to her skirt and her bra. I'm like 'what the hell are you doing?' The next thing I know she's trying to give me a lap dance and is kissing on my neck, then trying to get me to kiss her. I push her off and just look at her. She and her roommate laugh.

Is she fucking with me? Is she serious? Either way it went too far. It isn't just that Victor would beat the shit out of me, but more than anything else, I respected their relationship and would never do anything like that. What kind of respect did she have for the relationship, which, at this point, had been going on for around six months? Then, people started to show up, and she passed out in her room, still just in her skirt and bra. The party goes on without one of its hosts.

They had made arrangements with the landlord, I guess, and had access to the roof top deck. That is what took us so long to set up. When we finished, it was awesome. Tiki torches were up, and plain white Christmas lights were strung overhead. It was complete with leis and a whole lotta booze.

Victor showed up after his shift around two AM, and by then Britney had been up again for a few hours. Even after a four-hour nap, she was still wasted out of her mind. I didn't know what to say, but I felt like I should have said something. Instead, I got wasted myself.

The next day at work, I take Victor aside and tell him what happened.

“Oh... yeah, she does that sometimes.”

That's it. He's not bothered at all. He's not mad at me, and he's not mad at her. Not being mad at me was what I was hoping for, but wow.

He didn’t seem to care at all, and it wasn’t like he wasn’t taking the relationship seriously; he had bought her a ring. He later told me that he was mostly upset that she had gotten the apartment. After getting married, she was supposed to move in with him. He was still taking care of his mother and sister and wasn’t going to be moving out. His mother was old with a bad hip, and his sister was handicapped, I think. Anyway, he had his hands full taking care of them, and I think he thought that Britney would maybe be helping out with all that. She had been for the last six months and got along great with his family.

To make matters worse, Britney may or may not have had a coke problem, but it was none of my business.

Coke was almost as readily available as the booze. I generally didn’t need any help getting amped up, so I left it alone... for a while.

Jerry is having a party at his place, and I'm trying to get to know this new girl that they had just hired. Amber Lockwood. She's from Indianapolis. She's twenty-two, and this was the first time she had been away from home. She is absolutely beautiful: long red hair, green eyes, and a smile that could make you lose your balance. We're talking about Indy because I had lived there myself at one point. Then, Jerry comes and pulls me to the side.

"I got you set up in the other room."

"What are you talking about?" I thought maybe he thought I was ready to hook up with Amber right there at the party. Things are going well, but not that well.

"I set you up a bump."

I still have no idea what he's talking about but make my way to the room anyway.

"It's in the closet."

I walk in the closet, and there is this plastic-like plate with three lines set up on it. This is actually the first time I have ever seen cocaine. Without even thinking about it, I snort all three lines. Jerry later told me that I was only supposed to have only done one and laughed. I thought he would have been pissed at me for taking more than my share. That shit wasn't cheap. He seemed to know it was my first time and watches me with a grin on his face the whole night.

I had never been more alert in my life. Speed or any quantity of caffeine doesn't even come close. I remember talking really fast, and it was like my eyes were gonna pop out of my face. I must have had this extremely surprised look on my face the whole night. This was no condition to be in while trying to impress Amber. She had done some too and was right there with me, though.

I don't realize it, but I was drinking a lot more than usual. I don't feel the booze at all and keep drinking more and more. At around three in the morning, I start to feel sick. It's not the coke that has me sick; it was the ridiculous amount of alcohol I drank. The coke maybe made it possible to drink that much, but it wasn't the coke that got me sick.

It's like how I hate red wine. When I was about sixteen, I was at this wedding and got really drunk on red wine. So now I hate it, but it wasn't the wine; it was the fact that I drank three bottles of the stuff.

After taking a short nap on the bathroom floor, I get up and go back to the party. There are about seven people that are crashed out on the living room floor. The music is still playing loudly, but everyone is either gone or out cold.

Amber has left.

Billy and I would occasionally smoke some pot, but hard drugs were not my thing. Now, coke is just as available as pot and easier to get. The only thing that keeps me from becoming a fiend is the fact that it is pretty expensive, and I would never admit it to anyone, but I am kind of afraid of it. I only used when someone else was offering, which wasn't that often.

The next night we are all hanging out, and Amber wants to go home. She has her car but is pretty wasted. I've only had one drink because I just got off work, so I drive her home. When we get to her place, she invites me up, and I think it would be a pretty good idea to make sure she gets in OK. She has this fantastic one bedroom all to herself. It's huge with an all-leather living room set and artwork on the walls, some of which she had painted herself. The place is beautiful. All on Daddy's dime.

I walk her to her room, and as soon as she gets to the edge of her bed, she starts taking her clothes off. Amber has an amazing body, but that is not why I brought her home. My intentions are good. She gets down to her bra and panties and gets under the covers, then lifts the covers on the other side for me.

"Uh, I think I'll just sleep on the couch."

"The couch is really uncomfortable."

"I don't want you to think that this is why I brought you home."

She says nothing, and I just stare at her face. Not so reluctantly, I get into bed, but above the covers and still have my clothes on. I'm trying hard to be good here.

She rolls over, and we start making out. My God, she's not making this easy. Maybe I should just go for it. Maybe she's not that wasted. Maybe... well maybe.

No.

She is drunk. It would be wrong, so I get up and sleep on the couch. It's the most amazingly comfortable couch I've ever slept on. She's either never slept on the couch or she really wants me to stay in the bed with her. Oh well.

In the morning, she makes eggs.

I was just thinking that I hadn't seen Nate in a while when he shows up at The House. We do the usual handshake-hug thing and sit down with the crew. Alex brings Nate two Cokes. He drinks them so fast that it's just easier to bring him two at a time. Nate hardly ever drinks because when he does, he drinks just as fast and gets wasted pretty quickly.

"What's been going on?"

"Not much. Just working a lot."

"Same here."

"How's the job?"

"Paying the bills, but it just doesn't excite me."

Nate's a fast-paced kinda guy, and if a job is too slow, he gets bored, but he knows how much he needs to hold on to this one.

"How are things with mom?"

"She's cool, but I can take only so much of her preaching. She is relentless about getting me saved. Bible this and Bible that. Don't get me wrong; I love my mom, but enough is enough."

Just then, Victor leans in and says, "Check it out. This girl has been looking at you all night. Wait, wait here she comes."

This very attractive girl walks across the bar towards me, and I have no idea why. She comes right up to me and takes my hand. She heads towards the back of the bar where her group is. I'm just going along and don't say anything. I want to see where this goes. We get closer to her group, but she banks left and takes me into the men's room and closes the door.

I'm dumb struck, and I don't know what to do. She turns, backs up, and takes her pants down. Then, she backs up and sits on the toilet.

"Pee, if you have to."

So, I turn around to the urinal, and I start to pee.

She goes back to her group, and I go back to mine. Nothing is said.

Victor, Raymond and Nate all ask, "So... So, what happened?"

"We peed. It was ridiculous."

Everyone erupts in laughter.

Amber shows up after work with Joe. She already looks lit up. She's really out of control lately. Nothing but partying with anyone who has a little coke to go around, and guys were always willing to share with a hot girl. She's out every night, which I can't really say anything about because so am I. The difference is that she would show up to work lit. There is really never a time that she isn't. Eventually she hooks up with Joe. He generally has a steady supply. I missed my chance to have sex with this outrageously hot girl, but I had to be a good guy. It seems now that any relationship with her wouldn't have lasted long, mainly because I didn't usually have any coke.

It seems to me that as soon as I started drinking again, everyone else's drinking seems to increase. Maybe I am just more aware of it; I don't really know. The only one whose drinking slows down is Billy's. He still smokes a lot of pot, but only has maybe two or three beers when we hang out. I guess the other morning when he was dragged off by the cops had an effect on him... as you would hope it would.

I'm just noticing that when I went back to drinking, I went back hard, but now there is weed and coke in the mix.

Stacy drinks gin straight from the bottle in a ten-ounce martini glass. No ice, no mix. And he pounds them like water. He'd have around ten or eleven of these every night. Raymond is a bottomless pit and has now switched from scotch to high-proof bourbon. Victor drinks his Long Islands like Nate drinks Coke. Two at a time. He'd put away about a dozen or more each night. Britney doesn't really seem to drink that much, but she's always blasted.

Nothing seems to slow us down though. It's still the bar, work, somebody's place, work, the bar, and round and round. Money is actually coming in pretty well, but instead of saving it for my own place, it just spills out of my pockets. Something has to give. Despite having steady work now, I still can't afford a place of my own and going back to the high rise was out of the question. Billy and his mom were in no hurry to get me off the couch, but I'm starting to feel like I've been there too long.

"Amber's in the hospital."

"What happened?"

"OD, we think. Her mom and dad came in from Indianapolis. It doesn't look good."

"Oh my God."

When things would get out of control, I would try to get myself back into work. Jerry's is starting a brunch with a Bloody Mary bar. It needs someone to oversee it. I'm back to running the training team, and now I would be put in charge of the brunch. I ask Joe for a raise. Servers don't generally get raises. Usually tipped employees are paid about half of minimum wage and that never changes no matter how long you are with the company. I've only been back for about five months, but he agrees. I always got two dollars more than minimum wage when I was training someone, but now I would get that all the time. That seems like a pretty good deal.

More responsibility drew me into work and slowed down my partying.

The House put in this golf game where you slam your hand across this ball to drive the golf ball. The harder you hit it, the further it would go, and everyone was going for the hole-in-one. Victor missed the top of the ball and slammed his hand into the front of the game. The game survived, but Victor broke his hand.

Since servers need both hands for everything and there isn't much servers can do in a restaurant without getting their hands wet, Victor is pretty much out of work. He takes the time off and relaxes, but they need someone to cover his bar shifts. Guess who?

I was just waiting tables so far, but now I have a chance at the bar. It is where most servers want to end up. The money is better, and it's just that much more fun. You could make your own call on comping stuff and buying drinks. You don't need the manager to do stuff like that for you, and it speeds things up because management tends to be hard to find when you need them. There is freedom, fun, and money. The booze was the blood, the night was the power, and the weak were all around us.

I work the service bar on the weekends, and I don't mind because of the speed and intensity of it all, but before I could take main-bar shifts, I would have to train someone to cover my floor shifts. They hire Anna Woods, Britney's best friend. She had worked in the business for years and was easy to train, but at the same time, they hire her boyfriend to work the main bar. I get stuck with the service bar and get shut out of the main bar because Stacy is working Victor's other shifts. This all basically puts me back on the floor during the week, so what was the point of training Anna?

Three weeks later Anna gets promoted to manager.

I'm pissed about everything that is going on, but it's because I'm actually taking work seriously again. So much for that.

Work gets weird. On Friday and Saturday nights, Damen, Anna's boyfriend, would work the main bar with Raymond. Stacy starts picking up server shifts instead of bartending. It seems like a back step, but that's what he wants.

Every Saturday night, Anna would run the floor, and I would be in the service bar. We'd work till close then go across the street to The House. Then, right after they closed, Anna and I would walk back across the street to set up for brunch. Being scheduled to work every Saturday night and Sunday morning, there was no other way to do it.

If we were to go home after close, it would be three in the morning, and we would have to be back at seven to set up for brunch, which started a nine. With travel time from Bridgeport, I'd have no time to sleep.

Every weekend is like this, and it's killing me, but at least I'm being paid a little better to do it. My checks are getting bigger, and the checks were something I can hold on to and start seriously saving to move out.

Jerry's roommate is moving out at the end of the year, and his place is nice. My part of rent would be four hundred, and I could handle that. It's only early November, so I had some time to wait.

Anna is starting to get a little flirty with me whenever we hang out, and Damen isn't around. Damen only works at Jerry's on Fridays and Saturdays. The rest of the week, he is... well, he said he's a model. Anyway, he isn't around much. I don't like this guy, so if his girlfriend wants to flirt, I'm fine with it. She and I spend every Saturday night and Sunday morning together, so we have ample time to get to know one another.

I learned that Anna was hired in the first place to be a manager but went through the server training to get a taste of how things ran, to learn the menu, and to learn the system. She was from Wisconsin and had gone to school in Madison. They had a great hockey team and, she was a fan. So, we had something in common. I'm not really a sports guy, but hockey was the only sport that I played and was any good at, and the strangest appeal is that the Blackhawks emblem is the best in all of professional sports. Truth was, I wasn't that big of a fan. I just liked it because I used to play, and the uniforms are cool.

I played every sport growing up, but I was little and sickly, so I never did that well at anything. In grade school, we would play floor hockey, and I would be the goalie. I was good because I didn't care about getting hurt and would put whatever I had to in front of the puck to keep it out of the net. It was fun, and I was pretty good at it. The best part was that people really genuinely wanted me on their team. In most sports, I was usually picked last, if at all.

Anyway, my sophomore year of high school, I found out that the school had developed a hockey team. I taught myself how to ice skate and played that winter with friends out on the pond. I wasn't great. The following year, I tried out for the team. We did drills and wind sprints the whole first day, and I was so sick to my stomach. I was dry heaving in my helmet. I never worked that hard for anything ever. They needed a goalie, and I was just the right size to fit the equipment, so I got the gig.

I played two years, and although our team didn't do that well, I was in the papers with the amount of saves I was making. The league was small enough that every team made it to state. It was double elimination, and we lost our first two games, both eleven to nothing. Letting up eleven goals was brutal, but to have it happen twice, really sucked.

Somehow, though, I was noticed by scouts for The Indianapolis Ice... the farm league for the Blackhawks at the time. They invited me out to skate with them the summer after I graduated. Most of my equipment belonged to the team, and they wouldn't let me use it now that I was out of school. I begged all around to get the money to buy the rest of the equipment, but no one would budge. The shin guards alone were around fifteen-hundred dollars.

I hated asking for money, and more than anything, I hated asking my dad for money. He moved out when I was eight, and there was no real contact. I worked summers with him during high school, but he was more of a boss than a dad. Actually, come to think of it, he was a pretty reasonable boss, so maybe that was more like a dad. People told me that if I was going to get the money from anywhere, it would be from him. I just couldn't do it. I couldn't ask. I didn't go to Indianapolis, and I missed my chance to play for a semi-pro hockey team, the farm league for the Chicago Blackhawks, no less.

I could have been a contender.

Anyway, after telling her this story, that was really all the hockey we talked about. She seemed entertained by the story and gave me looks that led me to believe she was into me.,

I haven't seen Victor in three weeks. It was weird not having him as part of the crew. He made the night most of the time.

The rest of the crew and I are hanging out at The House on a Sunday. We were all pretty blasted when Britney comes over. She's off tonight, and I hadn't seen her for a few days, either. She walks right up to me, crying.

"I need your help."

"What is it?"

"I need you to help convince Victor to go to the hospital."

"What's wrong?"

"Just come on."

I gather up Raymond, Jerry, and Billy. Billy drives everyone over to Victor's. I don't even think about the fact that Billy is driving. It's three in the morning, and this is a pretty quiet neighborhood, but Jerry is pretty lit up and isn't very quiet.

We go through the alley and up to the back door. The light goes on before we get there. We're being louder than we thought. Then everybody shuts up, and we go inside. The back porch area is screened in and packed with stuff people would usually keep in the garage. It smells like old paint.

When I turn the corner and actually see Victor for the first time in three weeks, I almost fall over. Now, everyone looks sick when they first wake up, and we have just woken him up, but this is way worse. He's lost at least thirty pounds and is white as a ghost.

“Britney wants you to go to the hospital, so let’s go.”

“I’m OK. I got an appointment in the morning, and I’ll be fine.”

“Come on, let’s go. Now.”

We go back and forth for a while. Suddenly, I start to feel sick and need to go outside. I turn to Victor, give him a hug and say, “Love you, man. Get better, and we’ll see you back at work. Now I gotta go.”

I run out to the back yard and when the air hits me, I feel better and don’t throw up. I'm sitting in the grass when everyone except Britney comes out the back door.

“He’ll be OK. Let’s go.”

Raymond is pretty sober, and he and Billy talk to Victor for a while. They're OK with leaving, so we leave.

Back to the bar.

I’ve been locked up in work for about a month straight now, and I have tomorrow off, so I'm sleeping in.

The phone rings. It never wakes me up. It isn't my phone, and it's never for me, but this time, it wakes me up.

"Jeff, Ray's on the phone."

"Ok, hang on."

I get to my feet after only having had maybe two hours of sleep and make my way to the kitchen. I take the phone and answer with a cough and a groan then, "Hello. What's up?"

"He didn't make it."

"What?"

"Victor. He didn't make it."

"What are you talking about?" My head is starting to clear.

"Jeff, Victor's dead."

I drop to my knees right there in the kitchen in front of Billy and his mom. Billy must have sensed why I'm so upset and covers his face with his hands. His mom stands there, staring.

"He was fine. When we left, he was fine."

"He was worse off than any of us knew. Apparently, he had been sick for years. We just never knew. He never talked about any of it.

Come by Britney's place. We are all trying to keep her together. She's a mess."

"OK. I'll be there."

Billy knew, but he asks anyway. "What is it?"

"Victor's dead." When I say it, it becomes real.

Chapter Six: Only the Good Die Young

It's eight in morning, and everyone is at Britney's place. Billy and I are the last to show up. Her face is drenched with tears. Her complexion is an odd shade of gray. She and Anna are sitting on her bed with Anna holding her. She is inconsolable. I couldn't say anything; then, I noticed that everyone else is speechless, too. He was twenty-nine.

Everyone is trying to get her to eat something, drink some water, walk around, but she won't budge. Despite every effort, it seems all we can do is be there with her. At around ten, people start to leave. A few had to go into work. Anna and I are the last ones to leave, and we can do nothing but hold her. We stay all day. That night, Stacy and Billy take over. Just before going into work, we go around the corner to the bar where almost everyone else is hanging out. It's four o'clock in the afternoon on a Monday, and we are the only ones in the place.

"He was only twenty-nine."

The House staff couldn't believe it either. As far as anyone knew, he was just out with a broken hand. No one knew he had been sick in some way or another for at least a year. No one knew what actually killed him, but some thought that alcohol was somehow involved. He could have stopped drinking. He could have taken care of some of his stress. Britney could have helped out. Things could have gotten better.

Maybe if I had stayed sober, he would have come to me, and I could have helped. Instead, we all sit here, drinking to his memory. It isn't all sad though. Most stories about Victor include something to laugh about.

"Remember when he was about to get thrown out of that one club on LaSalle? The doorman came over and Victor was just smacking him on the back of the neck telling him that everything was cool. The doorman was so pissed."

"We got him out of there in a hurry after that. Remember when Billy took his keys and took the car for a spin around the block? I thought he was gonna kill him. I've never seen him so mad."

"He was pissed."

"He just slammed his hand on that golf machine. Then, he stood there for a while and kept drinking with the good hand. We had to make him go to the emergency room."

"At least that time we got him there."

We try to ignore that one.

"The day after he broke his hand, he showed up ready to work, and everyone was like, 'How are you going to churn out drinks with one hand?'"

We sit around telling Victor stories while progressively getting more and more drunk. Some stories would make us laugh, some would make us cry, and some would make us wonder just what happened.

I don't usually work when I'm drunk, but tonight it doesn't seem to matter. That night at work, it is eerily quiet. The whole staff loved him.

He died on a Monday morning, and the wake would be Friday night with the funeral on Saturday. They said they were waiting till Friday because the hospital wanted to rule out suicide. There's no way Victor would have killed himself. He might ignore all instructions on how to save his life, but he would never kill himself. They may have told him certain things that he could have done to get better, and he either found them impossible or just didn't think they were necessary. Either way, it seemed that he wasn't going to listen to anything anyone said. He was just going to live his life, and that's just what he did.

I cover other people's shifts at work while they take care of Britney, but while I'm consoling Britney and helping Anna take care of her, I miss two of my own shifts at the end of the week. I wasn't scheduled the whole weekend because I had asked off weeks before for my nephew's wedding. I would talk to them about the shifts I missed on Sunday, but now it was just about getting through the weekend.

After taking care of Britney one night, Anna gave me a ride home. When we got to my place, she took my pants off, and we steamed up the car. Nothing ever developed from it, and she stayed with Damen. We never talked about it again. I think we just needed the release.

I thought they would have to shut down Jerry's to accommodate all the staff that would be at the wake and funeral. He was very popular with the whole staff. It seemed like everyone was there Friday night and Saturday morning. Amber even showed up on Friday. She was out of the hospital, and her parents would be moving her back home to Indianapolis over the weekend, so she would miss the actual funeral. Raymond was somehow missing. He told me later that he just didn't do funerals. That was no excuse; this was Victor... these were all his friends... this was an important time to be around, and he wasn't.

Immediately after the funeral, I borrow Billy's car and drive out to Indiana for my nephew's wedding. I'm twenty-seven. I'm far too young to have one of my best friends die and then be going to my nephew's wedding. I'm way too young for this shit.

Wearing all black at a wedding is not very cool, but I don't have time to change. I float through the wedding and go right back home when it's over. Since I'm driving, I don't drink at all at the wedding. Besides, my family doesn't know that I'm drinking again. More than anything else, I just don't want to drink. I want to actually feel what I'm feeling.

That was Saturday. Today, I'm off, but I go into work to talk to them about the shifts that I had missed. Everyone missed a few shifts during all of this... a lot of which I covered.

Joe fires me.

"Are you kidding me? Everyone missed shifts this week."

"I expect more from you."

We argue for a while, but that's that. Joe keeps saying that he puts me on a different level than the other employees because of all the extra that I did. To me this is a reason to give me leeway, but to him, it's a reason to fire me. I am so pissed, but there is no sense in talking about it anymore. I've lost one of my best friends and now my job. Again. What a completely shitty year.

A few nights later at The House, one of my trainees from Jerry's recommends me to a place she used to work. I'm only out of work for a week.

In January, I move in with Jerry as planned, but he neglected to tell me before that his lease was up in six months and wasn't planning to renew it.

Oh well. It's a new year, a new address, and a new job. It's a fresh start, so I thought I ought to be fresh and decide to quit drinking again. This time things would be different. Jerry's apartment is up on the north side off Montrose, and the bar where I'm working is just outside of Boy's-Town on Belmont. It's harder to get to The House every night, so I would be hanging out there less and going to meetings more.

The job is cool. The place is called English Rose. It's an English pub and has a great set of regulars. When the regulars find out I'm friends with Kristen Harrer, the girl who got me the job, they make things easy for me. They welcome me quickly and tip well. Covering my rent is not going to be a problem. It's a small bar, seats around twelve people, and has a simple menu. The regulars come in at the same time every day in short intervals. They start at exactly five and then show up one by one every ten minutes until six. The same seven guys, and occasionally a wife or girlfriend, hang out every day.

The whole place runs with four people. Me at the bar, a cook, a manager, and Cindy McCormick waiting tables. It's routine, but the money comes in fine. Easy money is never something to complain about.

Cindy has a boyfriend but is really flirty with everyone. She shamelessly admits that that was how she earns her money. She dresses sexy, showing what she could get away with, and she knows everyone's names and plays the game well. For some reason, she's flirty with me, too. I wasn't giving her any money though, so what was the point? Just playing the game, I guess, but maybe it's more.

This is a two o'clock bar, so it's harder to make it to The House in time for last call. However, I'm not sure how much that matters these days.

The crew died with Victor. However, I would show up late some nights and hang out with Jason at the door. Now that I'm not drinking, I'm in no hurry to make last call. It's about seeing people and winding down from work. I don't even drink Cokes. I just hang around by the door for the last fifteen minutes that they are open.

A lot like at some other bars where Victor, Raymond, and I used to hang out, I was occasionally invited to stay after close. Instead of drinking free with the staff like in the past, I just sit there and watch them clean up, and we talk. I find out a little more about the staff. Dell is actually married to Amanda, one of the waitresses. It's a very incestuous business. They are the strangest couple, but I guess opposites do attract. Dell is outspoken and talks all the time while Amanda is quiet and keeps to herself. The quiet types are rare in this business, but she is one of the sweetest girls you'd ever meet.

Alex has a boyfriend, but they don't really get along, and she complains about him every night. He is one of Jason's best friends from high school, another small world thing. As far as this guy being a boyfriend, I think we all thought 'Why are they still together?' Some people just don't want to be alone, and they stay with someone they don't like just to have someone. I never understood that. I'd rather be miserable by myself than be miserable with someone else.

Jason has stopped working the bar at the place where I ran the kitchen. He just started bartending at The House on the weekdays while still working the door on the weekends. He has a natural charm that works to his advantage. He doesn't intentionally play the game like Cindy does, but it's in him.

Steven Milbrook is part owner and only works the bar on the weekends. He has a ponytail - a Deadhead and a Hippie all the way. A weed-smoking boss is pretty cool. He is really laid back and just oozes cool. He knows everyone who walks into the place. Regulars or not, he knows everyone. He is ultra-friendly and the consummate professional. He makes the staff wear ties and dress shirts to show some class, but the place is still really laid back. He sets the tone, and the staff follows. For some reason, it's hard to act like a fool when you're wearing a tie, so the whole staff maintains the same level of class.

It's a friendly neighborhood bar with a ton of regulars, mostly people in the business. Other places would close around two or earlier, and their staff would go wind down at The House. Its name fit. It was just that comfortable.

At this point, I've been coming here for around two years. They all know me and treat me well. I feel comfortable here, so I almost always make a point of coming by most nights, regardless of what else I have going on.

I introduce Cindy to the place, and she and her boyfriend would join me there whenever we could get there before last call. A cab was needed to do this. Cabs were not that expensive, but when you took them all the time, it added up.

I probably spent enough on cabs each year to have bought my own car. Keeping a car in the city seemed a waste to me. It wasn't just gas, parking, and maintenance. Tickets and towing were inevitable and made owning a car in the city more expensive than I could justify. Just covering the day-to-day bills was enough for me.

Cindy, her boyfriend, and I hang out a lot. Her boyfriend shows up every night at last call and stays with us while we close the place. Even though he's a bit of a loser, we are friendly towards one another, and at the same time, Cindy and I get close. It works that way with most jobs. There is that bond. Also, if you are friends with your coworkers, the job is just that much easier to take. Work is still a party and fun, which is why this business is so much better than a nine-to-five; at least, it is for me. I can't imagine doing anything else.

Staying sober in the business is challenging, but I've done it for years. Meetings on my off days, make it easier. In Chicago, meetings are a lot different than in Texas. In Texas, I had several meetings where everyone knew me, and I was comfortable enough to talk every once in a while. In Chicago meetings, I pretty much just listen, but I start seeing a lot of the same people. One guy shows up at a lot of different meetings and is like a local celebrity in his own right. Everyone knows him, and everyone wants to be like him. He isn't just sober. He shows that it is possible to be clean and still have fun.

Ryan Briar is his name. Last names are not usually used, but he says he had nothing to hide. Everyone knows him and anxiously waits to hear him talk in meetings. He always has something inspiring to say. He's, my age. The average person in AA seems around forty or older, but Chicago has people of all ages. Ryan is like the leader of the people under thirty. The way he lives his life makes you want to live yours the same way. He knows what not to say just as much as he knows what to say, and in only a few words, makes you feel better about your day.

I don't make it to a lot of meetings, but he's at about seven out of ten.

Cindy comes into work one night looking kind of down. She's finally broken up with her loser boyfriend. I never liked that guy. They are both former heroin users who still drink. Keeping clean is more important to Cindy than it is to him, and he went back to it one too many times. She drinks, and drinks a lot at times, but has been off the junk for three years. He just couldn't leave it alone.

Now that she's single, I want to find out if there is anything behind her flirtiness. There is.

Over the last few months of hanging out, we got to know each other pretty well, as one usually does with coworkers. The regulars were placing bets on how long it would take for us to hook up. They had been rooting for us even while she was dating the loser. We would have made a decent couple, but she had just broken up with her boyfriend, and I was not that kind of shark.

One night, she and I are hanging out with Jason, Stephanie Hunter, and Dan Plum. Dan works at the blues club on the same block as Jerry's and The House. Stephanie is Jason's latest girlfriend. Dan is married, but after months of hanging out with him, I still have never seen his wife, ever. This night is no different.

The five of us are hanging out at Dan's place and listening to music. Dan has a great collection of old blues records. They are smoking weed, and the contact high has me just as mellow.

At around six in the morning, Jason and Stephanie drive me and Cindy back to my place. It's like it was planned that way all along.

It's unusually hot for April, and it's just about to get even hotter. Cindy and I are making out on the way into my place and go straight for the bedroom. She slowly takes off her clothes, one piece at a time. It doesn't take long because she rarely wears much in the first place. Her skin tastes like strawberries. It's four hours later when we both pass out.

Raymond says that if your girl doesn't fall asleep after sex, you have more work to do.

After everyone finds out about us at work, Bob, the older regular, wins the pool.

A few weeks later, Jason tells me that his roommate is moving out and invites me to stay with him. Jerry's lease would be up soon, and

Jason seems stable enough that I could stay at his place for a while. Jerry turns around and renews his lease at the last minute and is pissed that I'm moving out, but Jason's is just the better deal. It's still four hundred a month for my part, but he would pay a little more because he has the bigger room, and it's his name on the lease. I think he is also just being a nice guy about it. He knew how much I was paying at Jerry's and didn't change that. It puts The House almost exactly halfway between our place and English Rose. It's a much better set up.

Jason's place is also only about eight blocks from an AA house where Ryan Briar is a regular. I see him at every meeting and his words just seem to make life easier. At this place, I feel more comfortable and actually speak once in a while. It makes a difference when you are actually a part of the discussion.

Cindy keeps a studio that is only a few blocks from our bar, but for some reason, we spend most nights at my place. I don't have AC, and it gets to be a very hot summer. We take a cab back and forth to work every day, but the cash flow is strong enough to support it. Most of the time we have the same cab driver, and he becomes our regular guy. To have your own personal cab driver is pretty cool.

One morning at the end of summer, Jason comes banging on my door.

"Hey, man. You oughta wake up and check this out. They are blowing up New York."

Cindy and I get out of bed and rush into the living room. The TV is showing this scene over and over again. It's like something out of a Jerry Bruckheimer movie. Two planes, one after the other, are crashing into the Twin Towers. The World Trade Center in New York comes down like it's made of sand. They also show another plane crashing into The Pentagon. There is a fourth plane that people think is headed for the Sears Tower that crashes into a field. America is under attack. It's the first attack on American soil since Pearl Harbor.

It just doesn't look real.

English Rose was on the first floor of a fifty-story high rise, and it was kinda scary thinking about being at work. The thought of being caught in that same scene in Chicago was terrifying. Somewhere around three thousand people lost their lives. Some actually made it out and some were pulled out of the rubble days later. I can't imagine what it would be like to be trapped or essentially buried alive. An unknown number were lost in the wreckage and dust. In Chicago we prayed that there would be no more.

The scenes played over and over again on TV for months and every time I saw it, it was like something out of a movie. It didn't seem real, but to every American it was very real.

Patriotism was at an all-time high, but we didn't feel safe for a while. The news kept saying to stay vigilant, but what could we really do? Everyone seemed to be suspect, and no one could be trusted. Things changed forever.

In November, I take Cindy to a family party. She met Nate at The House, and now she's meeting the family. Things are getting pretty serious. Everyone seems to like her, but even if they don't, they would never tell me. They would usually wait till it's over to tell me just how much they didn't like the girl.

On a rare night that Cindy is working and I'm not, I make my way to The House. Raymond takes me aside. "I ran into Cindy at a party." Raymond hasn't been around much and hasn't even met her yet.

"When? She's with me almost every night."

"Last Friday. You were working."

"Ok."

"I didn't know her, but as we were making out, she said that she was cheating on her boyfriend and that I knew him."

"You were making out?"

"Yeah, like I say, I didn't know who she was. We were making out hard, and I was just about to take her panties off when she told me that she was dating you. It stopped immediately. I just thought you should know."

There's nothing to say.

A few weeks later he tells me that he knows that she's cheating on me with some guy from Jerry's. Raymond seems intent on convincing me she's no good.

I don't really believe him, but the guy comes in, and I figure I'll confront him to find out for sure. Horse's mouth.

"Raymond says that you were fooling around with Cindy McCormick."

"Raymond said that?" He works with Ray, and I knew him through channels. He seems genuinely shocked. At one point, he even breaks into tears and swears that it isn't true, and he couldn't believe that Raymond would say that about him.

That's it for Raymond. I've taken all I can handle from him. He bailed on everyone when Victor died, and now that he's around again, he's making up lies about my girlfriend. We stop hanging out and talking. He's not around much anyway, so this is pretty easy to do.

Awhile later, I go into English Rose while Cindy is bartending. The guy is sitting at the end of the bar. Why is he here?

The manager comes over to me, all friendly, "Hey Jeff, do you know Mark? He's gonna be working here."

How is he supposed to start working here when there are no shifts available? Why isn't anyone saying anything? Why does the manager have this shitty grin on his face?

I look over at Cindy, and the look on her face says it all.

I look right back at her, "It's true, isn't it? You fuckin' bitch." I storm out and throw a bar stool across the room on my way out. It just barely misses hitting this glass Guinness sign.

Still pissed, I go to The House, pass Jason, and go right up to Raymond. We haven't spoken in over a month. I look him straight in the eye. When he's sitting, we're almost at the same level. Everyone can see how pissed I am. I reach out my arm, shake his hand and say, "I'm sorry, you were right all along." Then, I just leave while everyone is still staring.

The guy took my job and my girlfriend. Or so I thought. They did fool around but didn't become a couple. He did take my job though. It wasn't all Cindy's fault or his. The manager was a drunk and hated me. Half the time, I ended up doing his job. I thought that I had a chance at taking his job since I ended up doing it most of the time anyway. Instead, he found a way to edge me out.

He was one of those that didn't trust anyone that didn't drink. He would get so wasted while working that he would often leave early, and I would end up closing. Most nights I didn't mind not having him around. The cook would leave early after closing the kitchen, and when we got everyone out, Cindy and I would have sex on the pool table or in the office. We had sex on the roof of my apartment building once. We even had sex on the back patio of The House. She was crazy, and I shouldn't have been surprised by her cheating on me. I later found out that she had gotten back together with the heroin guy.

Despite everything, later that week, I go over to Cindy's place and confront her about everything. She opens up and tells me everything and apologizes, for what good it would do. We sit around talking for a while. She gets up at one point and tells me she has to go change her panties because our conversation is getting her all wet.

I figure we'd take advantage of the situation, and I follow her into the bathroom, and we have sex one more time. If she could cheat on me, she could cheat with me.

Afterward, I walk her to work and sit at the bar with the regulars while she starts bartending. The manager worked the day shift, so I wouldn't have to see him or Mark. She is all red and uncomfortable. I love it.

I realized later that I didn't love her. I just loved the regular sex and having someone around. So, this didn't hurt that badly.

When it was all over, all of my friends took their turn telling me how bad she was for me. Nice timing, guys.

A few weeks later, I'm hanging out at my place with one of the hostesses from Jerry's. She is hot, and I'm trying to work her to some extent. I call for a cab to take her home after getting nowhere with her. The cabbie is my regular guy. He is all ready to go straight to

English Rose when I tell him the address. He kind of looks back, then just takes us to her place.

"I'll be right back. I'm just going to walk her to the door."

"With anyone else, I would make them pay first, but for you, I will wait."

I get back to the cab, and he says, "I'm sorry. I didn't realize that was not your wife."

I just laugh. The other girl wasn't my wife either.

Another girl, another job, another address, another year.

Since Jason is now working bar shifts, he gives his door shifts to me. Steven welcomes me aboard, and all is well. After tip out, the job barely covers rent, but we make it work, and I look for another job during the week.

The House has a regular guy that does cleanup and takes in orders in the daytime, but he is leaving. Steven asks me to take over, as well as work the door on Friday and Saturday nights. It means six days a week cleaning with two nights a week at the door. I take it because I need it.

The hours are rough on the weekends. Friday, I did the cleaning job from 8AM to 4PM. I started the door shift at 6PM, so between 4 & 6 I would just hang out. Then after closing and finishing the door shift, I only had 3 hours before I had to be back for the cleanup shift, so I'd just stay. Basically, I'd go in at 8AM on Friday and stay till 4pm on Sunday.

It is brutal, but it pays the bills.

I do this for about six months. Then, Ken Lawler takes over the door shifts. Ken is Jason's cousin. He works for UPS during the day all week long then the door on Friday and Saturday nights. He seems to handle the hours better than I ever could.

I'm pretty strict at the door, whereas Ken is more easy-going. He seems to really want to get the hang of it and gets to know everybody pretty quickly. The regulars like him, and he starts hanging out at their bars when he can, just to get to know people better.

I don't mind the day shifts six days a week, cleaning up, and taking in orders. Sometimes, I take inventory and actually place the orders. I get to know the vendors and all the salespeople. It's more than just cleaning up; it feels like I'm a manager at the same time. It still isn't quite what I want to do, so I'm still looking.

I found a place that needs a five-night-a-week bartender, and Ken helps find someone to do the cleanup shifts. Steven understands that I am too much of a bartender to just be the cleanup guy, and Evan Hibbard takes over. Evan is a friend of Ken's from high school, and they still hang out. It always amazes me when I see people that are still friends with people from high school.

Ken and Evan are pretty good guys, and I feel like I'm not leaving Steven high and dry when I leave. I'm actually leaving this job on good terms.

My new bar is not technically a gay bar, but it has drag shows on the weekends. It attracts more gay guys than not, but it isn't technically a gay bar. I don't really know what that means either. It also attracts bachelorette parties. The manager is gay and is also the kind of person who doesn't trust people who don't drink. We get along fine, though.

I go to a meeting at the regular place that was a few blocks from home after having not been to one for about three months. Everyone is really quiet tonight. Ryan had just died.

Son of a bitch! What next?

They say it was just a freak accident, and he was shot in the face while cleaning one of his guns. The thing is, he knew better than that, and it was questionable that that was how it happened. Regardless, he had quite the following, and the place is packed. Everyone is there to talk about him and to mourn the loss.

I can't stand it. I've had enough. So, I'm off to The House to see friends and to order a CC and seven. Jason is bartending and doesn't even question it. I don't think he even realizes that I've been sober for the last nine months.

It's the same time of year that Victor died.

I also find out that my Godmother died this same week.

How are all these people dying while I, somehow, stay alive? With all of my reckless behavior and near misses, how am I still walking around breathing? What the fuck?

I may not have beaten my mother to the grave, but it seems that my plan is still in action and death would be sweet release. Somehow, I keep going to work and paying the bills and getting by. Why them? Why not me? Nothing seems to make any sense. Just another day. Just another messed up year.

Anyway, now that I am drinking again, the manager at my new bar is loving it. He would come behind the bar and pour Rumplemitze straight out of the chilled bottle down my throat. Occasionally, I would end up working with my shirt off. I'm not in very good shape, but no one questions it or seems to mind. My friends would sometimes come in and wonder what the hell is wrong with me, but who cares? I'm having fun and making about three hundred a night.

I sometimes get so wasted that I can't clean up at the end of the shift. The manager would tell me that it was no big deal and to have one of the kitchen guys do the cleanup. I would give them about fifty bucks for the help. No one complains.

A lot of nights after work, I would need to take a Silkwood shower to get the dirty off. I was a whore. I'm playing the game now, and I had never been like that before. I used to be all about professionalism. My style of bartending was based on speed and consistency. My style was friendly but serious. My style was by the book. Now I've sold out and fallen into the game. I'm doing whatever it takes to make money, regardless of morals and personal dignity. This job has reduced me to a slave to the game, but that's exactly what the manager wants out of me. He respects my style, but insists I at least look like I'm having fun. I am playing the part well.

I'm not friends with anyone at this place, so the usual fun with coworkers isn't there. Everyone is playing the game, and everyone is just out for their own money. I'm the new guy, but I'm getting the best shifts. They hate me for that and without the bond amongst my coworkers, the job feels like work for the first time in a while.

As long as the customers love me and the manager likes what I'm doing, the money keeps coming, but who have I become?

I would end up losing this job, too. I just have no idea how it went down. Being too drunk at work was never a problem, and I don't remember missing any shifts. It just happens as if on a schedule. The cycle is always the same. I'd get a good job and make decent money. I'd usually meet new people and have a lot of fun, but when the time was up, it was up. Time usually brought on what Nate called the "Jeff Echterling home game". I would start coming in late, I would start missing shifts, then I would just disappear. One day, I would come in for my last check, then just walk away. I don't know if I just got bored, or I felt there was nothing more that I could bring. It just ended. It always just ended.

I thought of Amber and how she got lost in the rush and the wildlife that sometimes went hand in hand with the business. I thought about how she was able to be picked up and dusted off and was able to start over with the help of her parents. I had no safety net. Somehow, I always found work and survived, but was just surviving all, I could hope for? Just getting by and barely living in a blind whirlwind life? I could maintain consistency in the recipes of hundreds of drinks, but consistency in my own life seems so far out of reach. I'm lost and out of control, but all I can do is keep going.

I go back to work at The House. I take over Evan's job like he took over for me. Steven is fine with it as long as someone is doing what needs to be done. Evan gets a job at another restaurant cooking, which is more of what he really wants to do. He is a chef, like I am a bartender. It is just in us. He is a lot like me and works a lot of different jobs. He is never satisfied and always thinks that he could do more. He has drive and ambition, plans and dreams. I'm just surviving.

Anyway, his leaving works out great for me, and I am only out of work for a few weeks. The money I made at the last place keeps the bills paid and lets me do what I want, but if I had been out of work much longer, it would have gotten tough.

Life goes on, and I get by.

This time, I take the cleanup job more seriously. I overhear Steven tell one of the vendors that he couldn't run the place without me. I feel valuable again. The rest of the staff calls me 'Super Stocker' because they wanted for nothing during their shifts. I have the place stocked tight and over stocked on days when I know they would need it. The floors never shined more.

I work my eight to four and get my hours in. I do my best work and am appreciated for it. I sleep well at night and feel good about myself. This is more than just surviving, even though it is not exactly what I want to do. The rush of the bar is what I really want. It would come. I just have to do what I have to do for now.

Victor is gone. The crew died with him. People are dropping like flies, but somehow, I survive. I am the one who has wanted to die since I was twelve, and yet I'm still here. Then again, Amber survived. Not that I wished her any harm, but if she had died, it would at least have been expected. It would have made sense.

Who goes and who stays is not up to me. It's not up to any of us. For most, life goes on even if it isn't quite what they want. I know a ton of people that just do their jobs and pay their bills. It's not about fun or excitement; it's about providing for their families and doing what they have to do. Their rewards come in different ways. Their reward is in their families and in enjoying the time with their kids and spouses.

I have no kids, and a wife was, at the very least, a long time away. I can't relate to people that have that kind of life. I just don't understand it. I don't think I ever will. This was never for me. Excitement has to be a part of it. Just grinding through life isn't in me. There has to be more.

More, hopefully, would one day be a steady job that was rewarding, a wife and kids, family life, and the whole shebang, but for now...

What's next?

Chapter Seven: Hot-Dogs, Whores & Haagen-Dazs

At this point, I've been working on and off at The House for close to two years. While working the door, it is a 6PM to 6AM shift. When picking up bar shifts, it is four to six. Whenever I worked at other places, the hours were pretty much the same. Working day shifts has always been a real challenge for me. I've never been a morning person. Whenever I work the cleanup job, I work my eight to four, sleep till around eleven, and then the night is mine.

The night is still a big part of who I am, but now it is just a matter of what to do with it. I can't stay out too late because I have to work in the morning, but that rarely stops me. I don't want to hang out at the bar, because I'll be there till close and just hang out till it was time to start work. There is never a shortage of people to talk to. I have to find something else to do with my time.

Most nights, I end up walking the streets trying to tire myself out so I can get a little more sleep, but mostly I'm killing time and, in a way, looking for trouble. I start out in the East Village where we live, about Grand and Ashland and walk-up Ashland to North Avenue, then east to around the Red Line. I don't know how many miles I'm covering, but this is a pretty fair distance. The length of the walk never crosses my mind. I just have to do something.

Along North Avenue, it is easy to find trouble. There are a lot of bars, and the hookers work that strip. I have never thought of actually using their services, but it's weirdly cool that it is available. I get propositioned all the time, but just shrug it off. There is action in the neighborhood and even though I'm not involved, being a spectator always holds my attention.

After a little people watching, I would usually turn around and take the walk home. I'd get back to my neighborhood anywhere between one and five in the morning. I'd grab something to eat, relax for a bit, then I would be off to work again.

My neighborhood isn't quite as exciting, but that is a good thing. There is a twenty-four-hour gas station that for some reason serves fried chicken. It is affectionately known in the neighborhood as 'The Chicken Shell'. They also always have a stock of Haagen-Daz.

I had developed a bad ice cream addiction when I lived with Jerry.

When I lived with Jerry up by Montrose, only a few blocks away, there had been a twenty-four-hour Baskin Robbins combo-ed with a Dunkin Donuts. It seemed an obvious combination to me to put a scoop of ice cream on one of the donuts, but I could never get them to do it. Living with Jerry and taking in plenty of second-hand pot smoke all day long, I had found myself at the place all the time. I was putting away about a half-gallon of ice cream a day. That was the first time in my life that I actually noticed myself putting on weight. I put on almost twenty pounds to bring me up to about normal.

Near our place in The Village is a hot dog stand that stays open till about two in the morning. I am pretty much living on ice cream and hot dogs - Chicago style hot dogs with the works, except that I'm not a fan of the hot peppers. I eat hot dogs and cheese fries with a giant Coke. That's my diet, and although I never exercise, I maintain my average weight.

One night, I wake up around midnight and head out for my walk. There is a hooker working our neighborhood. My mind is going crazy and as much as a part of me is saying, 'don't do it', I am going to do it anyway. I think maybe if I could do it in the comfort of my own home, it won't be so awkward. Somehow, it feels like it might be OK. Trying to work something out on the street always seemed impossible, but my own bed... well, it was possible. Do I really want to be that guy, though? Cindy was months ago, and my current lifestyle isn't bringing up many options.

I go for it.

When I approach her, she propositions me right away. Since we are only a block away, I ask if we can just go back to my place. She has no problem with that. There is definitely a condom used, and I am careful... as careful as you can be in this circumstance. I tend to take a while, and I can tell she is getting antsy and ready to go. So, we just kind of stop, even though I'm not even close. I guess if she has a pimp, and she is gone for more than twenty minutes she could get in trouble, and it's been like forty-five minutes. Despite not getting off, it is still a thrill. It is so wrong and a bit twisted, but that's a big part of what makes it exciting.

I try not to make a regular habit of this.

All those nights of wandering around watching the action makes it almost inevitable that I would eventually give in and try to be a part of the action. Just doing something out of the ordinary and outside my comfort zone... is a rush.

Most nights, I would just end up at the bar and stay all night. I would hang out after close, then start work at around 6 or 7 AM depending on what we are doing. As long as I start work by nine, I'm fine. On Sunday nights, it's a free-for-all because I don't have to work Mondays. It's a lot like when Raymond, Victor and I would hang out. All night runs. Bar, coffee house, work and sometimes a little sleep, then repeat. Raymond is a part of it all again and Jason is working there most nights so he would hang out, too. It would never be the same without Victor, but it is better and safer than my midnight walks.

We start playing poker and blackjack after hours with some of the guys from the blues club. Dan Plum would be there and Alfredo Romona. Alfredo is nuts. He is about 5'7" and around three hundred pounds. He works the door at the blues club with Dan. At one point, well before I met him, he had been shot in the head, but survived, and apparently now is just as nuts as he always was. It doesn't slow him down a bit. In fact, it seems to rev him up because I think it makes him feel invincible. He can handle himself in any situation with the utmost confidence. Every other word out of his mouth is 'fuck'. I swear a lot, but this guy... it is just a natural part of his everyday speech. He is who he is, and no one says anything about it.

There is also this guy called Knight. I don't think his closest friends know his real name. This guy dresses like he is the star of the show every night, and most nights, he is, or at least he is treated that way. Everyone respects him or maybe fears him a bit. He usually has a lot of crazy fine women around, but none of them hang out for long. He seems to like a bit of freedom. This guy is style personified.

So, Raymond, Jason, Dan, Alfredo, Knight, and I shuffle up and play cards at least three nights a week. Steven could never know. We would lose our liquor license. The front of the bar is all glass, and you can easily see in from the street. Despite the risks, we are throwing money around the table with every turn. Most nights, I lose my ass, but when we play blackjack and I'm the dealer... I rake. I'm paying my rent with my winnings.

We always play at a table in the back and never talk about it. It's like 'Fight Club'. No one else is part of it, and no one else ever knew. It's best that way, and we feel better about risking the license, although I think I'm the only one concerned.

The excitement again comes from the simple fact that it's wrong and dangerous. It satisfies my need for some kind of rush.

On a Tuesday morning, I am getting ready for work. I start to open the bathroom door, but it opened before I could get to it. Alex is standing on the other side of the door completely naked. I'm sure my jaw is on the floor and my eyes are bugging out of my head. We just stand there staring at each other for what seems like a full five minutes. She is frozen like a deer in headlights, and I'm in complete shock. Why she is there doesn't even cross my mind until later in the day, but the image of her standing there naked would be forever frozen in my brain.

As far as I know, she is still seeing Jason's friend, and this is probably something I should keep to myself. I don't tell anyone.

Although things are running reasonably smoothly lately, I am always on the lookout for another job. This time, I'm looking for management positions instead of bartending. I've worked my way into management at most of my jobs. The management part of the cleanup job feels good to me. I feel like I'm learning how things are done in Chicago, and I want to see if I can bring that to a full-on job. Can I be that kind of guy? Responsibility is another rush for me, and the more the better.

There is a new place opening up that likes my resume. I recognize the address. It is the 'not really a gay bar' place, but this time, it would be quite different. This place is set up to be anything but gay. Their bar staff aren't actual trained bartenders. They are all scantily clad models and dancers. Usually, you would get sued if you intentionally only hired hot people to work, but this place got around that.

They really aren't bartenders.

They would dance on top of the bar all in unison to various songs. Anytime those particular songs came on the jukebox, they have to get up there. They would stop pouring drinks and basically drop everything to put on the show. Their bartending skills were secondary to the show. The show drew the crowd, and the crowd was huge every night. If they only got around to making half the drinks an actual bartender would, it was still a great night in sales. They played the game, but I felt for them. Being the same place that I used to play the game, I knew what it was like to be a whore for the money. These girls were different. None of them seemed to mind it at all.

This place seats around two hundred people but somehow packs in over three hundred. My being a by-the-book kind of guy makes me uncomfortable with over-filling the place.

You see, a few years ago there was a club on the South Side that packed the place every night, and one night, things got out of control and people started rushing the door. Five to six hundred people all trying to leave at the same time. Someone upstairs yelled, 'bomb' after one of the security guards sprayed a cloud of pepper spray to break up a fight. People were in fear for their lives and because of the panic, and the narrow hallway to the one exit, people got trampled and dozens of people were hurt, and a few were even killed.

Overcrowding a bar is a serious offense now. The city polices this really closely and the fire department reset just about everybody's max capacity signs. These signs are taken seriously, and when it says two hundred and seventeen people, they mean two hundred and seventeen, not one more. Most places are required to have the doorman use a hand-held headcounter to track it all closely. A lot of places have learned how to fudge the numbers by now, and this place is great at it. It also helps that they have the fire department and some officials in pocket, I think.

This job wasn't easy to get. It was one of the most intimidating interviews I'd ever been in. They sat me in this tiny office with the whole management staff and all the corporate heads. Around seven people were packed into this small room, and all of them were hammering me with questions.

At one point, the head corporate guy asked, "How do you calculate liquor cost?"

I had to be honest, "The computer always does that for me."

They all laughed, but it was an uncomfortable laugh.

Turns out the old owner, the guy that ran the 'not really a gay bar' place, is still involved with this place. He remembers me and is a strong advocate for putting me on the staff. That helped a lot and may have been the deciding factor.

They are a chain but have never served food before. It is now required in Chicago that you serve food if you want to hold a liquor license. The House didn't have to serve food because they'd had their license long before the rule went into effect.

The fact that I'd opened a ton of places from the very beginning, coupled with my kitchen background, was another reason I got the job. I was hired to run the kitchen but was trained to run the floor.

The kitchen runs pretty smoothly for the most part, mainly because no one orders food. The menu is simple bar food, and I rarely have to pitch in to help out the cooks. Most of my time is spent out on the floor playing the part of another security guard and being accessible to the bar staff.

The security staff at this place is the same staff that works for one of those 'throw-chairs-fighting-screaming-tearing-clothes' daytime talk shows, and they earn their money. Horny, drunk guys can be trouble.

One particular night, I'm hanging out on the upper level around the back bar. One of the stupidest things about this place is that they don't serve water. If you order water, the bartenders would occasionally spray you in the face from the soda gun. I know this will be trouble one day.

Sure enough, this guy orders water, and the bartender hits him with the spray. He gets pissed and throws his drink at her. There is no security by the back bar, so now I have to be the one to throw him out. I hate doing it because I think I would've done the same thing in his shoes. He doesn't put up any fight. I think he knows he is in the wrong. I walk him to the door, and the front door security takes him out.

Later, the head of security finds out about this and decides to bitch me out on one of the days that the owner of the company happens to be in the office. He is dead serious that any issues that come up have to be dealt with by the security team and no one else is to get involved. I couldn't say anything because there is no break in his rant. Then, he leaves before I can explain my side. After he leaves, the owner and everyone else just stare at me.

"There was no security guard by the back bar. I just did it out of habit."

Nothing more is said about it, but the owner would remember.

A week later, I notice that I am scheduled 'off' on a delivery day. No one else knows how to take in the deliveries, so it's nuts to not have me there on that day, but I haven't had a day off since I started, so I take it.

I come in the following night for my next shift, and they have run out of almost everything in the kitchen. As it turns out, the manager who had been working the day before just sent the delivery back. He sent the driver away because he didn't want to take the delivery in. I can't believe it. This has never happened. I am fuming.

I start making all my phone calls and arrange for the delivery to come that night, which is pretty much unheard of. The rep is really cool, and we get along great, so he does me this huge favor.

Just after I hang up the phone, the owner comes in and fires me. I tell him that I fixed it, but he doesn't care. The manager who turned the order away is a friend of his from New York, and one of us has to go because of this. The fact that I have more experience and a stronger background doesn't matter. The guy is a friend.

Oh well, here we go again. I actually don't mind losing this one that much. This is one of the most corrupt places I've ever worked. They seem to have everybody in pocket or at least brag that they do. They do whatever they want, regardless of any rules, laws, or basic morals. Not to mention the fact that the owner is a huge coke head and would light up the bartenders to try and get laid. It's a whore house.

Before I left The House to go work at the whore house, Evan took over for me again. The timing always seemed to work out for both of us. I would lose a job, and he would find a job about the same time. Then he would lose a job, and I would find one. Whoever was out of work at what we considered 'real jobs' would work at The House. It was time to switch places again. He was working, I was working, and Steven was happy as long as the job got done, but how many times could we do this?

This time, I'm not taking the job seriously at all. I get the job done, but my heart just isn't in it. I cut back the hours that I would work and start hanging out more. This time, Evan and Ken become a part of it all. I feel I owe Evan because he's bailed me out so many times and, because of his help, we've always been able to keep each other employed. I haven't really seen that much of Ken before, but having been such close friends they kind of came as a packaged deal. They are funny together. They know each other so well that they finish each other's sentences and tell stories in unison. The few crazy events in their lives are constantly a part of the conversation. Even after hearing the stories several times, I still find humor in the way the two of them would tell their stories.

Truth is, before moving to Chicago a few years ago, they had lived kind of sheltered lives. Suburbanites completely. They were cool and great friends, but they were on a much different level compared to Raymond and Jason. They weren't losers by any means; they just lacked style and social skills that seemed so natural to guys like Ray. That was all fine. I could dial it down a notch for a while.

Since I am off on Mondays, they start inviting me to go golfing with them. I've never golfed before in my life, and I'm not making much money these days. I understand that golf is a pretty expensive sport. Ken insists on paying. I don't like being a leech, but he doesn't make me feel that way. It seems like they want me around, and it doesn't matter that I'm broke. This guy is generous to a fault. He is literally a shirt-off-his-back kind of friend. I actually saw him give the shirt he was wearing to someone because they said they liked it.

After we would finish a full eighteen, we would go to some nice place to eat. Again, he insists on paying. Golf and nice restaurants... it feels like we are big shots living the high life.

Most of the regulars from The House also work in bars. It's Ken's idea to go to their bars and kind of get to know them better. We are building better regulars and sharing the wealth like Raymond, and I used to do. The only difference between hanging out with these guys and hanging out with guys like Raymond is that, with these guys, there aren't really any chicks around.

I still play cards with Raymond and the guys most Sunday nights. Jason isn't working one Sunday. Dell is the bartender, and he isn't a part of the game, so we decide to take the game back to my place. Just as we are getting out of the cab, Raymond says, "Maybe we should ring the doorbell first. Jason's probably up there fucking some chick."

I hadn't even thought about it, but what if he were up there with Alex? No one is supposed to know. I think I've screwed up badly here, but there is no turning back. If we don't go upstairs, they would know that Jason is up there with someone, and they'd know that I knew. They wouldn't know it was Alex unless they were in the living room. As long as they were in the bedroom, everything would be fine.

When I open the door, they are either not there or in the bedroom. The place is dead silent.

We play cards for about three hours, and I am losing my ass. Despite knowing better, I go into my rent money and lose that, too. When I'm cleaned out, the game pretty much ends and everyone goes home, but before Raymond leaves, I pull him aside.

"Dude, I screwed up and lost my rent money. I'm totally tapped."

"Don't sweat it. How much do ya need?"

"Five bills. Rent and some walking around money."

He pulls out his winnings and peels off five bills without even a thought. He is usually flush, and it doesn't set him back any to help me out. He doesn't even seem concerned with when I would pay him back.

I have him paid in full in five weeks.

I hate borrowing money, so I only do it when I am truly desperate. Unfortunately, desperate times seem to come pretty frequently. When I think about it though, I haven't had to borrow any money in a long time. That is mostly due to the fact that there is no one I can borrow from.

As soon as Raymond is out the door, Alex comes out of Jason's room and makes a beeline to the bathroom. Apparently, she has had to pee really badly for hours and had almost hung her ass out the window, but everyone left just in time.

The next day, I'm doing the regular golf thing with Ken and Evan. Somehow my borrowing money from Raymond comes up, and Ken asks, "Why didn't you come to me?"

"Five bills is a lot of money."

"I trust you."

"Hopefully, I'm never in that spot again, but it's good to know I'm covered."

Jason starts giving up a lot of his Sunday nights because he is starting to cover more Fridays and Saturdays. So, with Jason out, poker pretty much stops. It's more than likely for the best because it seems my luck has run out.

One Sunday night, I'm finishing my cleaning and stocking when Ken comes in to cover Jason's shift behind the bar. Ken works a regular Monday through Friday, nine to five and is still working the door Friday and Saturday nights. I don't know how he manages those hours, but he is determined to work as much as he can at The House. Dell and Jason give up shifts all the time. I'd covered several in the past, but now that Ken is also bartending, he thinks he is 'King Shit'. It usually takes a long time to work your way from the door to the bar. Some places make you wait a full year. It only takes Ken about four months. Almost all doormen try to work their way onto the bar schedule. It is much more money and a lot more fun.

That night they even have him training a new waitress.

Jeri Proesel is her name, and she is ultra-sweet. Something in my head says that if I work it right, I could get her, and it wouldn't be that difficult. Not to say that she seems easy, but that she seems to like me just that much. When we talk, she has a grin from ear to ear and even if we aren't the ones talking, she seems to have her eyes on me the whole time. We talk the whole night.

The bar is pretty much a ghost town. Whenever Jason would trade away his shift, people just wouldn't come in.

Towards the end of the night, right around 2AM, the bulk of the regulars show up. Almost every one of them asks, "Where's Jason?" as soon as they walk in the door. They did the same thing whenever I was working, too. It drove me nuts. Like, 'What? I'm not good enough for you?'

A few leave right away, but most stay. They stay either because it would have been rude to leave, or because they just don't want to make the effort to go anywhere else.

Knight, Alfredo, and Dan come in just before last call as they usually do. Raymond is already there and laughing at how I'm trying to work Jeri. Knight asks us all if we want to go to a party. He seems to include Ken and Jeri. Ken bows out because he has to work in the morning, but Jeri is up for it. I wasn't going to go because I'd heard about Knight's parties. They were usually way on the West Side, they didn't start until five or six in the morning and sometimes went on for days. When Jeri set herself up to go, I took this as an opportunity to continue my game. So, I'm in. I don't really have much of a game, but this isn't too hard. I just have to keep her talking.

Knight takes off ahead of us then the rest of us pile into Alfredo's truck. As I figured, we are headed west. It seems like we are driving for hours when we end up at Alfredo's house. I guess he has to pick something up. I don't ask, 'what?'

Then, we turn around and head east. We get pretty close to going all the way back to The House when we pull up outside this club. There are people lined up around the block. I don't see any women, and a few of the guys are dressed in leather from head to toe. It's an IML (International Men of Leather) party.

Knight comes out and tells us to take off. It isn't the scene he thought it would be. So, we just go to breakfast.

After two hours of driving around, packed into this truck, we end up going to breakfast a few blocks from The House. Oh well. I am making headway with Jeri. We talk a lot and Raymond chimes in once in a while to help sell me. It doesn't take much. I can tell she is hooked.

After breakfast, Jeri and I go to the beach and talk some more. Most of the night, I've let her talk, but now she wants to know about me. I talk about my time in the restaurant business and a little about my hockey years. Then, I find myself talking about Victor and my mom. This is kind of serious stuff that I generally reserve for people I really care about. Getting deep, though, really works in my favor.

We leave the beach and go back to her place. She has two cats, and I'm highly allergic, but I am on a mission. She throws a movie in, but we start making out instead. I start to take off her clothes, and she stops me.

“Isn’t this moving a little too fast? We just met.”

“Sometimes it just works like that.” Shitty line, but right after saying it, she starts taking off my clothes.

I never take off my own clothes. I had had an ex-girlfriend years ago that accused me of date rape. She never said anything, nor made any effort to stop it. She never said anything and never gave any signs of not wanting to. She even took the top at one point. She just seemed to decide later that she really hadn’t wanted to. It hadn’t been our first time, and nothing seemed out of the ordinary, so how could I have known?

Anyway, I never take off my own clothes anymore. How could I be accused if they were taking that kind of action? I was really careful to not make any stupid mistakes. I didn’t want anything to be taken the wrong way. Sure, this time I was kind of playing a game, but she was playing along with no hesitation.

The sex is great. We start on the couch but move to her bedroom pretty quickly. We don’t want to give her roommate a show. It is early June and incredibly hot in her apartment. We are both sweating so much that it's like doing it under water. Our bodies are sliding across one another, no friction, no discomfort of any kind, just fluid motion. The noises she's making are freaking out her cats, and it's like we have an audience. They sit on the floor next to the bed, staring at us. When it's all over, I fully expect them to break into applause. Why not? I feel like applauding.

We both pass out. It's around three in the afternoon after an all-night run. Thank God I don’t have to work today.

After a long and solid rest, we wake up at around midnight and decide to go out again. We go back to The House, and everyone in there knows exactly what's up. Raymond kind of gives me a motionless, silent high five. I can tell he is proud of me. This is the kind of guy he hoped I would be. He feels that all I need is a little training. Ken is just shaking his head. Jason is trying not to laugh. Evan is a little lost, but Ken catches him up and then he tries to give me a real high five. I give him a look, and he knows to let it go.

Around closing time, we end up back at her place again. This time, we aren't bothering to pretend we are going to watch a movie, but also, this time, I can't stay long. I have to go work in the morning.

I get dressed and leave around eight. She is still asleep.

I am finishing up work around three when Jason comes in to open the bar, so I sit at the bar and hang out for a little while. Minutes after the bar opens at four, Jeri shows up and slides a bar stool right up tight against me. Ken comes in with Evan and invites us out to dinner. I don't want to look like a punk, so I won't let Ken buy this time.

Now she knows all of my friends and most of my life story.

When she gets up to use the bathroom, Ken and Evan start in. "What are you doing? You're just playing with her. She's cool, and we need her as a waitress. Don't fuck up."

"I'm not leading her on. We're just having fun. She knows that."

"Does she?"

She comes back to the table. It's uncomfortably silent. She's not an idiot, so she knows we were talking about her. To break the silence and change the subject, she says, "I'm training with Alex tomorrow night. Anything I should know?"

The only thought about Alex that comes to mind is that she looks great naked. I smile, but no one knows why.

Ken and Evan give her the breakdown on the kind of person Alex is and what to expect. I am actually impressed that they know so much about her.

Alex has been working with the company for years. She started at the sister restaurant on the North Side when she was eighteen and transferred to The House the second, she turned twenty-one. She's about to turn twenty-five, so with eight years in the company, no one has more seniority. You couldn't have asked for a better trainer. Not to mention Steven loves her. Dell has been at The House since it opened, but Alex is the favorite.

Ken and Evan head out, and Jeri and I head back to her place again. This time seems more intense than ever. It's like we are wrestling, and she's winning. I'm not into violent stuff, and it doesn't really go that far. She is just more aggressive than the last few times.

In the morning, it's the same thing, but this time, for some reason, I start to feel a little guilty. I start to feel like I am sneaking out. I start to feel like I am doing something wrong. The guys have gotten to me.

I'm working my shift as usual, and she shows up when the bar opens.

We started hanging out Sunday night at four, then we continue to hang out all day Monday, all day Tuesday and now it's Wednesday afternoon. Thursday, she has to work, and I am able to go home and try to think about what I'm doing. As much as I try to convince myself to shut it down before I hurt her... the sex is just too good.

I never ask her if she is looking for a relationship, and she never asks me. I convince myself that it's all going to be fine, and no one is going to get hurt. When the time comes, I'll do the right thing and let her down easy. If she starts to get too serious, I'll shut it down. If she asks any questions, I'll be honest. So far, it seems safe. I am comfortable enough with it all to finally get a good night's sleep.

Chapter Eight: Playing the Part

When I get home, Alex is there, this time fully clothed.

"So, what's up?"

"We're all going to Whiskey Fest tomorrow night. You comin'?" She successfully dodges my real question.

"Who's all going?"

"Me, Steven and Jason."

"It would be cool to hang with Steven. I might make an appearance."

The next day, Jeri and I find them at this bar on the North Side. The three of them are blasted out of their minds. They've been drinking whiskey all day at this event. Jeri feels the need to get caught up and starts pounding shots. She'd always been a big drinker, but tonight it's like she is on a mission. I think hanging out with Steven is just as uncomfortable for her as it is for me. He is a great guy and treats everyone as friends, not employees, but it's still weird hangin' with the boss. I am kind of doing the sober thing at this time, and I'm just drinking my Coke, trying to ignore the tension. Alex still has a boyfriend.

I have to wonder if Steven knows what's going on, but he may not be making the connection. We are all hanging out as coworkers and friends. No one is acting any differently. Jeri seems to know but asks me anyway.

"Are Alex and Jason a couple?"

"It looks that way."

"I thought she had a boyfriend." She and Alex have become fairly close friends. They work together a lot, but Alex hasn't given anything up. It is still on the down low. I may have given it away, but Jeri is not an idiot and has pretty much figured it out on her own.

The next day, Jason catches me before I lie down after work.

"Did you tell Jeri about me and Alex?" I'd never seen this guy mad before. I didn't think 'mad' was part of him.

"She kind of figured it out."

He is pissed but calm and collected. He says quietly, but with a stern undertone, "Look at it this way... it's not your secret to tell."

I have never heard anyone put it that way. I have to agree and couldn't say anything. We just leave it at that.

Stephanie Hunter, Jason's on-again-off-again-girl, still hangs out at The House, and anytime she's around, Alex has this look of disdain. Jason is hooked on Alex big time and couldn't care less about Stephanie. He still talks to her and flirts a little, but he flirts with every girl that comes into the bar. It's his thing. All the girls love him, but despite trying not to show it in public, he loves Alex.

A few days after Whiskey Fest, Alex breaks up with her boyfriend, but it would take another month before she and Jason would go public. By then, most everyone has already figured it out. They hadn't been that good at hiding it.

Alex's ex-boyfriend hadn't had a clue. He had trusted them both completely, but he knew his relationship with her was over long before she broke up with him. They hadn't really talked or hung out in close to six months.

There is a new regular at The House. When a person comes in everyday and gets to know everyone by name, they are considered regular enough. It always amazes me the amount of people that come in every day. They have real jobs and real responsibilities, but they still show absolute devotion to the bar. Guys like Steven and Jason make everyone feel very at home. Like I said before, the bar's name fits perfectly.

This girl is really talkative, smart, and very likable. Her name is Britney Harrison. No one had seen Britney Wallenberg very much since Victor's funeral. This Britney is blonde and sort of sophisticated for a twenty-two-year-old. She becomes fast friends with everyone, especially Ken. They seem to hit it off right away. Ken is far from a ladies' man, but his personality clicks with hers. They are both very chatty and know a little about a lot of things. They read a lot and watch the news and stuff. I never watch the news. There never seems to be any happy stories.

This girl is not really in the business. She works at a hotel, but I don't really know what she does. For a second, I wonder if she knows Nate. There are tons of hotels in the city, and it is ridiculous to assume they all know each other.

As it turns out though, they do know each other. They had worked together a few times over the years but were never really close. More like good acquaintances.

In this business, acquaintances are much more common. You couldn't get close to everyone no matter how hard you tried. And at this bar, we tried with everyone that came in. That was why there were so many great regulars. To me, though, despite seeing them every day, they were just acquaintances. Good friends were much harder to come by.

Although we still talk pretty often, I haven't actually seen Nate for a while.

Ken's birthday is tonight, and it looks like everyone is going. We end up at this jazz/blues bar off of State Street. As usual, we get through without paying a cover. Ken is getting really messed up, and Raymond seems to be challenging him to keep up. Raymond is like 6'9" and around two-eighty. He's also been a prodigious drinker for years. He could handle his stuff. There is no way Ken can keep up, but he tries.

Tries and fails.

Ken is sitting at the bar with Raymond, and I'm sitting in between Britney and Jeri at a rail behind them. I have to keep reminding Raymond to keep Ken alert, but he keeps dropping his head on the bar. It's never cool to lie out like that in any bar, but this time, it's worse because we know people here. We have to keep him from tapping out. The night is still pretty young.

All the while, I'm actually trying to get to know Britney better and blow off Jeri at the same time. The conversation is going well, and Jeri is preoccupied with the music. I love live music. It's one of my favorite things about living in the city, but I love women more.

I haven't been watching, but when I turn to check on Ken, his head is on the bar again and a pile of puke is forming on the floor. We have to get him out of here.

Jeri volunteers to clean up and asks the bartender for a rag and a mop. I could never have done that. I have a really weak stomach and end up getting sick myself whenever I have to clean up after someone. Unfortunately, I have had to clean up my share of that shit. It's just a part of working in a bar. My usual thought process is that if I'm not the one who over-served them, why do I have to do the cleaning up?

I'm a by-the-book bartender, and no one overdoes it on my watch, but when we are all hanging out, I don't care... Let people get as wasted as they want. That night, Ken is determined to get really wasted.

He succeeds.

While Jeri is cleaning up inside, Raymond and I are on the curb trying to get Ken a cab. He is sitting on a nearby stoop continuing to empty his stomach. A cab comes, and we throw him in. I go with him to see him home, leaving Jeri and everyone else behind.

The whole ride he is puking out the window. When we get to his house, the driver wants to charge us an extra twenty bucks to clean up after him. All it would take is hosing off the outside of the door. I'm sure these guys have to do it all the time.

Ken is lying in the street after falling out of the cab when he opens the door. I'm trying to get him to stand up, so I could walk him into his place. He is much too big for me to carry. The whole time I'm trying to get him off the ground, the cab driver is bitching at me.

"I paid the fare and tipped you ten bucks on an eight-dollar ride. If you want, I'll clean the shit up after I get him inside, but I'm not giving you another twenty."

He continues to bitch, but I'm not gonna give in.

I'm still trying to get Ken off the ground. He keeps saying, "Leave me here. I'm fine."

"I'm not leaving you in the middle of the street. Get the fuck up."

As much as he insists that he's comfortable and doesn't want to move, I finally get him on his feet, and with one of his arms over my shoulder, I lead him into his place. While we climb the stairs, he starts to drop and with everything I have, I pull him back up and push him the rest of the way. I get him inside, and he walks on his own. He goes into the bathroom, then finds his way to his bed and passes out. Part of me feels that I should stay and make sure that he's all right. Another part of me wants to get back to Britney.

I head back to the bar. They are all still there, but as soon as I show up, Raymond takes off. The girls and I head to the beach. It's four in the morning, and they decide to go swimming, fully clothed. They come out soaking wet and freezing, so we head to Britney's place, only a few blocks away. She makes good money and pretty much has to living in this neighborhood. It's only a studio, but it's a pretty good sized one and really nice. The two of them are laughing and talking and having a ball. I can't get a word in. They both pass out on Britney's bed, and I just head in to work.

I had bought some DJ equipment a while back and had been looking for a reason to use it. The House is a simple bar and has never had a DJ, but Ken and I convince Steven to turn Sunday nights into 'Industry Night' and I would DJ. Every night is industry night. The majority of the regulars work in the business and Sunday nights don't exactly draw a different crowd. It is really just an excuse to use the equipment.

The first night we do it, we make a big deal about it. We make fliers and promote the hell out of it with all of our industry regulars. It also lines up with the first anniversary of the club across the street.

A year ago, Jerry's had changed its name and changed the music and changed the crowd they catered to. The menu, now, is pretty much the same, but it is a very different place. They have about eighty regular employees, and it definitely helps us draw a pretty big crowd.

For a Sunday night, or actually any night, it's packed. We cut most of the lights and put out more candles. With the red candles and a few red lights, the place glows. We crank the music and really throw a party. It's a big hit, but the Sundays that follow are less than spectacular.

A few Sundays later, Britney comes in with a friend of hers. I just about drop to my knees. She is gorgeous. She's like a Playboy model except only about 5'5". She has beautiful blonde hair and blue eyes, a smile that takes your breath away, and she seems to light up the room. She also has like the perfect body, all the right sized curves in all the right places. I haven't seen anyone this amazing in... well, never.

I never could get a girl like that, but that's not going to stop me from trying. I'm still sort of with Jeri, but that's the furthest thing from my mind.

They come to the end of the bar and Britney introduces us.

"Jeff, this is Tiffany. We went to college together."

"Ah... hello."

I'm dumb struck.

After doing what I could to shake myself clear, we end up talking all night. Since I'm already taken, I seem to have almost super-human confidence. I don't have anything to lose. Maybe my pheromones are different. It seems to work in my favor.

She seems to like me... she really likes me.

I haven't hung out with Jeri since Ken's birthday.

In a little less than a week, it will be my birthday. Nate and I are a week apart, and Ken and I are two weeks apart. June is a big birthday month, and we always have a party. It's really just an excuse to do a lot of drinking. We rarely need a reason, but to the guys, that is the gift. The usual birthday routine is a nice dinner then a night of debauchery.

For my birthday, I talk to Steven about having Jeri work that night. We said it's because she is the new girl, and everyone else would be at the party. So, she has to work. It's actually just a set up so that I could talk to Tiffany.

The night before my birthday, Jeri has me over for dinner. She cooks this fancy meal with candles and the works. I rarely get real home cooking, so this is a great gift. After dinner, we have sex, another part of my gift. Sweaty, sticky sex, just like always, but this would be the last time. I just don't tell her that.

The next day, I meet up with everyone at the bar, and once everyone is assembled, we go to dinner. After dinner, they ask me where I want to go. I'm turning twenty-nine, and for my last year in my twenties, I want to go someplace stupid. We head to Division Street. We never hang out there. It's too collegey, dirty, and over-crowded. The clubs up there just lack any kind of style and are too chaotic to really enjoy yourself, but tonight, that is exactly the stupidity I'm looking for.

All of the doormen at these places are regulars at The House, so we don't have to worry about cover charges or getting carded. We just walk right in and then usually walk right back out. These places are nuts. We do find one place, one of the bigger places, that actually has a table available. Everyone is getting super wasted. You almost have to in a place like this just to fit in. Fitting in was never something we cared about, but this time, joining in is a big part of the fun.

Tiffany and I talk all night.

Morning comes around too soon, but for most, it's definitely time to go home. I walk Tiffany to Britney's place around the corner. She is staying with her until she finds a place of her own. At her door, we talk for another hour or so. When she starts to nod out, I get ready to leave. I'm hoping for a kiss goodnight but get none.

Even though I never considered us to be officially together, Jeri and I break up the day after my birthday. She doesn't take it well, but thankfully we don't really have to see each other that much. Since I work days and she works nights, staying apart should be easy. However, I still see her a lot whenever I hang out at the bar. Since we had only been together for three weeks, I didn't think it was much of a big deal when we split, but I was kind of replacing her pretty quickly.

Now, I'm concentrating all my efforts on Tiffany. Like I said, I never thought I could get a girl like her, but I'm still going to give it my best shot.

We spend nearly every day together, mostly with Britney and Ken tagging along. Girls feel safety in numbers.

One night, I decide to cook dinner for everyone. Outside of doing it for a living at times, I really don't do much cooking. It's supposed to be Cajun Shrimp Alfredo, and it turns out pretty well. I make the Alfredo sauce from scratch and season the hell out of the shrimp. I add brown sugar and maple syrup which makes the shrimp sweet. They taste like candy.

The meal goes over really well and at the end of the night and after ten days of working it pretty hard, she gives me a kiss goodnight. It's actually more like a ten minute make out goodnight. I'm feeling on top of the world.

A few weeks later, I seem to crash. I feel like shit and all I want to do is sleep. I stop hanging out and stay in for three nights in a row. Tiffany has invited me to join her and Britney on Britney's dad's boat to watch the fireworks on the Fourth of July. As much as I'm crazy about this girl and things are going well between us, I just don't have it in me to go. I also don't have a reasonable excuse for bowing out. I have to make something up.

I find myself writing this long and extensive letter which is nothing but an elaborate lie. I tell her that I have to have emergency surgery on an ulcer, and they have discovered some severe heart condition. I go so far as to say that I only have nine months to live. I go even further and shave my crotch where they would have done the surgery. I even try to cut myself so there would be a scar. It's insane, but I'm doing all of this as if it's nothing. I can't cut myself, but I'm still shaved, and I wear a bandage just in case anyone wants to see.

I then take it even further and send the letter to everyone I know. My whole family and all of my friends, everyone. It's the biggest lie I've ever told, and I now have to make it convincing to everyone. Whenever I have anyone read the letter, like Jason and Alex, I have a sincere look on my face and as long as I believe it... so do they. I have actually convinced myself that it's true.

Since I was twelve, I had hoped that I wouldn't live to see thirty. I had also hoped that I would die before my mother. Despite her beating me to the grave, I'm still hoping to not see thirty. This lie has to be true. I have to make it true, and I'm going to, regardless. This lie is so incredibly ridiculous, but everyone seems to believe it. I don't really know why I do it, but I'm in it now.

I have nine months to make it true, but for now, life goes on.

I start to feel better and am hanging out with Tiffany again. She wants to see the scar. It's been around two weeks since the supposed surgery. There is no scar. I tell her that it was a small incision, that it was laparoscopic surgery and that I healed really quickly. She seems to buy it.

Five weeks into us hanging out and up to now just making out, I try to make a move. She doesn't stop me or push me away. I start touching her all over and taking off her clothes. She is just as amazing as I had pictured her in my head. She has by far the best body I've ever seen in person. I go down on her then come back up to kiss her some more. As hot as it's getting, she makes no attempt to take my clothes off. Breaking my own rule, I start to do the job for her. She stops me. I could do just about anything to her, but we are not going to have sex. Not yet.

After another few weeks of fooling around, she decides that it's time.

I don't carry condoms, but even the sweetest of girls usually has 'The Kit'. 'The Kit' is a stash of condoms, usually dozens, lubricant, and a toy that they may or may not have named. Her kit is fully stocked. Sex with a girl that you find this incredibly attractive is just that much more amazing. We go for hours.

I end up not getting to work until eleven o'clock and have missed a few deliveries. That's bad, but they would come tomorrow. Work and everything are a distant second or even third to being with Tiffany. However, I'm flirting with losing this job.

A few days later, I ask her if I could call her my girlfriend. She is the most physically attractive girl I've ever been with, and, despite being a bit self-involved and materialistic, she would make for a great trophy.

She says that other than hanging out at the bar and at her place, we haven't been on an actual date. That is true.

Although I have no real money, I'm determined to satisfy her need to be taken on dates. I take her to the jazz/blues club that we all went to for Ken's birthday, and on another night, we go to a fancy dinner on Rush Street. We go walking on the beach, go rollerblading and go window shopping. I can't afford to actually buy her anything, but thankfully it's only window shopping.

In the middle of one of our walks, she takes my hand that she's holding and pulls me in to whisper in my ear, "I want you now."

We get back to her place in record time. She rarely initiates sex, so this time is fantastic. She's a machine and is screaming to scare the neighbors. Good screams, so no one has to call the cops on us. Lying there sweaty and spent, we forget the time and Britney comes home. She knows about us and kind of likes the idea that two of her friends are hitting it off, but she doesn't need the floor show. We get dressed quickly, and I'm off to work again. Late, as usual.

Sunday afternoon, I go home after work. I haven't actually slept at my place in a while. Most nights I sleep in between Tiffany and Britney at their place. When Britney is around, there is no play time, but I still feel like a pimp sleeping between them.

I change and decide to go rollerblading by myself. I skate all the way from home to The House. I roll up onto the sidewalk in front of the bar, and Steven comes out to talk to me. He is kind of pissed. Just like Jason, I've never seen this guy mad before. He gets kind of scary, all quiet and intense.

"Did you even work today?"

A little off guard, "Yea, I did."

"Did you do the bathrooms?"

Lately there was usually something that I missed. Sometimes I didn't stock as much as I usually did, or I might just touch up the floor instead of making it gleam. This time, I guess I missed the bathrooms.

"There's shit on the toilet seat."

Instead of making the effort to go in and clean it right then and there, I stand there as if it's nothing. I know better, but I just stand there. I'm in shock from his being pissed. I really don't care.

"Don't worry about coming in tomorrow." Then he turns and walks back inside.

Jason comes out right after. Even though he hasn't heard any of the conversation, he knows what happened.

"Are you all right?"

"I'm fine." I am fine. I really don't care at all. I'm not upset or even showing any emotion. I'm not stunned or in shock. It just doesn't affect me in any way.

"Hey, I'll float you rent for a while till you find something else."

"Cool. I'll be fine." Then, I skate away and go to the lakefront as planned. I skate all afternoon then skate all the way home. I'm sweaty, but not at all tired. I shower and go to meet Tiffany.

She has decided that our relationship has run its course.

Maybe she knows I got fired and knows I wouldn't be able to take her anywhere or really do anything. Sex alone isn't enough to keep us together. She needs more and deserves it. She doesn't say anything like that, but I think it might be in her head. She just says that it's over and delivers the usual, 'we can still be friends' line.

It doesn't faze me. I feel nothing.

Another girlfriend gone. Another job lost. No prospects and nothing in the future but planning my death, and I don't feel anything. I'm not sad, depressed, scared, worried, or anything.

I feel nothing.

Chapter Nine:
No Man is an Island

This time, I'm out of work for a while. Jason floats me the first month, and on the second month, I ask Ken for a loan. Ken actually seems eager to help out. He is a great friend.

I finally find work, but it's a fairly insignificant job. Short lived insignificant jobs are all I have for a long time.

My general mood is blank.

In November, I start noticing this new girl who is hanging out at The House a lot. Elizabeth Hackberry. Sweet and innocent-ish. Tall, at about 5'9". Dark, long hair that curls just enough. She's into Jason. She lights up whenever he is around, but she gets to the point where she respects his relationship with Alex. She doesn't like it, but she respects it.

The more I hang around her, the more she starts showing interest in me. Whenever I set up camp in my usual spot at the front of the bar, she always joins me there. One night, I take a shot.

"I'm heading home. You wanna go watch a movie?"

'You wanna watch a movie?' is pretty much like asking, 'You wanna fuck?' It's kind of rude and not really like me, but I don't really care.

"Sure, let's go." She's up for it, although I don't think she understands my code. We actually watch the movie. 'Ice Age' - a friggin' Disney movie. Needless to say, we don't have sex. We just watch the movie and talk a little. She seems shy. We end up watching a lot of movies over the next two weeks or so.

On Thursday night, Alex is covering one of Dell's shifts behind the bar. I come in late, and Elizabeth is there.

"You wanna watch a movie?" I ask but am not really feeling it.

"Yea, let's go."

I turn to Alex and look at her with a little disappointment, "We're gonna go watch a movie and NOT have sex."

Alex knows the code and laughs. I have no problem saying this right in front of Elizabeth. She seems almost clueless. Sweet, but clueless.

Only about ten minutes into the movie she just climbs on top of me, and we start making out. I kind of stop her for a second.

"You were into Jason. Am I second prize?"

"No. I'm way over Jason. He's got a girlfriend, and I don't push it when that's the case." Then this shy, clueless girl slowly takes off my clothes and climbs on top of me right there in the living room.

She is taller than me, and I'm usually uncomfortable with that. Taller girls seem to have an edge over me, and the playing field is unbalanced. It is sort of intimidating. This time it doesn't matter. She has an amazing body. Just as nice as Tiffany's. All the right sized curves in all the right places. How did I get two such hot girls in under a year? How did I get them period?

We start seeing each other a lot. Whenever we go out, she picks up the tab. She knows I'm out of work most of the time and don't have much money. She never makes it an issue. I feel a little worthless when I'm broke. I usually don't even try to get into a relationship unless I have something to bring to the table. I'm old fashioned. I try to be the gentleman and do the right things. She never makes me feel like less of a man. I feel great for the first time in almost four months.

I'm very comfortable with this girl, and I even take her to my dad's Christmas party where she meets the family. They all like her a lot, and she makes a nice trophy. I like showing her off.

Meeting the family is always a big deal.

At this time, I can't afford to go out much. I mostly spend time with Elizabeth and go to a lot of AA meetings. Going to meetings again is a little weird, but it makes me feel better about things. Other than having a pretty great girl in my life, life pretty much sucks, and, as usual, I attribute it to drinking.

I actually haven't been drinking much this past year or so, and I haven't been going to meetings either. I'm doing fine on my own, but after Tiffany and I split, I picked it back up some. Not much, though, because I just can't afford it.

This time, though, I'm taking my sobriety pretty seriously. I have a sponsor and am working the steps again. My sponsor, for some reason, doesn't like the fact that I'm in a relationship. He feels that I should keep things simple for a while. He really doesn't like that I spend so much time in bars.

I've been hanging out at The House for years at this point, and most of that time, I've been sober. They knew I went through swings, and they were, almost always, pretty understanding. They never asked any questions; they just went with it.

This New Year's Eve, I decide to wear a tux to the bar. It's the first New Year's in a while that I'm not working. I meet Elizabeth there, and she buys some sparkling cider for me so I can be a part of the fun... I guess. Fake drinking is almost as bad as real drinking. Midnight comes around, but I don't touch the stuff.

Midnight is usually pretty uneventful for me. This year I have someone to kiss, but I'm not really feeling the night.

Around one, Tiffany comes in with some friends. She seems to like my tux and walks right up to me and greets me with a hug. A long hug. She's rubbing my chest with one hand and has a grip of my arm with the other. She keeps saying how nice she thinks I look and won't back away.

Out of the corner of my eye, I see that Elizabeth is leaving. She is pissed, and I can't really blame her.

I run out after her.

"You could say 'hi' of course, but that was more than 'hi'. She so wants to fuck you tonight."

"What was I supposed to do, push her to the floor and say, 'Get off me!'? What she wants doesn't matter anymore. We broke up five months ago. I'm with you now, and that's all that matters."

"She touches you like that again; I'm taking her out."

I laugh and we go back inside.

It's not uncommon for me to have a few ex-girlfriends in the bar at the same time. Cindy comes in from time to time, Jeri works there, and now Tiffany. Tonight, they are all there, but I could not have cared less. I'm with someone, and all of the girls in the past don't matter. I never look back... at least not until after a little time has gone by. Most, if not all of the time, break- ups happen for a reason, and getting back together is something that I've never done.

A few weeks later, I'm still in and out of work and broke. There is some guy who is repeatedly punching holes in the walls of the men's room at The House. Even though I don't work there anymore, it pisses me off. I'm in there with Elizabeth one night when it happens again. This time, the guy is still in there, and we know who it was.

I'm out of my mind pissed, and I am going to beat the shit out of him. I start to go after him when Jason grabs me and takes me outside.

"I'll take care of it."

"I'm calling the cops. It's destruction of property, and we'll get him arrested."

"I'll take care of it," he says, this time in his stern, serious voice.

I call the cops anyway.

When they show up, I point out the guy, but Jason and Alex intervene.

After listening to me bitch for a while, the cops ask, "Who's the manager?"

"I am." Jason answers. Whenever Steven isn't around, the bartender is the manager. So, this is true tonight.

"What do you want to do?"

"I'm taking care of it. The guy agreed to pay for the damage."

The cops get ready to leave, but I'm still bitching. I just can't control my anger, and I'm starting to scare myself.

Alex chimes in, "You don't even work here anymore. It's none of your business."

I turn and start walking to the bus stop. Elizabeth chases after me.

I'm sitting at the bus stop for only a few minutes when I close my eyes and slump a little. Elizabeth has been talking the whole time, but I haven't heard a word.

I slump over and fall to the ground. I'm shaking like a leaf and crying uncontrollably. I can't open my eyes, and I can't stop myself from shaking.

My mind is racing. Jason and Alex don't give a shit anymore, and I'm pretty much no longer welcome at a place that has been the only constant in my life since I moved here. I'm running through all of these seemingly catastrophic things in my life. Nothing seems real.

Elizabeth is trying to hold me, and she starts crying too. I hear her say, "I love you." And I know she means it. I haven't heard those words since Dana.

I continue to shake and cry.

I hear people other than Elizabeth, and someone is poking at me.

"Get up."

"Come on man, get up."

Then, I feel them trying to pick me up. I have no strength. I'm totally limp. They try to make me stand on my own, and I fall to the ground. I feel one hand under my left arm, and I can tell that it is someone else's hand under my right. I'm being dragged. Then, I'm dropped again, and my face hits the curb. I'm lifted up and placed on a gurney. I start to realize what's happening, but I still can't stop shaking or crying. I still can't open my eyes.

I feel what seems like someone's knuckles pressing against my sternum. I raise my hand to push it away. It's my first voluntary movement.

I wake up a little while later in a hospital. Elizabeth is there holding my hand. I'm calmer now, and I open my eyes. I'm looking at her and trying to think of what to say.

There is a doctor standing on the other side of me.

"You seem fine now, so we're going to get you out of here." Then he walks away.

I turn to Elizabeth, and all of my catastrophic thoughts come back to me.

"As soon as they let me out of here, I'm gonna kill myself. I'm not fuckin' around."

She begins to cry and turns away. I fall back to sleep.

I wake up again, and I'm in a padded room. No kidding - a real padded room. There is nothing in there other than the bed I'm on, a small desk that seems to be a part of the wall, and one secure door with a small window in it. The door opens. Jason and Alex walk in.

"Are you alright?"

"I'm fine." Now I feel that I really am. I'm calm again. It has to be six in the morning. They tell me that the same cops that we were talking to in front of the bar were the ones that picked me up at the bus stop. No wonder they didn't seem to have much sympathy. It was the paramedics that dropped me on the curb, though. I still have a cut on my chin.

There is no getting out of it once the hospital thinks I'm suicidal. They put me in an ambulance and take me to Read, the county mental hospital. Once I get there, they strip search me and give me some paper-like pants and a shirt. They take out all of the stuff in my pockets and show me to an office. I sit down, and this woman starts to interview me.

"Were you going to kill yourself?"

"No." Before I can start to explain, the phone rings.

She answers, and after a while of listening in, I can tell that it's Elizabeth on the other end. She is calling to see if I'm all right and when and how she can visit.

I'm going nowhere that night, and after they give me something to eat, I go to the room they've assigned to me. There is someone else in the other bed. In these places, you never know just how crazy the other people are. I fall asleep pretty easily, though.

The next morning, I'm interviewed again, and I tell them that I was just drunk. I hadn't actually been drunk, but it seems to help explain my actions. I had been pretty out of my mind. I explain that I'm fine now, and I'd like to go home. That is all it takes, and I'm on my way.

They give back my things, and I put on my clothes. They give me a bus card and send me on my way. Generally, once you say that you're going to kill yourself, you are stuck for at least seventy-two hours. I got out in less than a day.

I'm in a part of the city that I don't really recognize, but I find my way to the bus. It takes me close to two hours to get home.

A few days later, Elizabeth comes into the bar to meet up with me.

"How are you feeling?"

"We gotta talk. Let's go get some coffee." Everyone knows that this statement usually leads to bad news, and she knows it too.

We go around the corner, and as soon as we sit down with our coffees, she starts to cry. The place is full of people, and she is causing a bit of a scene. I stand my ground and tell her that it's for the best and that I just need to be alone right now and get my life together. I really did need to get my life together, but I could have also used her help instead of cutting her loose. I didn't realize that at the time.

We go our separate ways.

I still see her all the time at The House, but she has joined forces with Jeri in hating me. They are really the only two girls I've ever broken up with. I was always the one being dumped. They hang out together and cut me looks every once in a while. It doesn't really faze me, but it does remind me that I can be a fool at times. That is not really news, though.

A few months go by, and things aren't getting any better. I still haven't found steady work. Short lived insignificant jobs, that's all. It's barely enough to cover rent, and even at that, I'm late most of the time. Jason is working a lot these days and doesn't really sweat me about it. Alex moved in a little while ago, and she is helping with rent, too.

My brother is getting married in a few months, and I'm not sure I'll be able to afford to go. It is going to be in Tennessee. He asked me to be best man and to DJ the reception. I have to be there.

Raymond has started a construction business in addition to his bartending. He takes foreclosed property and rehabs them a little, then sells them for a decent profit. Kristen Harrer is working with him as a partner, but he is actually just trying to work her.

I worked construction all the way through school with my dad, so I had a little experience. Ray hires me and promises me that I'll make my brother's wedding. That's all I care about. Rent is secondary at this point.

The work is pretty rough. The restaurant business is a cake walk compared to real manual labor. We work every morning until Ray has to get ready to go bartend. I don't know when or if he ever sleeps.

The money coming in helps a lot, though.

At one point, I am working in a bathroom stripping the old wallpaper, and Kristen is working on the tub. We've been talking a lot while working together, but there's nothing there. The next thing I know, I turn to say something to her, and she's right in my face. She has this look like she wants to pull me into the tub and fuck me right there. I haven't seen that look very much before, but it is definitely the 'fuck me' look. Our faces are within an inch of each other when I pull back. She just looks at me but doesn't say anything. She knows Raymond is into her, and she knows that he and I are close friends. She knows. We never talk or even think about it again. She knows.

It is actually a month until my birthday, but Raymond gives me concert tickets as a present. Concrete Blonde at the Vic. Awesome. I remember that Britney is a big fan of theirs, too, so I invite her along. Ken joins us, and Britney asks a friend of hers from the hotel to come with us. Kym Thelin. Another 'Kim' but this one spells it with a 'Y'. I love shows at the Vic. It is just the perfect size for a concert.

We have a blast.

A few weeks later, Kym comes into the bar just before we all go out for Nate's birthday. She ends up joining us and spending the whole night trying to work me. I'm not really interested in dating again at this point.

Nate gets really fucked up as is the tradition during our birthday month. Kym has a car, but she's kind of messed up, too, so I drive. Nate's still all the way on the South Side, so it takes us a while to get him home. Once we get there, he heads right in, leaving the door open behind him. Kym has to use the bathroom, so she goes in and closes the door. She comes out laughing. Apparently, Nate didn't make it past the kitchen floor.

As soon as she gets back in the car, she's all over me. She is kind of hot, so I'm not really complaining. She explains that I've made a good impression at the concert and that she's been into me ever since. I made a good impression because I just hadn't cared.

We end up back at her place. I have to drive her home. It's her car. She invites me in, and we go nuts. I'm not really 'that guy,' but sex with twenty-two-year-olds has been plentiful as of late.

It's now my actual birthday, and we pick a restaurant around the corner from Kym's place. It's a nice little Italian restaurant. Ken, Evan, Britney, Kym, and Jason are there. Alex has to work, but Raymond has no excuse. We have a good time, anyway. This birthday is more sophisticated than last year's. Thirty is usually a big deal, but for me, it is a really big deal. I wasn't supposed to live this long.

Most people have probably forgotten about all that.

A week later, Kym is having a party at her place. At first, it is all people I know and am comfortable with: Ken, Evan, Britney, Jason, and Alex. Then, some of Kym's old friends show up. Kym is already pretty wasted and gives them all big hugs. Long hugs. They are mostly guys. Mostly old boyfriends.

We are hanging out on the back porch, and the guys start telling stories. They are mostly really inappropriate stories about things they used to do with her when they were together. Kym is sitting on my lap and seems oblivious to the fact that I might be uncomfortable with this. They keep talking and laughing. Kym is laughing along with them.

No one says anything about how obviously inappropriate this whole conversation is. Jason, Evan, Ken... no one steps in, and if I say anything, I know I'll lose it. I've had enough, and I stand up, dropping Kym on her ass. I storm towards where the guys are sitting. I just blow by them and head to the next major street where I could get a cab.

My phone starts ringing immediately. After about five minutes of nonstop calls, I pick up on the next one.

"What?"

It's Britney.

"You gotta come back. Kym's a mess. She can't understand why you left and hasn't stopped crying this whole time."

"She doesn't get it, and no one there seems to get it either. I don't want to know about my girlfriend's past sex life, and I definitely don't want to hear it directly from the guys that she was with. They were just pushing me to say something. They were trying to see if I would do anything. They wanted a fight."

"They all left. She really needs you to come back." I can hear her balling in the background.

"Come on, Jeff. She really likes you. I haven't seen her this hung up on anyone in a long time."

I feel like I'll regret it, but I have the driver turn around.

When I get back, Kym is passed out in her room and most everyone has left. Ken and Britney are the only ones left. They are both telling me just how upset she was and how much she likes me. I'm still kind of pissed, but I could use someone who cared, and I've screwed up in this situation before.

They leave and I lie down next to Kym. She must have felt me get in the bed and she starts to wake up.

“Thank you for coming back. You know I love you, don't you?”

We've only been together for a few weeks. I can tell she is waiting for me to say it back. I just can't.

My brother's wedding is in three days, and Raymond hasn't called me to work so far this week. I've been calling him every day, but he doesn't answer. I end up having to go to his house and ring the bell.

“Hey, man. What's going on?”

“Just too many hours working the bar.”

“I'm not really sweating the work, but my brother's wedding is in two days, and you promised to help me get there.”

“You'll get there, but right now I gotta sleep.” Then he just closes the door in my face. I'm not feeling very good about this at all. He has never really let me down before. He hadn't shown up to Victor's funeral, and he hadn't shown up to my thirtieth birthday party, but other than that, he'd always been there. He always made good on what he said. That is one of the things that makes him who he is.

It's the day before the wedding, and it's going to take like seventeen hours to get there. I have no car; Raymond was supposed to get me a rental. I have no money; Raymond was supposed to set me up. I call several times. I have to leave in like two hours. I show up at his place again. He isn't home. I go to his job. He isn't there. I have hit all of his hang outs. He is gone.

I am about to lose it.

"Take my car, and I'll give you my credit card for gas and stuff."

Kym is smiling from ear to ear at me. I'd been sweating this all week, and now it's clear that Raymond isn't going to help.

"I can't take your car and giving me your credit card is just nuts."

"You are also not going to miss your brother's wedding."

She kisses me and hands me the keys, still with that big smile on her face.

I have about thirty dollars of my own cash. I'm pretty sure I should only use Kym's credit card to pay at the pump for gas. I'm running way behind schedule to make it there the night before the wedding, but I'm going to make it.

I pull up to the townhouse my family has rented for the weekend at around two in the morning the day of the wedding. My sister lets me in, points out the couch and goes back to her room. I don't sleep at all.

The wedding is beautiful, and everything goes off without a hitch.

On the way home, just as I'm going through Indianapolis, it starts to rain. I've never seen it rain like this. It is coming down in sheets. I can hardly see in front of me. Cars are pulling off to the side of the road all along the highway. I'm going about twenty-five miles an hour, and I have a truck's taillights clear in front of me. I'm following just close enough to keep him in my sights, but not close enough that I wouldn't be able to break in time.

I lose track of the lights, and I reduce my speed to about twenty.

A flash of lightning lights up what is happening ahead. The truck in front of me is turning over onto its side. It's on its side and starts to slide to the right, almost as if it's getting out of my way. There is a parked pickup truck to my left, and the truck on its side is sliding off to the right. I barely make it in between them. All of this just in that one flash of lightning.

The road ahead is clear, but I've missed my turn off. Panting and in shock that I survived, I call Kym. I try to tell her what's happened in a way that really tells of the danger, but in a way that won't scare her; just to show my amazement in having gotten through it. She tells me that I should pull over, but the rain has let up now, and it's all clear. The only thing is that I'd be about two hours late getting the car back. I am on a completely different highway at this point, and it's too late to turn around. I'll have to go a little south into Illinois then head up I-57.

A few days after I get back, Kym and I are driving to her place after hanging out at the bar. She is pretty drunk, and it looks like she's sleeping. She stirs a little and without turning to look at me, asks, "What would you do if I were pregnant?"

I almost lose control of the car on Lake Shore Drive. I collect myself so I won't freak her out and calmly answer, "I don't know. I can't take care of myself right now. How could I take care of a kid?"

She doesn't reply or even react. She just goes back to sleep.

Now it's two weeks since we've had sex, and we've hardly even hung out. I've been staying at her place most nights, but she just lies there and barely acknowledges my existence. She's been really moody and distant.

I suspect that she may have had an abortion, but I'm not about to ask.

It only takes another week. She tells me that it's over.

This time it hurts a lot.

I try calling almost every day, but she doesn't respond. I head to the bar and ask Britney if she's seen her. She insists that she hasn't, but I'm relentless.

"OK, she is camping in Wisconsin with Robert. She'll be back Monday."

I had meet Robert. He was always hanging around. He had tried to get Tiffany when I was with her. He's a slime-ball.

Monday, I try calling, but she doesn't answer. I take the last few dollars that I have and jump on the bus. I get into her neighborhood around one in the morning. I see her room from the windows out front. I see the light on in her room under the door. She's home. I ring the bell over and over again. Finally, the bedroom door opens.

It's Robert wrapped in a sheet.

I step back from the door and scream, "KYM, YOU BITCH! ROBERT, I'M GONNA KILL YOU!" This all seems far too familiar. I continue to call out their names and yell.

Kym comes to the window and tells me to leave, or she'll call the police. I yell a little more but give up after she goes back into her room.

I start wandering the streets. I can't get on the bus because I don't have any more money. I find myself right around Wrigley Field, and I am beyond exhausted at this point. There is a pay phone, and I dial 911. I tell them that I'm going to kill myself, and they insist on hearing my plan. I don't really have a plan; I just want to die. They aren't going to help unless I tell them my plan. I see a broken bottle nearby and tell them that I'll cut my wrists with the broken glass. That's enough to get them to come.

They show up, and I am heading to Read again.

This time I do the same thing. I tell them that I was drunk when they picked me up, which is true this time, and I tell them that I hadn't really planned to hurt myself. They let me go again after staying the night.

I would have missed my own brother's wedding if it hadn't been for her but being replaced so quickly hurt... hurt bad.

It's been close to a year since I've had a decent job, and I'm three months behind in rent. Jason is understanding, but not that understanding. Besides, he's going through some shit of his own. Alex caught him cheating on her and moved out all while I was in Tennessee. For whatever reason, he'd take any opportunity to have sex, regardless of the situation. If some girl showed him that she wanted to... well, he was up for it. He hadn't really gotten any in high school, so he was making up for lost time. He wasn't going to miss any chances, despite his real feelings. He really loved Alex.

Alex told me that he also slept with Elizabeth in February. It had only been a few weeks since I'd broken up with her. Not fuckin' cool.

I talk to Elizabeth about it, and she tells me that they had both gone to this convention, and they had been staying at the same hotel. She had gone for work, and he was there for school. He had been taking a few classes with the little free time he had.

Anyway, she tells me that she felt like she didn't have a choice in the matter and that she didn't really want to. She wasn't really upset about it, but she had felt really used.

I believe her. She still really cares for me and wouldn't have lied.

I'm probably more pissed at Jason than Alex is, but I'm not really in a position to do anything about it.

A few days later, Jason asks me to move out. He says it's not personal; it's just out of principle. I haven't paid rent in three months; anyone else would have done the same. Despite everything, at around two years, it had been my longest running address since I'd lived with my mom.

I have no idea what I'm going to do. If I were still with Kym, I could have maybe moved in with her. If I'd had a job... well if I'd had a job, I wouldn't be in this mess. I've had a few good interviews lately, and I feel like I'm right on the verge of working again, but it's all too late for Jason.

With no real place to go, Ken comes through and offers up his couch. Thank God.

I get a call back from this one place, and they want to fly me out to their corporate headquarters and interview with the owner. This is nuts. This is like never done, but if they are going to these lengths, I figure my chances are pretty good.

I hate flying. This is the first time I've even been in an airport since September 11th. I am nervous as hell. Not just about the interview, but the whole experience. There ends up being some issue with the plane, and we land in Kentucky instead of going straight to Cincinnati. This is all I need.

I call and explain the delay, and they say to call when I would be getting back on the plane. Rather than picking me up and doing the interview in their offices, they are now planning to just do the interview in the airport. This seems like no big deal, and it makes it possible for them to keep their other appointments.

I tank the interview. I can't intelligently answer one question. I look like a fool. Then, I turn around and go home.

I call the guy the next day and try to explain why I presented myself so badly in Cincinnati - the flight issues and the timing; I was rushed and uncomfortable. All those little things built up together, and I just wasn't in the right frame of mind. I pretty much beg for the job.

Two days later, he offers me the position. I jump all over it.

I live with Ken for a total of five weeks before I'm able to get a place of my own. This place is a transient hotel downtown. It's only four hundred a month, and they only want two-fifty up front. It's three blocks from my new job and not far from The House.

Life is coming together.

I've been working there for about six months when I meet Lisa. She's a friend of Ken's from The House. Just like a lot of times in the past, I don't intend on doing anything. The road to hell is paved... well, you know the rest.

Ken buys us all Blackhawks tickets. Lisa, Ken, Evan, and I go to the game. We are having a blast, but as a chain smoker, I can't sit through the whole game. At both intermissions I go to their designated space to smoke, and Lisa comes along. She's a smoker, too, so it doesn't look weird to the guys. We talk some and get to know a little about each other. I'm not interested.

After the game, we go bowling, then to a bar and play darts. We hang out all day and all night, then end up at Ken's place. We sit around playing cards on the floor, laughing and talking. Ken and Evan never fail at making me laugh.

I go outside to smoke out of respect for Ken's smoke free place. Lisa comes along. As soon as we get out the front door, she kisses me. Kisses me hard.

After our smoke, we go back inside and continue with the card game. Around five in the morning, we are all spent, and we start heading home. I don't know where Lisa lives, but Evan lives in the same building as I do. Evan wants to stop at McDonald's, but Lisa and I say we aren't hungry. As soon as Evan goes inside, Lisa pulls me into a cab, and we go to her place. It's only like four blocks away. We are lying on her bed, making out. I start to undress her, and she stops me.

"I'm too tired, but soon."

We fall asleep, holding each other.

We hang out every chance we get for around a week or so.

Tonight, she says she wants to go hang out with a friend of hers and sing karaoke. I invite Nate to come along, too.

We sing and laugh and joke all night. Even sober I sing three love songs, and we try to do a duet of Leather and Lace, but I screw it up because I'm trying to sing Stevie's part. I would normally never do that, but this girl is something else. As much as I hate karaoke, it's a blast and I know I've scored big points.

On the way to drop off Nate, we stop at Leon's for BBQ. When I lived with Nate down here, we ate there all the time, but I hadn't been there in years. It smells great.

Lisa blurts out, "Nate, after we drop you off, I don't know what to do first. Eat or jump his bones."

We eat first, which really speaks to the quality of the food, but it's hard to perform your best on a belly fully of BBQ.

I start to get really into her and want to get serious. She does not.

We are kind of wrestling and play fighting one night: laughing and playing. I get kind of tired of it and tell her I'm done, but she keeps hitting me.

"Look, I'm not playing anymore. That's enough," as firmly as I can pull off.

She keeps hitting me.

"Seriously, I'm done. Stop."

She keeps hitting me.

This goes back and forth for a while. I finally get fed up and grab her arm.

"If you don't quit, I'm gonna break this arm," I say seriously while twisting her arm back.

I can't believe it. I am not this guy. I let go, and she can tell by my face that I am just as shocked as she is. I'm probably more scared than she is. It doesn't matter. It's over. I can't blame her. I can't believe I did that. What's Ken gonna say when he finds out?

She would never tell anyone, and we would never talk again.

I kind of fall into a funk after that. I'm disgusted with myself. I stop hanging out at the bar, partially out of fear of seeing her there. I sleep a lot. Then, the Jeff Echterling home game kicks in. I start going into work late, then sleep through a couple of shifts. When I wake up and realize what I've done, I hate myself. I don't leave my room for three days, only going out for food.

I finally get myself together enough to go in for my last paycheck. They really liked me there. The management team and all the employees, they really liked me. They couldn't believe what happened, and I don't lie: I tell them that I haven't been sleeping, and I had taken some stuff to get to sleep. I ended up sleeping for close to two days. They kept saying that if I had called, I'd still have a job, and they would have understood. I knew the story, but that never changed anything. When I was down and out, there was no logical thought.

I'm out of work again, but this time, I have a little savings along with my last paycheck, so I have enough to make a move. My relationships are a mess, and I don't feel comfortable at The House anymore. Things are just a mess, and something has to give.

I talk to my brother about moving to where he is. He's married now and has kids, so it wouldn't be like all the other times we'd lived together. Regardless, he's up for it and seems excited to have me around.

My mind is made up, and I start getting my things together. I tell everyone my plan and, in a way, make my peace with it all.

Jason, of all people, decides to throw a going away party for me at The House. Jeri, Kym, Lisa, and Elizabeth are there. Elizabeth is the only one that really talks to me. She is also the only one that actually seems upset that I'm moving.

After the party, she comes home with me. She makes me not want to go, but things are set. I would leave in a week.

A few days before I'm going to go, I'm hanging out at a diner when Nate calls.

"What ya up to?"

"Just getting a bite to eat."

"Where are you? I want to see you."

I tell him where I am, and he asks me to wait for him. He shows up with a friend from his church. Nate has recently found religion. He had hated it when his mom would preach at him, but now he's studying to be a preacher. I guess she had had an influence after all.

He starts in, and I can't believe it.

He is talking about my getting saved and accepting Christ. I've not lived a saintly life by any means, but I'm no heathen either. I have my belief system, and he has his. We always respected that, but never talked about it. It's just never comes up.

Remember, I was raised catholic, and not a 'two time catholic' - you know, the ones that only go to church twice a year for Christmas and Easter. We were the real thing and went all the time.

Now, he's trying to save me. At one point, he puts his hands up and starts praying over me. I want to say, 'What the fuck are you doing?' but I don't want to embarrass him in front of his friend, so I just let it happen.

I don't really react, and I let it go, but I can't believe that this actually happened. He was my closest friend and had never pushed his beliefs on me. We rarely even talked about our individual beliefs. They actually didn't differ that much. I don't need to be preached to. Certainly not by him.

Things are now weird with everyone. Ken: what if he finds out about what happened with Lisa? Evan: well, not so much. Raymond: because of how he screwed me. Jason: for the whole 'kickin' me out thing, plus his sleeping with Elizabeth. And now Nate. Not to mention all the girls that have had their individual effect on my life in the last few years.

I've lived in Chicago for five years, and I've fucked up at every turn.

It is time to move on.

I pack my few belongings into a rental and head east.

They say, 'Go west young man,' but I've always been a little backwards.

Chapter Ten:
Mosaic

My brother and his family welcome me with open arms, but it only takes a few weeks before they are ready for me to get my own place.

I still don't jell with people that have normal lives no matter how close we are.

I'm anxious to get out on my own, too. I'm excited about getting this fresh start going and making the best of this new beginning, but my thoughts frequently turn to Chicago.

All my thoughts and actions are floating through time with thoughts of Chicago popping in and out. Nothing seems connected. It's all just sorta happening.

I find work after only a few days in town. The Cork and Tap is a chain, and they have a location here in Asheville.

I've worked at a ton of other locations. Several in Indianapolis, one in Crestwood, the Gurnee location where all the shit went down with Dana, and then again in Texas.

My background and history with the company make it pretty easy to get hired.

I start as a server and never really make any effort to do anything else. One night the bartender has to go home sick, and they ask me if I bartended. I said, "No."

I don't care to make that move. They don't know about my cooking experience either, and I like it that way. The job becomes routine really quickly.

I get a place of my own within a month, and it's nice. A big one bedroom, furnished, and within a comfortable walk to work. The rent is right, and it feels good to be starting anew.

I see my brother here and there but spend most of my time alone.

I'm making decent money and living on my own, but there just isn't any pop to life.

Walking the streets here isn't nearly as exciting as it was in Chicago. There's no real night life and no danger.

One night, I'm walking around downtown, and these guys try to rob me. All I say is that I'm from Chicago, and they leave me alone.

Another night, I see this girl walking around in front of this hotel across the street from the restaurant. Her flip-flops light up as she walks. It seems like she wants some attention. She crosses the street and comes to where I'm waiting on the bus.

I just got off work, and I'm not really feeling the walk home.

The buses out here don't really run too often, and the whole system doesn't compare to Chicago, but tonight, I'm too beat to walk, so I'm trying the bus.

It becomes clear pretty quickly that this girl with the light up flip-flops is working.

I'm up for whatever so I say, "What's going on?"

She answers, "Looking for a date."

Yep! Hookers really use that phrase, but the really amazing part was that hookers were working out here in the hills.

I don't think to ask if she's a cop. I'm not that much on my toes. We walk back to the hotel, and she tells me to wait in front for a second. She goes into the office and talks to the person at the desk for a minute then comes back and gets me.

We go around to the back where her room is and go in.

This time doesn't take me too long. She is very talented.

In general, life out here is boring, and all I do is think about Chicago and go over everything in my head - Over and over and over and over again. Everything that I had done: all the girls, all the friends, all the jobs... everything.

Even though I'm working, making good money, and living on my own, I can't help feeling like I have nothing.

All I do is think about my whole life and what it's worth.

...I remembered a conversation that I had had with Jerry.

Jerry starts, "Have you ever wondered why they have the servers in most restaurants and bars wear all black or just black and white? Friday's and Applebee's used to have you wearing bright stripes, but they're wearing all plain colors now, too.

'Office Space' made fun of the whole 'flair' thing; now, no one does it. Promoting individuality is a thing of the past. Everyone wears all black or black and white... plain, nondescript colors.

They want us to fade into the background, to be insignificant servants. They don't even call us waiters and waitresses anymore. It's just the all-inclusive 'server'. They did it under the guise of political correctness, but I think there's an ulterior motive. Server – Servant –Slave.

That explains the 'all black.'"

Knowing that he had a point, but not really wanting to feed that train of thought, I tried to derail it a little.

"So, how do you explain why black people don't tip? And if they do, it's two bucks, even if the bill is two hundred."

"Payback."

"Payback? Really? So, because they were slaves two hundred years ago... now we're all slaves?"

"Kinda." He gave me this strange look.

I countered, "Even you, everyone, no matter what color they are or where they are from... they hate waiting on black guests. They're needy, demanding, rude, and they tip for shit if they tip at all.

Don't look at me like I'm a racist, just because I'm white, and don't try to say that I don't know what it's like because I'm white. The whole 'reverse racism' thing is bullshit.

Racism is racism, no matter who it's coming from.

I've seen plenty of racism myself. I know what it's like to get hassled for being the wrong color in the wrong place. So, don't try to pull that shit on me.

The tipping problem is not a stereotype. It's the truth about eighty percent of the time. You can't deny that. Most stereotypes are based on a certain amount of truth."

"I don't think you're a racist."

"I never assume that every black guest is going to stiff me, and I never assume that all white guests are going to treat me right. I always assume every customer has the potential to be an asshole."

Jerry comes back with, "I'll even add to that - that the more money they have, the more of a pain in the ass they are. 'No Tippin' Pippen' is not just one guy's opinion. The guy earned that reputation. It happens all over.

All the hip hop stars, the athletes, any brother with some cash. They aren't happy with all that money. They need to feel powerful and important. Truth is that athletes and pop stars don't change the world, but they feel like they do.

They throw money around to impress, and they think they deserve the best. They think we owe them something because they can drain a ball from twenty feet out.

They ain't nothing but entertainers. They're high-profile strippers. Entertainers who we seem to be constantly throwing money at. We are the ones paying for their extravagance."

"So, we are feeding the beast that kills us? It's our fault?"

"Yea, as long as anyone does anything that makes them feel important, they are going to insist that everyone treats them as if they are important."

"So, I get what you're saying. People that have money and fame and whatever feel superior, and that's why they insist on being demanding and a pain in the ass to wait on. What about those that don't have the money, fame or whatever? When they go out, they want to act like big shots... like they are famous and deserving of pampering."

"That's why I treat everyone the same no matter who they are or who they think they are.

I don't change my style of service for people with money or people that I've seen on TV. Everyone is on the same playing field as far as I'm concerned. I treat everyone the same."

"Yea, you treat everyone the same. You treat everyone like shit."

...the quick reference to strippers reminded me of a story an old manager of mine told.

He and a friend were at this strip club, and when the friend went to the bathroom, he noticed that the stripper had purple eyes. Very rare.

She came over by him. He tipped her and asked about her eyes.

She said, "Yeah, they're purple." Then, she took his lighter and held it up to her face, so he could see them better.

When his friend came back from the bathroom, he waved her over again.

He said, "Check this out." ... and she leaned down to show her eyes. This time, it was my manager that held up the lighter.

Not really paying attention, he lit her hair on fire. She went right back to dancing with her head ablaze.

Don't worry, she wasn't hurt. It was just kind of a funny story. I think.

Time goes by kind of slowly around here, and I think about old friends.

...I remembered another conversation that I had had with Elizabeth while we weren't dating.

"How long do you plan to keep that up?"

"What are you talking about?"

"The act."

"Are you trying to say that I'm fake?" She jokingly hinted towards her breasts.

"No. I know first-hand that those are real, and they are fantastic. But I also know that you are real and have the potential to be just as fantastic."

"We're not talking about my tits, are we?"

I answered, "No, that's the one thing you don't hold back. Everybody knows they're real, and you don't miss a chance to use them in your favor. The thing is that you think you're playing people by using your tits and acting like a childish moron, but you're the one getting played. You act all helpless and naïve, you flaunt your rack and manage to get people to do stuff for you, but they are only doing these things for you because they think they've got a shot at getting you into bed. You're no slut by any means, but you play the game.

They still think you're an idiot.

The more you act like that, the less trust and respect anyone has for you. You might think life is easier having things done for you, but no one will ever have any faith in you when you actually want to exert yourself and do something on your own.

When you have an idea or something you want to do differently at work, you know it's a better way of doing things, you know it will be more effective and more efficient... no one is going to listen because all they see you as is a set of tits that talk."

She tried to hide her tears. "Why are you always such an asshole?"

I said, "Because I know the truth. I know you're not an idiot.

I know you are very intelligent. You have great ideas for improving your office. You can sell more than any of those tools you work with, but you let them walk all over you.

They steal your sales because you're afraid to let them know that you have a brain.

All I'm saying is 'cut the act'. Start letting everyone else know what I've known since I met you. You are smart, strong, independent, motivated and goal oriented. You have more potential and business sense than most people twice your age. Don't let them see you as a twenty-two-year-old set of tits. Don't act like a childish idiot anymore. Be who you are.

You are a mature, intelligent, independent adult that doesn't have to answer to anyone because you can take care of yourself.

Let them see that and you will get the respect you deserve."

She responds with, "What about you? What about the asshole act? Are you going to let people see that you are actually a nice guy?"

"No way. I get a certain respect because I'm an asshole. If you see somebody that is always smiling and is the nicest guy on the planet..., what do you think most people's first impression is? They think they can take advantage of them. They think they are morons and pushovers. I'm neither, so I don't smile unless I have a damn good reason, and I'm only nice to the people who deserve it... people that have earned it."

"You're a hypocrite. People don't respect you for being an asshole. The best you can hope for is that they fear you and what good does that do? Once people get past you at the door, they go straight to the bar and bitch about you being a jerk. The guys don't really take them seriously because they know the real you, but you gotta start trusting other people to know who you really are."

"Maybe this is who I really am."

"You're hiding just as much as you say I am."

***

All men should strive to learn before they die – what they are running from, to, and why. -

James Thurber

***

...Once, I was running to catch the Brown Line at the Chicago stop. I was just about to miss it when I put my hand in the door as they were closing, but they didn't open back up.

My hand was stuck, and the train started moving. I was walking then running along the platform trying to get my hand out. Yelling and screaming for them to stop.

I was only about ten feet from the end of the platform, and I thought I might have to jump onto the outside of the train and ride it to the next stop.

I thought I was going to die.

With about five feet of platform left, I broke free.

These days, my mind just drifts, and stuff pops into my head that doesn't have anything to do with what is actually going on in my life right now.

...today I was thinking about how Victor broke down mixed drinks to a customer who complained their drink wasn't strong enough and thought they were being cheated.

"Here's the thing, sir... You ordered a mixed drink, and with mixed drinks, the mix tends to lessen the taste of the alcohol. They are basically designed to either mask the alcohol taste or to make it taste better. If you only want to taste the alcohol, just order straight alcohol. No ice, no mix, nothing but straight alcohol, and then if you can't taste the alcohol, we'll know the problem."

"The problem is you short the drinks. I can't taste the alcohol either."

Victor answers, "You, sir, ordered a Long Island Iced Tea and you're not supposed to taste the alcohol.

Not sure if you were paying attention to the whole break down of how mixed drinks work that I just explained to your friend, but please, both of you listen close.

Every drink here gets 2 ounces of alcohol. If you want 4 ounces, you have to pay for 2 drinks. A Long Island Iced Tea is made with 4 ounces automatically here, and that's why it's so expensive, but we still put sweet and sour mix and Coke in it so we can actually call it a Long Island Iced Tea. Again, and pay close attention this time, if you just want to taste the alcohol...

Don't order a fucking mixed drink; just order straight alcohol.

...Victor also broke down tipping to this one table a while back.

"Have you ever had to pay extra for shipping and handling, or pay for labor when you get your car fixed or any other service charges for any other service? Well, tipping is a service charge that isn't on the bill. It's left up to you, because society doesn't think that you're an asshole."

The mind drifts again.

...Two topics that should never be discussed across the bar are politics and religion.

Guns fall into politics, but I got into a conversation about them anyway.

I wasn't promoting gun control or taking any real sides.

I'm sick of hearing that 'Guns don't kill people. People kill people.'

Obviously, someone has to pull the trigger, but a gun's only purpose is to kill. It was invented, designed, and made for one purpose. To kill. That is its only job. A gun can't be used for anything else.

Yes, a gun could be used for target practice and other sports like trap shooting, but all of those are just methods of honing the skill of killing.

A gun could be used for hunting. That's killing.

A gun could be used for protection. Well, it's protection with the threat or the intent of killing.

Guns have only one purpose.

No one really took my point. I guess I'm not that good at debating any issues. I can talk about any subject, but never could debate anything. I don't know enough about anything to really take a stand on it.

I'm a neutral bartender, and I generally stay out of it when the conversation gets hot.

...Another thing that falls under politics is abortion. It also falls under religion, so it's probably the most taboo topic for any bartender.

As a catholic, I was firmly against it and felt that killing was killing no matter what stage of life someone was in.

Then, I spoke to a few girls that had had abortions. Their reasons seemed sound, and although I don't remember exactly what they all said, it had an effect.

Now, I feel that I have no right to tell anyone what to do with their own body, but I also feel that if someone has multiple, multiple abortions that something should be done.

I'm not a woman and I can never imagine what they go through, so I have no right to say abortion is wrong.

This is one point though: If someone stops breathing on their own, they are considered dead. Respiratory failure.

Babies don't breathe on their own until after birth.

Just a thought, not a stand.

...I also find myself thinking about how I've always felt that love doesn't exist.

Love doesn't exist in the traditional sense, and certainly not in the storybook way that is talked about in books, movies, and TV. Love is nothing more than an emotion, and like all emotions, it comes and goes. Nothing is forever.

Just like any other emotion (like fear, anger, or sadness) you are never afraid, angry, or sad all the time or for the rest of your life. Those emotions come and go. So, love, being just an emotion, also comes and goes.

No one is ever in love all the time or forever. Nothing is forever. That's why so many marriages and relationships never really last. Love doesn't exist. Everyone I've ever loved has hurt me or left me or was taken away. That's just the way it goes. I guess I've been bitter, angry, and upset, but I was never any of those emotions all the time. No emotion is felt all the time.

Love doesn't exist, and nothing is forever. In reality, instead of saying, 'I love you', it seems most people should say, 'You mean nothing to me, but I like having you around for now. At least until you're gone or until something better comes along.' That's what is really going on, and that is what I strongly believe.

The truest test of love is how you feel when the other person isn't around. When you're face to face, it's easy to feel close. If love does exist, it has to be felt by two people. If only one person feels it, it just isn't real. It's like two different people having two different keys, and both of them have to use their keys at the same time to launch a missile. If the other isn't there or feeling that same way, nothing happens.

Love is like Santa Claus or the Easter Bunny or the Tooth Fairy. They are nice enough ideas and seem innocent enough, but in all reality, they are just lies.

...Another time, I was talking to someone else about plastic surgery.

"What do you think of fake tits?"

"I look at it the same way I look at video games. They aren't real, but they sure are a lot of fun."

You would never buy a used car that was all bondo.

I don't understand all the nip/tuck stuff.

This might be a little out there, but bear with me.

Have you ever seen any of the Invisible Man movies? In all the movies and books after a while, he starts to go a little crazy, and depending on the movie or book, sometimes he goes a lot crazy.

He loses his self-image after not being able to see himself and starts doing all kinds of things that are completely out of character for him. He no longer feels human. He feels immortal and immune to legal and moral consequences. He doesn't know himself anymore and loses it.

I think this happens with too much plastic surgery, too.

Look at Michael Jackson for example. He looks nothing like his former self. He's lost his self-image and essentially has to create a whole new one.

This happens to a lot of people who change themselves too much. They have no idea who they really are, and no one else seems to know them anymore either. They have to become someone else. Not seeing themselves as they used to be is like not being able to see yourself at all. You lose yourself.

It's different if you are disfigured in an accident or burned or maimed. In these cases, it's a medical necessity. These times are the only times plastic surgery or altering yourself seems justified, but if you just don't like something about yourself... it's a matter of accepting who you really are.

You can change your appearance with makeup, but to me, most women look better without it. You can change your weight with exercise and diet. The most important changes come in changing your outlook on life and the way you think of yourself.

You can become a better person without any medical intervention.

Some people who start changing themselves surgically become addicted. Like being addicted to tattoos or even addicted to working out, it's all unhealthy. Changing yourself on the outside means nothing if you're the same person on the inside, but most of the time, who you really are is lost.

Hollywood and shows like Nip Tuck or The Swan, and all kinds of stupid TV shows and movies make it all seem totally necessary and completely acceptable. They make it seem like something you have to do. It's nothing more than peer pressure and conformity to the media masses. It's giving into what you think people expect of you. It's really a sign of some serious emotional problems and insecurities.

Actors spend their lives wearing tons of makeup and dressing and acting like someone else. When they take on the whole plastic surgery thing, they lose themselves even more. Who they really are is a mystery, even to them. We watch all kinds of shows and read all kinds of magazines to find out more about celebrities, and we notice and are entertained by their bizarre behavior in real life. As much as we try to find out more about them, I wonder how much they really know about themselves.

When your job is to be a million different people, how could you hold on to who you really are? A lot of people can do it, but there are plenty who can't. Those are the ones we find so entertaining because of their craziness in real life, but when you really think about it... who can blame them?

Self-image is a major issue, but only you can truly know yourself, and if you don't, you can't expect anyone else to.

If you change yourself too much on the outside, you lose yourself. It gets to the point of not being able to see yourself at all.

***

Inside yourself or outside yourself, you never have to change what you see, only how you see it. - Thaddeus Golas

***

...I once thought of legally changing my name to Current Resident just so I would get more mail.

...I actually overheard someone say this from across the bar:

"It's not 'rack opinion,' it's 'rack and pinion'. You're not judging someone's breast by how their car handles."

...Another thing I overheard:

"If bad things didn't happen to good people, the blues wouldn't exist. If good things didn't happen to bad people, hip hop wouldn't exist."

...I was standing in line at Rock 'n Roll McDonald's, and there were three people talking behind me. Two guys and a girl. They were dressed to the nines, and what each of them were wearing cost more than what I made in three months.

The girl relays her order and heads to the bathroom.

After she leaves, one guy says, "She's pretty cool, smart and fun." The other agrees. "Do you plan to see her again?"

"Probably not. If for some reason I can't nail her tonight, I don't think I'll waste any more time on her. She's a fucking bartender."

He actually said exactly that, as if being a bartender made her unworthy of him. I guess according to this guy, we are subhuman.

...I thought about when I was managing at this one place in the South Loop, and the employees all really respected me. When I spoke to them, they got what I was saying and appreciated the fact that everything I was asking them to do, I had once done myself.

It was another opening and since I'd done so many, I was running the training. I was really on my game, and things were rolling perfectly. I was making my mark at that place, and the owners and other managers appreciated it, too.

One of the other managers was kind of jealous and didn't like that I was doing all the talking in the training sessions. She was actually being kind of a bitch about it all, so the next day, I let her take the reins. She did just fine, but acted like she was deserving of more credit than was due.

"So, what do you think of me now?"

"Wow. That was impressive. You were strong, demanding, succinct, powerful and in those pants, it kinda looks like you have balls."

At this point, I can't help but think of Huck Finn...

***

Persons attempting to find a motive in this narrative will be prosecuted; persons attempting to find a moral in it will be banished; persons attempting to find a plot in it will be shot. - Mark Twain

***

...Another one of my random nonsensical thoughts that runs through my head these days.

There are basically four things that bring people together: money, sex, intrigue, or boredom. That's it. A lot of people think that intoxication is a factor, but I see that as only a catalyst for one or more of the basic four.

If you see two people together that don't seem to fit, one or more of those four basic elements are in play. A lot of people see some loser dude with a woman that is out of his league and immediately assume he must have money. A lot of people see a good-looking guy with a sub-average girl and assume that the sex must be amazing.

Truth is, every relationship, good or bad, short lived or long lasting, is based on and started with one or more of these four basic elements. It's not gender biased either. It's not that guys are dogs or girls are gold diggers; both guys and girls are motivated into relationships by the same four things.

Let's start with the more innocent of the four. Some might say they got together because they were genuinely interested in the other person. They found them intriguing, or they shared a lot of common beliefs and interests, such as they like the same books or movies or TV shows. They have similar political opinions. They have similar backgrounds. They work in similar fields. They have a lot in common.

Or it's the exact opposite, and they have virtually nothing in common, but it sparks interest. This is the whole 'opposites attract' thing. The intrigue draws them together. They hear the other talking about things that they have never experienced. Or, they see behavior they don't understand and maybe want to fix it or understand it better. Wanting to fix or change someone is dangerous.

Overall, intrigue is a fairly innocent jumping off point, but not enough to keep things going. You eventually learn what you set out to learn, and the interest fades. One or more of the other four have to come in to play to keep it going.

You might stay together out of boredom or fear of being alone. You might stay together because of financial security, which is money. You might stay together because the sex is good. But intrigue or any one of the four all by itself is not going to make it. They only stand alone in the beginning to start things up. Individually, they aren't strong enough to maintain a solid relationship.

One of the others is sex. A lot of relationships are started simply because there is a sexual attraction. I don't understand people who want to separate physical attraction from sexual attraction. I can only assume they think that if you say 'physical' it sounds better than 'sexual'.

Sometimes you might find someone that is not necessarily physically attractive, but they are intriguing. This sometimes makes them sexually attractive, but if you think someone is physically attractive, nine out of ten times you also think of them as sexually attractive. It's just that simple.

If you say, "Wow, they're hot," or "They are really good looking, but I wouldn't sleep with them," you're probably lying. No one is going to turn down sex with someone they find exceptionally attractive. If you find someone attractive in any way, it almost always means that you would have sex with them, even if you just think it.

There are plenty of times that you may find someone sexually attractive, but maybe they don't have any money, or they aren't that interesting, or you're just not bored enough to ignore the rest. There has to be at least a few of the basic four working together.

There's also the simple fact that if the sex isn't any good, almost no combination of the four is going to keep things together.

Now money. So many people are afraid to admit that money plays any part in their relationship. If you think it doesn't, you're crazy, and if you say it doesn't, you're lying. Financial security is important to everyone. You don't necessarily have to be a gold digger or spoiled or materialistic or looking for a sugar daddy or sugar momma, but money always plays a part.

Females are usually the ones that get hit with this one, but it's the same as any stereotype. It's true often enough to keep the idea alive. Men think about money just as much, if not more. It is always an issue.

There are insecurities that go with maybe not making enough money that definitely affect relationships. Too much money, and the gold digger suspicion is there.

Anyone that flaunts their cash flow as a way of attracting people is just as guilty as the gold diggers. They have no right to complain because they brought it on themselves.

Expensive clothes, nice cars, jewelry, a nice house or condo or apartment, a good paying job or an impressive title... it all means something, and it is a part of most relationships starting out. It means comfort and stability at the very least.

Movies, TV shows, and especially commercials show people buying big expensive things for their loved ones: the classic first date of a really expensive dinner and maybe champagne, the glamorous and expensive diamond ring, which has become the so-called symbol of love. Money may not always be spent to impress or attract, but it's always there. It's always an issue. In the mildest sense, it is at least security and comfort that matters to everyone.

Once again, money alone is not enough to maintain a relationship. If interest, sex, or boredom aren't also in play, it will never make it. 'Money can't buy love,' may be true, but it can hold them together if enough of the other elements are in play.

If money can't buy love, then why is the universal symbol of love a big fat expensive diamond ring? You can't spend the rest of your life with someone unless the ring is there. How would you know if someone was married if there wasn't a gold band or a diamond? Money is always an issue, but it can't be the only or most important piece.

It is however, the one of the four that people will try to make stand alone. More people will settle for money alone than they would sex alone or intrigue alone or boredom alone.

The poor tend to experience the least infidelity. Financial security in their case is motivation enough to try and stay together. That is unless someone comes along that can offer more.

The rich get cheated on all the time because money is not enough, but if some of the other four are in play, it can work out fine.

Money may be the root of all evil, but you can't do shit without it.

Why is boredom on the list?

Have you ever been in a relationship just because you didn't want to be alone? You've at least known someone who has. If we were meant to be alone, there wouldn't be billions of people, and Adam would still have all his ribs. We need other people in our lives to keep life exciting, even if we only find them partially entertaining. We want other people around, and at times, we aren't very picky. We just need someone, anyone.

Boredom in a relationship inspires people to look for more. Some sort of interest, good sex, or financial security has to play a part, or it's doomed.

Boredom is often a reason people get together. We may have just been bored when we talked to someone that turned out to be intriguing, sexy, or financially secure. Boredom can also be a good thing at times. It inspires people to shake things up.

Boredom, sex, money, and intrigue all play their parts in getting people together and when used properly, in a comfortable combination, can keep people together.

Or, at least, that is what I've seen.

All I have done lately is think about bizarre things and remember things about Chicago. Sometimes I get too deep into thought, and I don't make any sense, not even to myself. I try to think of funny things to break it up.

...there was a night at the bar when this girl came in all happy and said, "I'm going to be an aunt."

I don't really know why I said it, but without missing a beat I said, "I'm gonna be a caterpillar."

...I was in the mall once looking for a Leatherman but would have accepted a knock off. I went to the sports counter where they had a ton of knives and Leatherman type tools. I asked to see one, and they took it out and handed it to me. I opened it up and thought I'd check to see if it was sharp and ran it lightly across my thumb. I started bleeding like a stuck pig all over the glass display case.

"Does this mean I have to buy it?"

...I remember Kym telling me a story about her friend's first day working at a new hotel.

This guy came up to her part of the counter and was speaking some language that she didn't understand. It was a hotel that catered to international clients, and most of the employees spoke multiple languages. She did not.

She noticed that there was a German flag next to her station and realized that that was supposed to mean she spoke German. She took the flag down and put up the American flag.

The guy just smiled, shook his head and understood the situation.

Then, he started speaking Spanish.

...I think about Elizabeth a lot. I remembered a time that we had just woken up at my place and I rolled over and took a drink from a glass on the nightstand.

"Is that the martini from last night?"

"You want some?"

"No. How can you drink vodka first thing in the morning?"

"It's one o'clock in the afternoon."

...Another time this girl was talking about her favorite show at the bar, and someone over heard and asked me, "What's Sex in the City?"

"It's an instructional show that teaches women how to be materialistic, pretentious cunts."

...I remembered the first time I heard someone use the phrase, "wishful drinking."

...Winters in Chicago were brutal at times, but that didn't stop girls from standing in line at clubs wearing as little as they could get away with. They thought it was sexy. Oh yea, a runny nose and a thick phlegmy cough is just crazy sexy.

...There were those that wore the tight leather or latex pants thinking that was sexy. After a night of dancing and sweating, when you got them off, it was like an explosion of stir-fried salmon egg salad.

...Some girl they called 'Penny,' was actually 'Grace' or something.

I asked, "Why do they call her Penny?"

Someone answered, "Two reasons... she's cheap, and it's short for penicillin."

I think I'd heard that one before, but it's still funny.

The random thoughts go on and on in my head.

...Something I hate is when fringe minorities and fanatical groups get together and decide that something is bad and bitch to the government. Then, the government makes the law or rule for everyone to follow just to get these groups to shut up. What happened to majority rules? What happened to democracy?

Drugs kill and are illegal, but the war on drugs is a joke.

Smoking kills, drinking kills, and guns kill, but these are all legal. They all bring in too much money to really do anything about.

California has banned smoking, and it's going to hit Chicago soon enough. Foie Gras is being banned. Trans-fats are being banned. Anything that some people feel is bad gets banned, and it affects everyone. We, as Americans, have the freedom to indulge or stay away. It's our choice. Sure, tell me these things are bad for me. Warn me. But don't just ban it all. Leave me with the choice.

You know who did a lot of banning? Hitler.

They say second hand smoke affects everyone. Just don't stand by me. Trans fats are the leading cause of some heart issues. If you're that concerned, don't eat the stuff.

But the one that really gets me is Foie Gras. This one is being banned because of the treatment of the geese.

Who really gives a fuck about geese?

Geese, cows, sheep, chicken or any other animal... these animals aren't American citizens; they have no Social Security number. They don't vote, they don't have the right to vote (and hopefully never will), they don't pay taxes, they have no rights. Animal rights are just bizarre to me. As far as I'm concerned, if it's not human, and it doesn't speak... eat the fuckin' thing.

It's called 'dominion' It's in the Bible. Being food is their contribution to human life. It's their purpose. They give up their lives to keep us alive. And what's more important: our lives or theirs? Our health and well-being, or theirs?

Nearly everything can kill you. They say nearly everything is unhealthy, but does that mean that a democracy should just take it away to avoid the possible liability of someone dying from it?

All it is, is a sweater tied around your waist on a warm day. Its only purpose is to cover your ass.

...Racism is a constant issue that will probably never go away. As long as some stereotypes continue to be real, the wrong assumptions will be made.

I overheard another part of a conversation. Not the whole conversation so I really can't judge what they were saying:

"I hate that nigger rap."

"That sounds like a plastic or foil used to wrap niggers."

Ignorant, but kind of funny.

...One of Nate's favorite stories was when he was working at a restaurant in the city, and there was a dishwasher that lost it.

At the end of the night, everything goes back to the dishwasher. Everything from the front of the house and everything from the back. I've been there, and it's really overwhelming.

This guy couldn't take it, and after everyone else finished up and he was left alone with this pile of things to wash... well, he decided the best way to get through it was to just throw everything away.

He threw away the fryer baskets, the parts of the broiler, pots, pans, silverware, plates, bowls... everything that was left at the end of the night. Then, he just polished up the stainless steel around the dish machine and told the manager that he was done.

The manager went back and saw a clean, empty dish room and told him that he could go.

The next morning was trash day, and the dumpsters were emptied.

They had to close the restaurant.

Needless to say, the guy never came back. Not even to get his last check.

I loved telling the story to managers. The only question they'd ever asked was, "What's the guy's name?" but I bet they check the trash every night now, too.

...Sometimes all I hear is part of a conversation or just one statement, and they are often completely out of context.

I heard, "Stop threatening to punch me in my pussy."

Another time I heard, "...then there was a romantic explosion on my stomach."

Or, when someone said, "Tootely Noade." Without stammering or stuttering, and as if it were a real word. Tootle like 'poodle' and node like 'road.' 'Totally nude' is what she meant to say, but she stood her ground and swore she'd said it right.

...I was never much of a fighter. In fact, I've never really been in a physical fight in my life. I've never thrown a punch. I'm kind of an asshole, so this is pretty hard to believe for most people.

I've had to wrestle a few people to get them out of the bar, but it has never really gotten to a point where it was a fight. Most of the time, all I had to do was ask people to leave. There was something about my tone of voice and my demeanor that made it pretty easy. They would just leave. It might take a little while of talking, but they usually went peacefully.

One night, I was working the door. It was Halloween. I mentioned before that there were three clubs on the same block as The House. One held close to seven hundred, and the others held around two hundred each. So, at two in the morning, you had over a thousand drunks getting put out onto the street all at the same time.

That night, a little before two, I saw a guy come out of the club next door. His face was covered in blood. There had to have been a fight inside, and he had gotten the worst of it. He had started to just walk away, but then I noticed him heading back into the club. Bad move.

He came flying back out of the place with his girlfriend and three guys beating the shit out of him. Then he was on the ground, pinned against this car right in front of me. The three guys were still kicking and pounding on him. They were kicking his girlfriend, too. No one is allowed to hit a girl in front of me, so I got involved.

My only goal was to back them away from the guy and his girlfriend. I made a decent wall in front of them, and they were left alone, but I had to maintain my shield, and I was getting punched and kicked in the process.

We happened to be on a part of the sidewalk that was cracked really badly and was hollow underneath. I was standing right on top of the crack. There were a ton of people pushing and shoving and swinging all around me. It had to be at least thirty people. And the sidewalk started to give and dropped about a foot. If it broke through and we fell under it, someone was going to die.

Just then, I was pulled back from behind, leaving the bloody couple unguarded. It was someone else that was trying to break up the fight.

As I was pulled back, I noticed that the whole street was in a brawl. Out of the close to a thousand people on the street, there were probably three hundred fighting. There were several groupings that had set up their own fights, each with around twenty people involved. There was no way to stop this, and all I could do was step back to the front of the bar.

The cops showed up. Looked like fifteen or more squads and a few trucks. Around fifty cops started storming into the crowds, beating everything in sight.

It broke up about ten minutes after the cops arrived.

It was incredible.

...There was this girl who told me she was going to fuck me to death.

"Well, I'm twenty-eight (at the time,) and most of my family has lived into their eighties.

So, you better get to work."

...This other girl said, "I want some cosmopolitan ice cream."

"You mean Neapolitan."

"No, I mean cosmopolitan. It's Neapolitan, but with vodka."

...I was at some Greek restaurant, and this table got up to pay their bill. The manager ran their credit card and had them sign. Then he said, "I'll give you your card back after you clean the floor under your table. I watched you deliberately fuck up the floor with mud, food, and garbage and stomp it into the tile." He holds up his phone and says, "Do you want to see the pictures? You can call the cops and say that I stole your credit card, or I can call the cops and have you charged with vandalism. Your call."

I couldn't believe it! It worked. They swept up their mess before leaving.

I wish I could do that when a family brings their kids in, and there are crackers and all kinds of crap on the floor around the highchair.

...There was this one guy I saw at The House that had this tattoo on his wrist that looked like a watch, and it just said, 'right fucking now' where the hands would be.

Boredom isn't the lack of things to do.

It's the lack of motivation to do it.

All the things you hear in a bar and all the crazy experiences and stories... it reminded me of Chicago and all the friends I had there.

I have to go home.

I'm learning that it doesn't matter where you are if you're not happy with who you are.

*** - Timeless - ***

I've been brought up on charges of killing time

I await the sentence for my crime

She was found on Sunday, October 28

They tried to save her, they were too late

Arrested immediately no questions asked

A likely suspect, a messy past

A lonely wanderer not any plans

Much too much of her on my hands

She died without a sound

Not enough of her to go around

A million holes were in her heart

One for every relationship that fell apart

One for every opportunity lost

For every penny that she cost

Too much or not enough of her spent

Someday, I'll realize what it all meant

It all started long ago

A lesson my parents tried to show

Said, "Slow down, and that your time

Life's a mountain you must climb

Be careful and spend her well

Not to purchase or to sell

Give her freely to family or one good friend

To someone special, be proud to lead"

Said, "Not to worry or wonder when"

But, things were different way back then

When she and I first met

On us your watch you could set

All the fruits of life we once tasted

I blame myself when she got wasted

Every time I would stop to think

She always took another drink

If ever I meet her in another life

I would not hesitate to make her my wife

Never leave her side

Never looking for a reason to hide

Because, despite what happens good or not

I just remember she's all I got

Chapter Eleven: Committed

I leave Cork and Tap on good terms. I actually put in a two week notice and work it all the way out. I haven't done that too often. I also give my landlord notice, and everything is fine with that, too. I wasn't fired, and I wasn't evicted.

This is progress.

My brother will miss me, but unlike all the other times, I'm not leaving him high and dry. His life is set and comfortable these days.

I haven't really made any close friends out here, so I don't have to worry about leaving anyone else behind.

I make arrangements to stay on Ken's couch again until I get on my feet. I pack my stuff into a rental and headed west. Homeward bound.

I've moved a lot my whole life, and this move, this time, is going to be final. Chicago is home. It's always been. I was only in Asheville for four months, and it never felt like home. I lived in Chicago for five years, which was the longest I'd lived in any one place since I was eighteen. I was thirty-one now, and it's time to settle in and start building some stability.

Only a few days after moving home, Steven agrees to let me start covering bar and door shifts again. I would never work the cleanup job again, but he must have liked my bartending. It isn't long before I'm covering at least four shifts a week. Two door shifts and two bar shifts. I'm making good money and am able to move off Ken's couch in a few weeks.

It's another transient hotel in the North Loop. The rent is my standard four hundred, and it's right across the street from a grocery store, and the Red Line was basically just down stairs, only five blocks from The House. The location is great, and the rent is just right.

I keep the window open all the time, and the nonstop sound of the streets below is soothing in a way. It's a busy street, only a block away from the State and Division intersection where there are around ten popular bars just on that one block. There is always something going on.

Every once in a while, I would hear loud crying and moans of pain. There is this homeless woman that sits at the bus stop just across the street and right outside my window.

I've dealt with a lot of homeless in my time in Chicago. Mostly, I've had to keep them away from the front of the bar and keep them from bothering the customers. I do find myself talking to them every once in a while, and even know some of their names. Some are obviously street names, but a lot use their real names.

They all do what they had to do to survive, and strangely enough, most are reasonably happy.

This woman is very different.

She isn't begging for money or trying to play on anyone's sympathies. She's just in extreme emotional pain. I know it isn't physical because ambulances come every once in a while, and sort of check on her. She never accepts any help. I watch her sometimes, and I see people offer money or try to talk to her. She always just calmly turns them away. Then, she returns to her crying.

I feel for her, but there is nothing that I can do.

Eventually, I drown her out and don't even notice her anymore, but often it's a reminder of how things could always be worse.

I spent my whole life in and out of pain while hoping for death, but now I want to live. I don't really know what's different, but it feels good.

Life goes on, and I'm working and maintaining pretty well. I set out to work as much as I can and don't spend much time at home.

Dell was always good for giving up shifts, but over the years, he and I had never really gotten along. I would come in to hang out, and he would have me take over the bar. Then he would go to the basement and take a nap. Everyone had a tab, but nothing was written down. He either kept everything in his head or made up the total when people would cash out. That was what I had to do... make up a reasonable tab.

There was also a time when I had to throw someone out, and Dell later decide to overrule me and let the guy back in. We were co-workers, and you always backed up your co-workers, no matter what. I was pissed and had to throw the guy out a second time.

I don't remember what the guy did, but it was bad enough to make me have to get him out. The second attempt was a bitch because the guy kept looking at Dell to override me again. He finally supported me after seeing that I wasn't backing down, and I got the guy out.

It shouldn't have been that hard. Jason, Alex, Ken, Steven... everyone else would have backed me up.

I was by-the-book, and he was from the seat of his pants. We clashed.

Dell's main shift is Thursday night, and it is busy. Friday and Saturday nights are considered amateur hour, but Thursdays are big with the cooler regulars, and the general crowd is better.

I cover the whole shift, and at the end of the night, I count the tip jar. There's close to six hundred dollars. I count the drawer, and everything like seven times to make sure it's right. No wonder he can afford to give up so many shifts. In one night, he makes what most make in a week.

One night, I'm hanging out with Evan while Dell is working, and Jeri comes in. In the time that I had been gone, she had found another job somewhere but still comes in once in a while.

That night she's pretty drunk.

She pulls up a stool and slides in right next to me and starts in about how much of an asshole I am.

Evan tries to keep things calm.

Since the time we had been together, which was more than two years ago now, I've apologized about a million times. Tonight, I find myself apologizing again. I mean it, and I'm sincere. I had treated her like shit and had been dishonest and almost cruel. I had used her, and she knew that.

I sit and listen to her all night.

Dell closes the bar at four and gets everyone out, but me, Evan, and Jeri are allowed to stay. When closing up and doing all the cleanup, it's nice to have a couple of people around just for the company. Most shifts are worked alone, and after twelve hours of having plenty of people to talk to, when four o'clock rolls around and everyone leaves, it's a shock to the system. Most of the bartenders keep one or two people around after close. Most nights, other employees like me, Ken, or Evan, would hang out, and we are the ones that usually stay. It's almost never non-employees, but occasionally some of the better regulars hang out.

Dell finishes up and joins in the conversation. He seems to be egging on Jeri in her rant. I can see the entertainment value. I'm laughing along through most of it. After two years, my guilt has pretty much subsided. Evan keeps trying to change the subject, but finally gives in and joins the fun.

We leave, and Dell locks up. We are standing on the sidewalk out front, and Dell decides to wrap it up by pushing the two of us together. "There you go. Hug and make up. It's all good now."

Just as we are pushed together, neither one of us makes any effort to hug it out. She is still ranting, and I'm annoyed by the hours of berating that I have just taken.

We separate, and she comes out swinging, landing a few good ones. Dell and Evan are trying to hold her back and calm her down, but aren't doing a very good job. As she is flailing about and landing one or two, she reaches around Dell and takes a swipe at my face, cutting me with her nails just under my eye. I'm bleeding now and pissed, but I just walk away.

It's been two years since we've dated, and we had only been together for three weeks. I've apologized a million times. I had admitted I was wrong.

Evan and Dell seem to calm her down, and she walks the other way. Dell goes home, and Evan catches up to me. We go into a nearby diner and sit down for breakfast. I'm still bleeding a little.

Just as our food arrives, she comes in yelling at me again. She's causing a scene and is pretty much out of her mind, but notices that the cook is walking towards her to get her to leave. She leaves on her own after throwing a fist full of silverware at me.

Man, this girl can hold a grudge.

That's pretty much the last anyone sees of her.

I find out later from Alex that she's moved to Colorado to be with her mom. Good for her. A fresh start in a new place usually helps.

I've gotten to the point where I'm covering the door every Friday and Saturday night. I've done it for like five years at this point, and I've gotten to know most of the regulars, so I don't card them, but new sets of regulars pop up all the time. Not having worked all week long and not having been around for the last few months, there are a lot that I don't recognize. Plus, if they've never made any effort to be friendly with me, they don't register.

Even though they don't know me, they seem to feel that I should know them and try to walk right in without showing me their IDs.

It is a pretty standard practice in the city to card everyone. Even people that are obviously in their fifties or even older have to show ID. Everyone that enters a bar has to have an ID on them. It's the law and has been common practice in the city for years. A lot of people that are obviously of age get kind of pissy about it, but that's just part of being a doorman.

The regulars that I don't recognize get really pissy. They bitch about it like, 'how could he possibly not know who I am.' They might be in there every night, but if they don't know me, how can they assume that I must know them?

We could lose our license pretty easily if we don't follow the rules. Then I, and pretty much all of my friends, would be out of work. I'm not going to let that happen.

One night I'm working the bar with Steven, and one of his friends comes in with a girl that looks pretty young, but I'm not working the door that night and friends of the owner get certain leeway.

I overhear her telling someone that she's only eighteen. I get up next to Steven and tell him what I've heard. He gets her out of there immediately. He doesn't mess around either.

Another night, the owner of the club next door comes in with someone that looks young. I don't card the guy because I recognize him, and he is obviously of age. I card the girl, but she says she doesn't have an ID.

If you present a fake ID, you could have it taken away, and it's a bitch to get a new one. So, most people underage just say they don't have one. How many adults don't carry their license around with them?

The owner guy gets pissed that I won't let her in, but she knows she's in the wrong and doesn't pass the threshold. This guy looks like he wants to fight me, but I'm holding my ground. I'm not risking all of my friends' jobs for anyone.

I gain the nickname: 'The Nazi.'

It doesn't bother me. I know I'm just doing my job, and most of the staff know that I'm protecting theirs and appreciate my sternness.

Jason even says that he always feels more comfortable whenever I'm working the door.

Someone else had been working the door one night, and this girl had been underage, and she got served. It had been a sting, and we got fined a ton of money. A second strike and we could have our license suspended. A third strike and we could lose our license all together.

I'm not really liked at the door, but I'm able to get more bar shifts. They like me as a bartender. I ring big, and the customers like the fact that I'm fast and attentive. I am told more than once by regulars that I'm their favorite bartender because they never have to wait for anything. They may say it to everyone, but I'm in there enough nights, hanging out, to see just how slow the other guys can be.

Another thing that Dell is big on is 'comping.' Most of the guests are regulars and/or people in the business, so you take care of these guys, but he would cut their bill in half or run it even less. Someone could come in and hang out all night, and their total bill would be like ten dollars. Ken and most of the other bartenders do this too, but not as badly.

I charge for every drink, and none of the regulars ever complain. I even charge Raymond full price all the time. Nate only drinks Cokes, but sodas cost us nothing, so he never pays. Employees get half price anyway, so there is never any need to comp them any further.

Regulars don't need to be fully comped every time. That's not how you build regulars. You will get the reputation of cutting bills in half, and you will get a bunch of freeloaders. A respectable guest accepts a bill for every drink they've ordered. Sure, we'd hook them up once in a while, but not all the time and not to a ridiculous low.

So, I'm not the most popular bartender all the time, and I'm probably the least popular doorman, but I still get plenty of shifts. I'm covering my bills, and I'm comfortable enough to not have to always be looking for another job.

I'm going on six years of being associated with this place. I've always respected Steven, and I love the whole staff. They are my best friends. The majority of the regulars are great, and the money is good.

I'm settling in here, and I like it. I like it a lot. I'm finally home again.

Things are good.

Chapter Twelve:
2005

I've been back around three months now, and I'm right back into my regular routine of working and on off days, hanging out. It's a little nuts to spend so much time where you work, but this is where the people I care about are.

I'm not walking the streets; I'm not drinking and I'm not partying at other bars. There are no poker nights anymore, and overall, I'm being good.

Jason is working tonight. Even though he had had to kick me out of his apartment, we are still good friends. I understand that he did what he had to do, what anyone else would have done.

When I come in to take my regular spot at the point, there is this girl sitting on my stool. It's not that busy, so there are plenty of places to sit, but don't people know by now that that is my spot? I don't give that much special consideration to other people, and I don't expect it myself. It's more funny than anything else. And she is hot, which pretty much gives her carte blanche at this place.

She's talking to Jason, and he seems to be working his game, but reluctantly.

I sit down on the stool right next to her, and Jason sets me up with a Coke. Jason introduces me: "Jeff, this is Julie; Julie, Jeff."

Julie Hartzell: nice, sweet, kind, and sexy. She's probably 5'6" with long dark hair... thin, but not too thin. Her face is beautiful, and her giant smile makes it even prettier. She doesn't wear much make up. I love that. She works in the business and is with a bunch of people from her restaurant. They have all been some of Jason's regulars for a while now. They know Ken, too. Since they are in the business, they work pretty much every weekend, and those are the days that I generally work, too, so I've never seen them before.

She seems into Jason, but isn't really paying him that much attention. Maybe because he starts to get kind of busy. She is, however, paying me plenty of attention. She hardly acknowledges her group and seems very content to just sit and talk to me.

We cover seemingly every topic in only a few hours. She is really smart, but shows it without making you feel stupid. She knows a little about everything and talks intelligently on any subject. We actually don't spend much time talking about our jobs. That's usually all I talk about. Work is such a huge part of who I am.

The entire time we talk, I'm trying not to beam and trying to keep my emotions in check. She's awesome, and I feel myself falling for her, but I'm trying to be careful.

She notices early that I don't smile much, and I try to explain that I never smile much. It's just not a part of me. I smile, but only when I have a very good reason to. Right now, it's actually hard for me to not be hurting my face with a giant grin.

She's so interesting; everything about her is fascinating. She has lived an amazing life and has been through a lot. Her mom was only seventeen when she had her and raised her by herself. Her dad had died early on, and she didn't really know him. I can relate to losing a parent. I can relate to most of her stories, and she seems to relate to mine.

Even after just talking to her this one night, I feel like I know her pretty well, and she knows me pretty well, too. And even after knowing a lot about me, she still seems interested. Generally, if someone knows too much about me, they get scared away. I never minded when they got scared away. I'd rather be upfront about everything than to have to deal with shit later.

She also isn't looking to fix me or make me a project. I've had the girls that want to make a project out of me, and they get bored pretty quickly. Either it's stuff they can't fix because no one has been able to (and several have tried) ... or they realize that nothing is going to change me, and they give up. Then, it's over. Those never last long.

She likes me for who I am and even says that she doesn't try to change anyone. She takes people for who they are, and if there's stuff that should be changed or fixed, then it's completely up to that person and that person alone.

I really like the way she thinks and the fact that she says exactly what's on her mind. There are some girls that speak their minds, but it often turns out that their minds are twisted. 'Better to stay silent and be thought a fool, than to open your mouth and remove all doubt.' She is smart and conscientious. Her opinions are based on something, something real.

Before I can get up the courage to ask her out, the bar closes, and she leaves with her group. Jason has me stick around, and I have to ask him, "Is there anything between you guys?"

"Nope, we've just talked here and there."

"Is she someone that you would want to hook up with?"

"Nah, I kinda got my mind set on someone else."

I feel like I should ask him more about the girl he had his mind on, but I was only interested in one thing.

"I really dig this girl. When do they usually come in?"

"You want her number?"

I don't ask why he had it or even care. I program it into my phone and go home to get some sleep.

I send her a text when I wake up: 'Do you want to go see a movie Wednesday night? I'm thinking about seeing 'Meet the Fockers'. It's supposed to be pretty funny, and I might even smile.'

I don't give my name in the text, and she won't recognize my number, but I hope she remembers just how much she was on me about smiling.

She remembers.

She calls me and says that 'she would love to see the movie,' not 'she would love to see me.' I'm getting ahead of myself. The date is on, and that's all that matters. It's actually the first time I've asked someone out on an actual date. Most of the time, I meet girls, and we end up together after hanging out a few times.

She arranges for me to meet her at this bar by her place, and we then would go from there. We are going to meet about two hours before the movie.

When I get to the bar, she's kind of dressed up. All black, snazzy flowing pants and a kind of ruffled top. It's a cold November, so she has a fancy black coat to match everything. She's wearing a little more make up than before, but she looks amazing.

I wear all black, too. All black is the standard 'going out' clothes. I want to look good but don't want to seem like I'm trying too hard. I'm very glad to see that she seems to be doing the same thing.

I order a cocktail. I want to be loose, but I also want to maintain my composure, so I'm drinking slowly. She has one of the drafts.

Micro-brews are really big in the city. That's pretty much all The House carries.

They know her here, so the tab is very reasonable.

We have no problem filling the two hours. We talk and talk. In fact, we are actually running late for the movie. We take a cab and get there in just enough time to get popcorn and drinks and find good seats. I hadn't notice it at the bar because of all the smoke, but she has this wonderful perfume and smells amazing. I wonder if it is one of those pheromone enhancing perfumes. It makes her even sexier.

The movie kind of sucks, but I hadn't been paying close attention.

Afterward, we head to a bar that I used to work. I know it will be dead, and we will be able to talk without distraction. I don't know the bartender or recognize any other customers. I thought I'd see someone I know. Being known around the city used to be one of my things. I thought it might impress or at least look good.

She orders a martini this time and the bartender spends way too much time looking at her ID. We get our drinks and go into the back where they have these comfy chairs, and we can talk privately.

I really open up to her. I feel so unbelievably at ease with her.

She opens up, too. She admits to me that she's only twenty. She also tells me that no one in Chicago knows. I can't believe it. I had never carded her because she had never come in on a night when I was at the door. I had assumed that Jason or Ken had.

She shows me her ID. It's a really good fake, but if anyone looks at the name and then hears her being called Julie, she'd be busted. The name on the ID is Maryann. She tells everyone that her middle name is Julie.

If I hadn't heard her name, it would have fooled me, and I'm the 'ID Nazi.'

I don't really know what to do with this information. How can I go to bars with her? We can't ever hang out at The House, but I couldn't tell on her either. She's been going there for months and has never been questioned. If I say anything, it would get both Jason and Ken in trouble... anyone that had ever served her would be in trouble... in trouble with Steven. But what about the license?

It's not just because I like her - There are a lot of factors in play.

I don't know what to do. It's a stalemate in my head. I'm too into her to touch the issue. It's too late. I would never make this concession for anyone else, but no one knows, and it has to stay that way. She'll actually be twenty-one at the end of May. Six months is a long time to keep a secret.

I'll keep her secret as it is, but the only way I can justify it to myself is to pretend she's never told me. If there were to be a sting or if anyone questioned it, I would swear that I had had no idea. I'm the only one in the whole city who knows the truth, and it will stay that way.

She looks at me with her almost glowing green eyes and asks, "Why didn't you hold my hand during the movie."

"I have no idea."

Then she leans in and kisses me. This one kiss, this amazing kiss, soft and gentle, sweet and strong... this one kiss is better than any sex that I've ever had.

We kiss for what seems like hours, and it may have been. The bar lights go up. It is a quarter to two. We decide to head to The House.

Far from private, but at least it is still open. The night couldn't end yet.

We get to the bar, and Jason is working. When we sit down, he comes over with this big grin on his face.

"What's up?"

"Nothing."

"What's up with the grin?"

"Just seeing you guys together… I know you've only known each other for three days, and it looks like you've been together for years."

We are holding hands and smiling from ear to ear. I guess it shows.

Some of her friends are there, too, and one of them comes over and almost word for word says the exact same thing.

We leave after last call, but I'm still not ready for the night to end. She isn't ready either and asks, "Where do you live?"

"I'm about five blocks from here."

"Let's go." And she leads the way, clutching my arm the whole time. It's freezing outside. It's only November; it is going to be a rough winter.

We get to my place, which is just one room with a desk, a mini fridge, a TV stand, and a bed.

Still standing in the middle of the room, we kiss and hold each other. This girl is just… just… there are no words. I've never felt like this with anyone, ever.

We slowly and carefully take off each other's clothes. Holding her gently, I bring her to the bed. I am kissing her all over, and she tastes like peaches. With her clothes off, her perfume seems stronger, and I am in heaven. We never turn off the lights, and after a few hours, her sweat covered body glistens.

I don't even remember falling asleep. I only remember waking up with her in my arms and never feeling more at peace.

In the morning, she starts to stir a little in my arms. She's waking up and seems as at peace as I am. In only three days, she knows almost everything about me. It feels like we are just plain meant to be together.

This time of year, is usually rough, but I've never been happier.

The holidays are coming.

People think of New Year's Eve as the busiest bar day of the year, followed closely by St. Patrick's Day. Actually, the day before Thanksgiving can be even bigger. Then, just about every day after Thanksgiving is busy all the way through to New Year's, but after New Year's things dry up pretty badly until St. Patrick's Day. During January and February, bars are ghost towns. Luckily this place has enough regulars to keep things popping all year round.

With us being not too far from the 'Mag Mile,' the holiday season is great. People seem to get into the practice of throwing money around, and the spirit of the season makes most extra generous. Then, after New Year's, they realize just how much they've spent and get really tight.

Smart people in the business start to save up during the holidays to make the first few months of the year easier.

I'm not really that smart, and I've never been good about saving, but this year I'm trying.

It's the Saturday after Thanksgiving, and I'm working the door. The night is going pretty smoothly, and it's nice and busy. The tip out should be good.

Closing time comes around, and the place is still packed. They were supposed to call last call at 4:30, but it's a quarter till five when they finally get around to it. They were supposed to turn up the lights at about a quarter till or at least ten till. They finally put up the lights right at five. We have to have everybody out now.

I start to go around and collect everyone's drinks.

"I gotta take these. We're closed. You gotta go." I'm being nice about it, but no one else is making any effort to get people out. I figure that as long as I get all the drinks off the tables and the bar, we should be OK if the cops come by. Still, no one is helping. Jason, Alex, and Dell are working, and they are usually pretty good about this.

Most of the people that are still here are the really good regulars, but there are over a dozen of them, and that's far too many to be hanging out after close.

I start yelling, "You have to go. We are closed." I'm loud, but not an angry loud.

The last drink I take away is Knight's. It's twenty after five. His hand isn't on the glass, and I slide by him and grab it without anyone seeing. Now all the drinks are clear, so I feel a little more comfortable, but there are still way too many people in here.

After cleaning a few glasses, I start to come from behind the bar past Knight, and he stops me and puts his hand on my neck. He is apparently pissed that I took his drink. He feels like I disrespected him in front of his friends, but no one would have even noticed if he wasn't making an issue of it.

"I took everyone's drink. I have to, or we'll get busted."

He is not appeased and starts to squeeze my neck a little. I push his hand away. He puts it right back and presses his thumb against my jugular. I push his hand away again, this time with a little force. He starts to put it back again, and I give him a little shove to get him off me. We start shoving back and forth pretty roughly.

Jason starts to pull him off me and takes him to the door. Finally, someone is actually helping, but did it have to take almost getting into a fight with one of our best regulars? I am following pretty closely. After all, it is my job to get people out.

I'm following too closely.

This whole time, Knight is trying to get at me while Jason struggles to keep him under control. Knight is a big guy, and he is pissed. He takes a few swings at me, then one connects. He gets me right in the eye. Now I'm pissed. I'm just doing my job. I can't believe it. He's a friend, and this is way out of line.

I'm screaming now, "GET THE FUCK OUT!" Not just to Knight, but to everyone.

I'm still following them out when Dell gets in front of me. "Please don't go outside."

I'd been hit in the face, and I can tell from his tone that Dell thinks I'm the one in the wrong.

I stop at the threshold, and Jason is trying to calm Knight down outside. I can still hear him screaming at me.

I turn to the whole bar and with everything I have in me, I yell, "GET THE FUCK OUT NOW!"

Dan, one of our better regulars and another guy I consider a pretty good friend, yells back at me, "Dude, you gotta get the fuck out of this business."

"I don't care who you are. If you don't work here, get the fuck out now."

No one is moving, and still, no one else is making any effort to get anyone out. It looks as though I'm never going to override three employees that have worked here way longer than I have, and I'm getting more and more pissed. I am about to completely explode.

Dell and Jason are still outside trying to calm down Knight. He still wants to kick the shit out of me and probably sees no reason for anyone to stop him.

Alex is behind the bar talking to the regulars that are still hanging out. It's now a quarter to six.

I've had it. I can't go outside, and I feel like I can't stay here. No one seems to care whether I am here or not. There are still around a dozen people besides the staff still hanging out. No one has a drink and the excitement is pretty much over. There is no reason to still be here. Maybe they are scared to go outside, too. A lot of people fear Knight for whatever reason.

I finally mutter 'fuck it' and storm out. I blow right past the crowd outside and head home.

After I get home, I realize my mistake. I've basically abandoned this job. I'm gonna get fired, but do I really want to work at this place anymore? The staff and the regulars clearly have no respect for me. I mean nothing to them.

I have to keep this job somehow. So, I go back.

Everyone is gone now. It's a quarter after six.

Evan had been in there the whole time, and I hadn't even noticed. He is doing all my cleanup and breakdown for me.

I sit at the bar on the end. Jason is closing out his drawer.

"Dude, what do I do now?"

We go into the basement and talk for a while, but I don't feel any better about my chances of keeping this job or of ever being able to show my face in here again.

I have to talk to Steven.

Evan had seen the whole thing, and he has had trouble getting people out at closing time, too. He also believes that the rest of the staff should have done their part in helping get people out. They always did when Steven was working, but did nothing if he wasn't.

Evan understood the situation and agreed that it was a problem that had to be dealt with. Steven should know how no one backed me up and just how hard I had been trying to do my job.

He suggests that we set up a lunch with Steven to tell him everything.

Evan would be there to back me up this time.

Steven meets us on Monday at a deli in the South Loop by where he lives. He already knows all about it. Apparently, Dell called him that night at around six in the morning. Just getting Dell's side of the story doesn't help me at all.

Evan and I tell him what happened from our point of view, but he is not listening. The issue is dead as far as he is concerned.

I still don't know if I have a job.

Evan calls me the next day and tells me that Steven has asked him to work the door this weekend.

I guess I'm out.

I show up right when the bar opens the next day. Jason is working and Steven is in the basement.

When Steven comes up, he tells me, "You know that I never fired you. I just don't want you working the door anymore."

No more cleanup and no more door shifts. This only leaves me with occasionally picking up bar shifts. It's not going to be enough.

I'm probably on Dell's bad side at this point, so I don't think he'll be asking me to cover any of his shifts. Ken is probably gonna get them all.

I guess I have to start looking for work.

Looking for work during the holidays is pretty much impossible.

Julie had worked all weekend and I haven't had a chance to tell her about it all.

Tuesday afternoon, I call her and tell her everything.

"Are you afraid that the guy will come back at you some other night?"

"I don't think so." I haven't really thought about it. "No, he's a friend. He'll get over it pretty quick."

“So, what are you going to do?”

“I just don’t know. I have been saving, and I’ll be alright for a little while, but I still have to hope and pray that there are a lot of bar shifts to cover. You know no one is hiring this time of year.”

“You’ve made it through worse. You’ll be fine.” We say goodbye, but just before she hangs up, she says, “I love you.”

She hung up before I could say it back. I really do love her.

She comes over Wednesday morning and stays with me for the next three days.

Just before she starts to get ready for work on Saturday, I kiss her on the forehead, look her right in her beautiful eyes and say to her quietly, “You know, all my life I’ve been hoping for death, but a few months ago, I decided I want to live... now I know why.”

This girl means the world to me.

I'm able to cover a few Sunday nights for Jason, and my money is holding out.

The bar is usually closed on Christmas, but Steven always said that if someone is willing to work, we would be open. Evan and I both volunteer to work. Evan would work the early shift, and I would come in and close. That way I could still make Christmas with my family.

We tell everyone that we would be open. Every other place is closed on Christmas, so any place that actually is open should do pretty good business. Based on all the people that we talked to, it looks like it will be a good night. We even ask Raymond to sort of work the door if it's necessary. He doesn’t have anything else to do and is up for it.

I go out and buy Julie a nice charm bracelet for Christmas then ask her to join me and meet my family. Her family is in California, and I know she isn't planning to go home this year. Not enough money for a plane ticket. Maybe that would have been a better gift, but I want her here with me.

She had made plans months ago to go skiing with some of her friends. She hasn't really seen much of them lately because we've been spending so much time together. I would miss her, but it sounds like she'll have fun.

I show up at the bar at about ten after spending Christmas with my family. Raymond and Evan are there, but the place is empty. It has been dead all day. At the very least, we are hoping for a later rush. People would be leaving their family parties soon, and most of them would need a drink.

A few people start to come in here and there, but it's only a hand full.

Then, Alfredo shows up, and he definitely needs a drink. Apparently, it's been a rough day. His family life is a bit strange. He'll be good for a thirty-dollar tab and a twenty-dollar tip.

Just about a half an hour after he arrives, this woman comes in and is heading right to him.

Before she gets to him, he pulls me in and says, "Hey man, don't put her drinks on my tab. She always assumes I'm gonna cover her."

I have no intention of putting anything on his tab, but that's good to know.

I recognize her. She is one of Knight's girls... maybe his wife... I don't really know. She orders a drink and starts talking to Alfredo. They seem to know each other pretty well, but I've only seen her a few times.

Then she starts to leave.

She is just about to open the door, and I call out, "Excuse me, but do you want to pay for your drink?" I'm not loud about it, and no one else hears me.

She starts to go off. She's bitchin' and screamin' and waving her arms all over the place. Then she starts in with, "He's a fuckin' racist."

Raymond tries to calm her down, "I've known him six years, and I consider myself one of his closest friends and his best friend for the last ten years is black. You're assuming he's a racist because he's white, and he's calling you on something. He's not judging you; you're judging him. The man's not a racist."

This doesn't calm her down. In fact, it seems to rile her up. She gets out her phone and makes a call. She starts pacing up and down the bar, cutting me this look of death.

I hear her tell the person on the other end, "I don't care what you are doing. You gotta come here and take care of this guy."

Only about twenty minutes later, this guy shows up, and Raymond catches him outside before he comes in. Then, they both come in and ask me to come to the end of the bar where no one is sitting.

The guy asks me, "So what happened between you and Knight?"

"Oh, that was like a month ago. I'm way over that."

Raymond says, "Just tell him what happened."

The guy asks for a beer. I give him one and start to tell him what happened. When I finish, he drinks the rest of the beer and takes off. The woman had taken off while we've been talking. Neither of them has paid for their drink, but I'm so freaked out by this time that I don't care.

After they've been gone for a while, Raymond takes me aside again: "You know what that guy was here for, don't you?"

"No."

"He showed up to kill you."

I'm dumb struck. I guess there are reasons for people to be afraid of Knight.

"I patted him down at the door, and he had a gun. He patted me down, and we talked for a second."

I'm still standing there stunned. I've never been that close to death.

After we close, the three of us go to breakfast, and Raymond tells me exactly what happened. Evan sits there, stunned. None of us believe it.

When Raymond had met that guy outside, I guess they had talked about Raymond's military background, and the guy had relayed his own history with the military. Then, he revealed that he was an off-duty cop that had known Knight for twenty-five years. The woman was Knight's wife, and she told him Knight's side of what had happened after Thanksgiving.

The guy had been sleeping and hadn't wanted to leave the house, but apparently when Knight's wife says jump, he's gotta jump. He'd been on their payroll for a long time.

Raymond always talked about everything that he'd done with the military, and it all seemed very hard to believe. He was always pretty drunk whenever he would tell those stories. I believe them now. I still don't know exactly what he said to this guy to get him to leave me breathing, but I thank God Raymond did what he did.

Two days later, Julie and I go to meet Raymond at one of his spots in Bucktown. She hasn't met him yet, but as soon as I introduce them, she grabs him with this huge hug.

"Thank you."

"What did I do?"

"You saved his life. You saved my life."

The next day, she moves in with me and insists on helping with the bills. She makes good money at her job and works a lot. I feel funny about it, but I'm in no position to make an issue of it. It already feels like we're married so this would all work out fine.

As she is unpacking her stuff, she shows me a picture of her mom. Her mom is actually only six years older than I am. I am eleven years older than Julie.

I look at the picture and say, "Wow." I shouldn't have said it out loud.

She gives me a playful smack, and we laugh about it.

Despite being basically banned from working the door, the bar always has two doormen on New Year's Eve, so Steven asks me to be the second. Evan and I would work the door and tag team bar-backing. Alex, Ken, Jason, Dell, and Steven work the bar. Everyone works New Year's.

Around eleven, Julie gets off work and is walking up the street to meet me. This guy is following her. When she gets to me, the guy backs off a little, but not much. He's talking up a storm and making no sense.

I ask him to leave, and he blows up.

"You think you're bad? You a bad man? You a tough guy?"

I ignore him and hold Julie behind me.

The guy is ranting and raving, pacing back and forth. Then, he starts to reach in his pocket.

I tell Julie and Evan to get inside.

I'm staring this guy down and watching very closely.

He opens his coat to show me the gun.

I take out my cell phone and call the cops. Calmly, but not taking my eyes off this guy, "There's a man pointing a gun at me." I give them the address and hang up, all the while never taking my eyes off this guy.

I probably should have gone inside or taken off running to draw him away from the bar. I should have done something to protect myself. Instead, I am staring him down. I have one eye on him and one eye on the gun. I'm not sure what I'm supposed to do in this situation, and I could get myself killed if I do nothing or anything. People in the bar could get hurt. My friends. Julie. If anything happens to her... I would rather die, so I stare this guy down.

We start to hear the sirens, so he takes off.

I am amazed that my pants are still dry. I take a deep breath and thank God... again.

No one else saw the gun, and I bet that everyone except Julie thinks I'm out of my mind. I guess I was out of my mind to stare down a guy with a gun.

On New Year's Day, the bar is closed, and Steven takes the whole staff out to eat at this restaurant in Lincoln Park. I've been going along for five years now. The place has an all-you-can-eat snow crab special on New Year's Day. I am dangerous when it comes to all-you-can-eat.

Julie can't stay long. She has to go into work. She leaves after about an hour.

After lunch, Steven takes me aside and starts talking about Christmas. I wonder if he's heard what happened. Raymond, Evan and I had all agreed to never talk about it.

"You worked Christmas with Evan?"

"Yea."

"Why?"

"You said if we wanted to work, we could."

"After paying you out, it cost us money to be open that day."

"We told everyone about it, and it sounded like there would be a lot of people. There just wasn't."

"You know I always let you work here because I felt sorry for you. How else were Jason and Ken supposed to get paid back? You're always out of work and looking for a hand out. Well, I can't help you anymore."

I don't say anything. He just walks away.

I couldn't have said anything if he'd stayed. I am in complete shock.

This is bigger to me than almost getting killed.

He feels sorry for me? I dedicated myself to this place for six years, and he feels sorry for me? I had considered him a friend, not just a boss. I had considered all of them friends. This place is like home to me. I help out and work more hours off the clock than some do on the clock. I've been in there nearly every day for six years, and that's it? I am cut down and thrown out like I'm nothing. I have risked my life for this place. I have given my life to this place. Everything in the last six years has involved this place. Now nothing? After everything I have done for this place, and he just feels sorry for me. Now that's it? I mean nothing to these people after six years. Six years.

Julie tells me that she'll cover the bills.

It's the dead season, but some places look to clean house and hire new people during this time. So, looking for work doesn't seem that bleak.

Without Julie, I'd be losing it. I'd be completely falling apart. I wouldn't have the strength to look for work. I would never have left my place. I would have slept all the time. I would have completely given up.

I have to get back on my feet. I can't afford any down time, and I am more motivated than ever. It is all for her now, and I am not going to let her down.

A few weeks later, I'm having dinner with Evan and Ken.

I have pretty much vowed to never set foot in The House again, so we aren't going to be getting together there. We go to the diner down the street.

I think about asking Ken for another loan, but I haven't paid him back from the last time. He's done a lot for me and has never made an issue of it. He's paid for everything and has loaned me money a couple of times over the years. I owe him a lot. I couldn't ask him this time.

Evan breaks the uncomfortable silence by asking, "How are things going?"

"Shitty, but I'll survive. I've been through worse. Thank God for Julie."

"You really love her, don't you?"

"I'd marry her today if I could afford a ring."

He thinks about it for a minute then Evan tells me, "You know I bought a ring like ten years ago, and I think I still have it."

"An engagement ring?"

"Yea."

"And you would just let me, have it?"

"You'll pay me back someday. I trust you, and I know how much you love her. I just have to find it, and it might take a while. I'll let you know."

Two weeks later, Julie loses her job. They had found out that she is underage.

Now what are we going to do?

Despite everything, we are closer than ever. We cling to each other and make each other strong. We have to get through this. We will get through this.

I'd been down before, but it had always just been me I had to worry about, and most of the time, I could not have cared less about myself. This time, I have to keep it together. I have to get us through this. Everything is for her. We'll be together forever, regardless of what happens.

She says every night that this is just something that we have to get through. It's a test. Every night, we hold each other close and pray like we've never prayed before.

We'll get through this no matter what.

I have to do something. I've put out a couple dozen applications and resumes, but haven't gotten one interview. Julie isn't having any luck either.

I go to Raymond. I haven't asked him for anything in close to two years, and when I have borrowed from him, I've paid him back immediately. As much as I hate asking for money, I really have no other choice right now.

"Yea, I'll help you out. I just gotta move some things around. I'll get back to you."

Great. He's gonna come through. I can breathe now.

Two more weeks go by, and he hasn't called, so I call him. He's not answering. I try at least twenty times on the phone, and I go to his work and his hangouts, and I just can't find him anywhere. I can't believe it. It's just like the week of my brother's wedding. I can't believe he's doing it again.

He is willing to step in and save my life, but he's backing out of this? I can't believe it. He's like my only hope.

I call him every day for a week, leave several messages but there is no response.

That's it for him.

I've had enough. Six years and no more. I just don't care anymore.

He's dead to me.

I have no other choice... I have to ask my dad. He's the only one on Earth that I have left to go to for help. I've burned all the other bridges. The rest of my family has done plenty for me, and I don't dare ask for anything else from them. I couldn't, even if I wanted to.

Julie has no one that is in a position to help. Her friends and her family don't have it like that.

I call my dad and pray for the best. It seems that every time I call him, I need help, but I haven't asked for help since high school.

"Dad, I'm in trouble. I lost my job, and it's been like a month now, and there just isn't anything out there right now. I'm behind on rent, and I'm gonna run out of food pretty soon. I wouldn't ask if I wasn't desperate."

Dad comes through. A month's rent and a little extra for food and stuff.

It is February fourteenth. Valentine's Day.

I go to the store to get some food, and I pick up four roses for Julie. One for each month that we've been together.

When I get home and I give her the roses, she starts to cry.

"Hey, it's gonna be all right. We're doing OK now."

"I know, but we just don't know how long we have to make your dad's money last. How much longer can we keep doing this?"

"We'll do it as long as we have to."

I get down on one knee and hold her left hand with both of mine. I look her in her teared-up eyes, "You know I love you. I will always love you. I want nothing more than to be with you for the rest of my life. You are everything to me." She is still crying, but now there's a smile on her face. The smile I fell in love with. "I know I don't have a ring, but I'll get one. Evan is gonna give me one. Anyway... I love you with all of my heart. Will you marry me?"

"Yes."

Now we're both crying.

She falls into my arms and nothing else matters. We jump into bed and make love for hours. Take a break for some water and a smoke... then right back to it. We make love for two days, never caring about anything else.

I never say 'make love,' but that's exactly what happens. This is real love. I've never felt like this, ever, with anyone, never ever before. She makes me feel like anything is possible. As long as we are together, nothing can hurt us.

It's almost the end of March, and we're running out of food and cigarettes. In probably two days, we'll be completely out.

Three days later, we are out of food, cigarettes, and money. We are still both unemployed, and things are looking bad. I couldn't ask anyone for more money. There is no one left to go to. I don't know what we are going to do.

When I get home from job hunting, there's a carton of smokes and several bags of groceries.

"Where did this come from?"

"Now don't get mad." That's usually a good sign that I'm not going to keep myself from getting mad. "I sold the bracelet you gave me for Christmas."

I'm not mad. I'm not really anything.

It's now the middle of April, and there's nothing left. This time, I come home from job hunting, and Julie is on the bed crying in the dark.

"What's wrong?" as if that isn't abundantly clear.

"I talked to my mom today. She said she can afford one plane ticket." She is staring at me, crying. "I have to go home."

It doesn't really take much thinking about. It's the best thing for her. She should be with her mom. She shouldn't have to suffer like this.

She'd be able to find work in California pretty easily. She could work with her mom almost immediately. The plan is that she would save a lot by living at home and would send me a plane ticket as soon as she could. I would continue to look for work and save also. One way or another, we would be together again.

I have to take her to the airport in four hours. We are lying in bed holding each other. Then, I begin to shake all over. My heart feels like it is going to jump out of my chest. I start to cry uncontrollably. My eyes shut, and I can't open them.

Julie puts her hands on my shoulders and tries to hold me still. “Jeff! Jeff! Jeff! Open your eyes! Say something! Should I call an ambulance? Jeff! Jeff! Jeff!”

I’ve had panic attacks before, but this is like nothing I’ve ever experienced. This is horrible. I'm shaking, but can’t move. I'm crying, but can’t open my eyes. I can hear her, but I can’t respond. I can hear her start to cry, too.

The bed jumps as she jumps to the floor and goes for her phone to call 911. When she leaves my side, I can feel it, and I start to come around. I open my eyes, and I try to sit up.

“My God, are you OK? You scared the shit out of me. Do you still want me to call an ambulance?”

“No, I’m OK now.” She holds me until we have to leave. I don’t ever want to let go.

We get to the airport almost late, and you just can’t screw around at airports anymore. She can’t miss this flight. Every part of me wants to tell her not to go, but I know it's for the best, and I know we would see each other again. We start kissing, and I never want it to stop. She pulls away crying and says, “I have to go.”

“I know. I love you.”

“I love you, too.”

There isn’t time for a long goodbye, and I know I couldn’t have handled one anyway. Watching her leave is the most pain I’ve ever felt.

The train ride home is agony. I'm on the Blue Line headed to Division, and it's a long ride. I'm in the back car, and there are only maybe three other people around. I had held it together in the airport. I try hard to not cry in public, but today on this train, I just can't stop myself. With every stop, more people get on, and I still can't control my tears. It doesn't matter. Who cares what people think? I just watched the greatest thing that has ever happened to me leave.

I know that I will do everything in my power and beyond to be with her again, and she is going to work towards the same goal. I can't fall apart. I have work to do.

I'm falling apart anyway.

The next day, Evan shows up with the ring.

We call each other every day until my phone gets cut off because I haven't paid the bill. Not having a phone is going to make it harder to find work. We send emails every day, but after my internet gets cut off, I have to go to the library, and I can't get there every day. It's hard to stay in touch, but we give it all we have.

She finds work right away and is starting to save. I get a job the next week, but it will be three weeks until I see a paycheck.

We realize that we need more than just a plane ticket. We need enough for us to live on our own. Neither one of us quite has enough yet for me to make the move. Not yet. We have to save a little longer, but I'm not even covering my bills. Saving seems impossible, but I'm willing to sacrifice everything to see her again.

Ken and Evan make sure I don't starve to death in the meantime. I give up smoking for the time being because I have no money to buy them, but living through this stress without it is hellish.

Birthday month comes and goes, and I don't even realize it.

One of Julie's co-workers goes into The House and tells Ken that Julie was underage. He is pissed, but he doesn't show it. I think he knows I am going through enough.

"You of all people to have someone underage in the bar."

"I know, but there were a lot of reasons to keep it a secret. Did you ever card her?"

"No, I first started to notice her on Jason's shifts, so I never bothered. I assumed that he did."

"He probably did. She had a great fake. It would have fooled me if I ever carded her, but I'm the same as you... I saw her on Jason's shifts. After I found out, I didn't want to get anyone in trouble. Her or Jason or anybody. I would have never stopped anyone from carding her, and if I was asked... well if I was asked, I probably would have lied, but I was never asked."

I could tell that he was thoroughly disappointed and thrown. If it were anyone but me... the ID Nazi. He lets it go, but it would have a permanent effect on our friendship.

Trust is a big deal.

Now asking him for any help is really out of the question.

The new job is a place that has just opened up, and as new places often do, they like the fact that I've done so many openings. They hire me on the spot. I'm bartending, but not really making any money. The place is too new and too slow. The business just isn't there, and the money is barely coming in. I'm able to keep myself alive and start buying smokes again, but rent still has to wait.

I make occasional small payments, enough to keep the eviction notices off my door, but I don't know how long I can get away with it. I have to start making more money. It means a second job or at least a better one.

I make it through to July, but something has to give soon, or I'm going to be out on my ass.

I haven't heard Julie's voice in more than two months, and I haven't gotten an email from her in six weeks.

I am interviewing all over on my days off.

One of the best options is an ice cream shop, and yet another brand-new place.

This one has been open for about a month but doesn't have a manager. They hire me the day I show up for my second interview. I would be making 35K a year, but for an indefinite amount of time I would be the only manager. So, I would be working nearly every day, and God knows how many hours. Still, it would be way better money than where I am currently working.

I'm able to work out a two week notice with the other place and make a little more money before starting the next job.

There are only three days between jobs.

I get my phone turned back on with my last paycheck but blow off rent again. I call Julie as soon as it's turned back on. It says I had the wrong number. She must have changed it to a California number after she moved. I go to the library and check my email to see if she maybe sent me the new number. There are no emails.

I planned a camping trip with my family weeks ago. It would be a nice break from reality. The new job doesn't have a problem with me taking the first weekend off.

I start on a Monday. They start at nine in the morning. Not too bad. I could get up early enough and make it there by 8:30 and still get plenty of sleep. Or so I thought.

I stay until close. Nine in the morning till midnight every day. I get home at around one, and it takes me close to two hours to get to sleep. Regardless of how wiped out I am, I still need some winding down time before I can finally fall asleep. That has always been the case, ever since I started working in the business.

I get around five hours of sleep a night. I've gotten used to closer to ten.

I have to do what I have to do.

By the end of the first week, the hours are killing me, but I have the weekend off for my camping trip. I really need a break at this point.

The next Monday, it's back to the same hours. By now, I'm broke again and for the last two weeks, I've been living on ice cream and hot dogs, the only food they serve. At work, I can eat for free, but don't always have time. I have to make time at least once a day to eat something.

Friday, the paychecks come in. I fish mine out first, and it's only two hundred and fifty dollars. Payroll is a week behind, but two hundred and fifty dollars for a week of fifteen-hour days? I can't live on this. I can't live on just ice cream and hot dogs much longer, and I can't get caught up on rent with only two hundred and fifty dollars a week.

I start to have a panic attack, and they are usually pretty bad. Too bad to have at work or in front of anybody, let alone in front of employees. I have to get out of there in a hurry, so I won't lose it in front of everybody.

I call the owner's partner. She is the only one I can get a hold of. I make up some family emergency to give me an excuse to leave immediately.

She says that I should just go, and she'll get there whenever she can.

I put the rest of the paychecks in the desk drawer and leave out the back door saying nothing to anyone.

I go to a Currency Exchange by my house and cash this tiny check immediately. I'm still freaking out.

As soon as I leave the place, I get a call from the owner's partner. She asks where the paychecks are, and I tell her. I guess it was kind of stupid to not tell anyone where I had put them, but if she had looked around for a second, she would have found them on her own. The office locks, so they would have been fine in the drawer, but I guess I should have put them back in the safe where they belonged.

I get home, and there is a thirty-day notice on my door.

I start the whole shaking all over thing, and this time is almost as bad as when Julie left. I wake up a few hours later, and I feel a little better, but not much. I'm still wondering what to do and how I'm going to pay my bills. I have no reason to believe that the second check will be any bigger. I can't get caught up on rent with what I'm making. I'm starving and I'm going to be evicted. I just don't know what to do.

I'm freaking out, and I have to get out of here. I have to go somewhere... do something. I have to leave, but where can I go?

At the last minute, I call my sister and ask if I could join them camping again this weekend. They go every weekend. They are only a few hours from leaving, but she says she will wait for me. It takes a little over an hour to get out there.

At least this weekend, I could eat.

When my mother died, I got her family ring in the will. It was supposed to remind me of the importance of family. A lot of the family thought that I would just disappear after my mom died, and my mom thought the same.

So, I got the ring. It wasn't worth any money, but its sentimental value was through the roof.

I take it camping with me this time and give it to my sister. I tell her that I'm afraid of losing it.

I'm hoping the weekend would calm me down, but there is no such luck. I act as if everything is fine, but inside I'm still going nuts.

I'm not going to have time to get another job before I'm evicted, and if I keep this job, there won't be any time for a second one. I am simply not going to be able to prevent getting kicked out.

So, what am I to do? There is no one left to stay with. There is nowhere left to go.

I get home Sunday night. I could go back to work tomorrow. I decide to sleep for three days instead. I'm screwed either way. I can't find a win in this situation. I have to accept that I have less than thirty days before everything goes to shit. I'll be homeless, broke, and alone. There is no chance of every seeing Julie again. There is no way to get out there. I don't even know if she still wants me. I still haven't heard from her.

I give up on the week and give up on the job, and I don't leave the house all week.

The next week is payday again, so Friday I go in to pick up my last check. I haven't been there in two weeks, and no one has called this whole time. When I get there, they don't have a check for me.

I call the owner, but can't get through. I call him like ten times, but there is no answer. I finally get a hold of his partner and ask why there is no check for me.

"We didn't think you were ever coming back."

"That shouldn't stop payroll from cutting me a check for that week."

"We took you off payroll."

"You still owe me for that week."

"You have to talk to Michael."

"I haven't been able to get a hold of him."

"He's out of town until next week."

"You don't understand. That's not acceptable. I'm out of money, and I don't even have any food."

"You have to talk to him."

I write out a thorough letter breaking down what they really owe me.

At fifteen hours a day for ten days at 35K a year, I should be getting a little more than twenty-five hundred dollars before taxes. I'd take two grand.

I email this to Michael and his partner.

After another twenty calls, I finally get a call from the partner again.

"I have your check. You can come in at two."

Michael had gotten the email.

I get there at 1:30 and wait till four. When she arrives, I give her my keys and she has me sign some paperwork. I figure that it's the basic exit interview stuff, and I sign without reading it. It's like seven pages of shit.

Then, she hands me an envelope and gets up to leave.

It's only a hundred and twenty dollars.

"Whoa, this is way off. You owe me two grand."

"You just signed an agreement to accept this final amount."

"You know you just screwed me out of two thousand dollars. What makes you think that's OK?" I'm livid, but try to keep my cool.

"You signed. We're done here."

"How can you be OK with this?" I'm genuinely floored that anyone could do this with a clear conscience, and I'm trying to appeal to hers, if she has one.

"Talk to Michael."

I know I'm not going to get anywhere with her and storm off.

I call Michael another twenty times, but there is no response.

I have to eat something, so I take what I got and head to the Currency Exchange.

When I get there and hand them the check, they take it into the back.

They come back to me and tell me, "We can't cash this. There was a stop payment on the last check you cashed here, so we have to hold this one, and you owe us another hundred."

I'm losing it.

I call the partner again, and after three attempts and an hour have gone by, she answers.

"Don't tell me to talk to Michael this time. Why did you stop payment on this check?"

"When we couldn't find the payroll last time, we assumed that you stole it and had all the checks stopped."

"I told you where they were within an hour after I left. They never left the office. You had weeks to accuse me of it and sort it out, but you never even told me that you suspected that. What the hell am I supposed to do now? And if you fuckin' say 'talk to Michael,' I'm gonna fuckin' lose it."

She hangs up.

Now I'm through the roof pissed. I call Michael again and still no answer. This time, my messages aren't so polite. I'm cussing him out, and I tell him that I'm going to sue, but the truth is there is nothing that I can do.

I leave about ten threatening messages, then give up and go home...while I still have one.

I'm lying-in bed, going over my options... as if there are any. At this point, I haven't slept in two days, and it doesn't look like I'm going to get any sleep any time soon.

I have no other options. I can't starve to death. I can't end up homeless. I can't let myself get screwed this badly. If I don't do something, I'm going to die.

I'm going to get what they owe me.

I had made a copy of the keys before I'd turned them in. Something told me that I would need them. I change my clothes to all black so I would be hidden from the cameras a little. The cameras are set up everywhere, but the whole time I had worked there, they weren't hooked up to anything. The alarm never worked either. I could dodge the cameras even if they had hooked them up, but if they had fixed the alarm... well, I'll just deal with that later.

I go into The House to set up an alibi, and Ken is working. I haven't seen him in like a month, and he's happy to see me, but he's super busy. He'd say that I was there all night. I stay for about an hour, getting up my nerve, then tell him that I'm going to the blues club, and I'll be right back. I make a short appearance at the blues club, then get on the bus.

When I get into the neighborhood, I start circling the place.

There are still employees in there.

My mind is racing, 'Get out of here. Don't do this. You can't get away with this. Just get out of here.' Over and over and over again in my head. The more this goes on in my head, the closer I get to actually doing it.

After a little more than an hour, I circle again, and the employees are all gone.

With 'get out of here' still running over and over in my head, I get to the door and unlock it. There is a camera facing the door, but my head is down. I pass by the alarm board, and it isn't on. I head to the office. I'm in the basement, and I keep the lights off. I have a small flashlight that isn't too bright that I had gotten from Jason as a gift a while back. It's just bright enough for me to see where I'm going, but not so bright that it draws any attention to me.

I go right to the safe. I don't have to worry about fingerprints because mine are already all over the place, and they can't date fingerprints. My mind is still saying, 'get out' over and over again. There is a camera on the safe, but it's dark, and I'm bending down the whole time, so there is no way of seeing my face. Besides, the cameras don't work... or so I assume.

I open the safe. The combination hasn't been changed. I'm taking too long and moving too slowly. I don't have time to count out just what they owe me, and I don't have time to clean it out either. I grab the drop bag, close up the safe and head for the backdoor, but are there cops waiting for me outside?

I'm out. I've done it.

It's all clear.

Now, I just have to get out of the neighborhood and get back to the bar.

I have the bag in my pants and the keys still in my hand. I drop the keys into the sewer and keep walking. It's about five blocks to the bus and six to the train. The train is faster, and it stops right at my place.

When I get off the train, I head up to my room. I take the money out and count it. It's almost four thousand dollars. It's more than they owe me, but they deserve this. I take the panel off my computer tower and stash the money inside. I take the envelope and bag with me, and on the way back to the bar, I toss it in a dumpster that isn't in my neighborhood.

When I get back to the bar, I stay the rest of the night. I even hang out after close with Ken. When he is all finished, we leave together. Then, I go home and sleep. I haven't slept in days, but tonight I'm able to sleep.

The next day, there are a half a dozen messages from Michael.

"You don't actually think you can get away with this. I have friends, and you will be dealt with."

He is a firefighter and does have friends on the police force, but he couldn't prove anything.

He calls again. I'd be stupid to answer. This message is pretty much the same with the addition of, "I'll kill you, you little shit."

I'm pretty sure that I'm in the clear, but I can't help but think, 'what if they got the cameras working?' There is no way my face was seen by any cameras. I'm freaking out a little anyway.

I take the money out of the computer, take two hundred out then strap the rest to my ankles. I'm heading for the train. I'm leaving town, just in case.

I take several different trains: the L, Metra and the South Shore line. I go all the way to the South Bend Airport. The end of the line. There is a Greyhound station there, and I could go anywhere. Planes require an ID, but the busses don't care. It's the safest way to leave.

The bus doesn't leave for three hours, so I decide to kill some time in town.

I get a cab and go to a strip mall near the airport. There's a barber shop there and I get my hair cut. I have them shave it all the way off. Then I go to the movies to kill some more time. Then, I take a cab back to the airport and get on the bus.

I'm heading back to Asheville. I could start over there, but I don't want to make my brother an accessory, so I'm not sure about seeing him.

I thought about going to California, but I don't know exactly where Julie lives and at this point, I don't think she wants to see me. It's been close to four months since we've talked and I haven't gotten an email in at least three months. We'd lost touch, and it seems that she wants it that way.

The bus station in Asheville is right across the street from The Cork and Tap where I used to work. I go into the restaurant to see if there is anyone I recognize. There isn't anyone I remember.

My mind is free. Free from any thought at all. Rational thought is long gone. I don't seem to have a care in the world. I'm not happy. I'm not sad. I'm not scared. I'm not anything.

I decide to see my brother after I eat. It's the best meal I've had in more than six months.

When I get to my brother's place, he isn't home, but I'm not really on any time schedule, so I sit on the curb and wait.

My mind is racing all over the place. I can't believe what I've done, and I have no idea what to do next.

When he pulls up and his headlights hit me, I can see the shock in his eyes through the windshield. No one in my family has any idea of what I've been through this year. I'm sure he has no idea what I'm doing here and, truth be told, neither do I.

"What are you doing here?"

"The truth is, I just don't know."

We go onto his back porch, and I tell him everything.

He and his wife are floored.

"Are you going to California?"

"Yea, twenty-sixth and California."

He has no idea what I'm talking about and I just hope I'm wrong.

"What are you going to do now?"

"I don't really know. I thought about restarting out here. I thought about moving on to somewhere else... anywhere else. But the more I think about it, I think I should go back."

"Are you out of your mind?"

"If it looks like I just took off, it's pretty suspicious, but they have nothing on me. I would just have to lay low for a while and not spend any money. I would have to move, but there's another transient hotel just around the corner, and I'm pretty sure I could get in there. If I get caught up on my rent and stay it would look suspicious too. The money will carry me for a while, but I just have to be careful."

"What are you going to do tonight?"

"I'm gonna stay in a hotel and probably head back in the morning."

"Why don't you just stay here?"

"I don't want you involved. It would be harboring a fugitive. I've already told you too much."

"Just stay here."

"No, I gotta get going."

"Then why come by in the first place?"

"I was still sorting things out, but while I was waiting for you, I made up my mind and while we were talking about it all, it's now pretty clear to me. I gotta go back."

"I think you're crazy, but you gotta do what you gotta do."

He gives me a hug, and I head to a hotel.

The hotel across the street from The Cork and Tap will be fine.

I check in and go to my room. It is only eleven o'clock, and I'm sure I won't be able to sleep. So, I go to the phone book and decide to go to a strip club. I call a cab and head out. When I get there, I set out to get really drunk, but no matter how many I put away, I don't feel anything.

The place closes, and I get a cab back to the hotel. It is two in the morning, and I'm not even close to tired. My mind is still racing. I'm going to sit by this lamp post and watch the traffic.

This rather large black guy comes up to me and asks me if I want something.

"Uh, no. I'm just sitting here." Then I think about it, and I figure what the hell, "You know any girls?"

"Yea, I got some girls. It'll be one fifty."

I had taken five hundred off my ankles to go to the strip club, so I still have money out. I don't want to get robbed, but I'm not really thinking about it. I'm not really thinking at all.

He waves over this girl, and I give him the money. He whispers into the girl's ear, and she looks stunned and a little disgusted. Then, she looks me up and down and smiles at me.

He takes my hand and pours about a dozen small white rocks into it. This is the first time I've ever seen crack cocaine.

"Dude, I'm not really interested in this. I just wanna get laid."

He takes most of them back, then tells me to give the rest to the girl.

Is that the deal?

You buy a hundred and fifty dollars' worth of crack and you get a girl free? Or is it the other way around? Package deal. Buy one get one free.

Anyway, the girl follows me to my room. It's around the back of the hotel.

When she gets into the room and I close the door, she stands there looking confused. I give her the rocks as I was instructed.

"I don't smoke." She takes them anyway and puts them in her purse. "Are you a cop?"

"If I were a cop, I would have busted your friend outside when he handed me the rocks. Are you a cop?" It's always smart to ask. I heard that if they lie, then it's entrapment.

"No. What do you want to do here?" She seems really shy and uncomfortable.

"I thought that was pretty clear."

"I've never done this before. I'm just friends with Jake through channels. I was hanging out with some friends drinking here. I had no idea what he was going to ask me when he waved me over. Initially I thought, 'no way,' but you're kinda cute. I'm just not sure." She probably says that to everyone, but I kinda believe her.

"Well, if you don't want to, maybe he knows someone else."

"No, I want to. I just don't know how to get this all started."

"Why don't you start by taking off your clothes?"

"You first. I figure a cop's not gonna get naked."

I take my clothes off, and we start.

It's been over an hour now, and I'm expecting a knock on the door. I'm expecting Jake to come get her.

She is great, and it feels really good. I start to forget about anyone coming around and get into it. When I finish, she gets dressed and leaves really quickly, but before she closes the door, she smiles at me and says, "Thank you."

I don't sleep at all. My mind is still racing. I'm going over everything in my head again. Again, and again and again.

The bus leaves in a half an hour.

I'm out of here, and I'm heading home again. I have no idea what I'm really doing, and a big part of me just doesn't care. I'm going through the motions, like I did when I was taking the money... going through the motions.

I can't seem to feel anything.

Before I'd left, I'd taken out five hundred dollars for the trip and turned the rest into money orders. I had hidden the money orders on the inside of these birthday cards and mailed them to my address in Chicago. I thought it would be better if I didn't have the money on me.

I take the direct route home. It's a long ride, and all I do is stare out the window the whole time. Close to eighteen hours on the bus, and I don't nod out once. I just stare out the window listening to my CDs, but don't pay any attention to the music at all.

When I get home, my key still works, and all my stuff is still there. I had been afraid that I would get booted while I was gone. Everything is just the way I'd left it. I hadn't taken anything when I left. Just the money, and the clothes on my back. I had bought some CDs and a CD player somewhere along the way. Even though I already had one, I felt like I needed something to break up the road noise.

It'd been a long trip. Pretty much a day to get out there, the day I stayed, and another day to get back. I'm pretty exhausted, so I lie down, but don't really expect to sleep.

It's ten in the morning.

Just as I start to doze off, there is a knock at the door.

"Who is it?"

"Jeff, we're detectives, and we would like to ask you a few questions."

"Is this about the ice cream shop? That guy just won't stop calling. It wasn't me."

"Can you let us in?"

"Hang on, I gotta get dressed."

I let them in, and they show their badges and tell me they want to talk to me at the station and ask me to come with them.

I should have explained to them that I haven't slept in more than three days, and I'm in no condition to talk, but I don't think about it. I'm just going through the motions.

We get to the station at Belmont and Western, and they take me into a room and start questioning me.

"I know what this is all about, and it wasn't me."

"Do you want to speak to a lawyer?"

"What do I need a lawyer for? I haven't done anything wrong. Are you charging me with something?"

"No, we just want to talk."

We talk for over an hour, and there is nothing. Then, they say that they have me on tape, and another guy comes in and starts to read me my rights.

I cut him off just as he is talking about the right to remain silent. "Hold on a second. Are you arresting me?"

"Yep. Do you want to tell us what happened?"

"Ok, OK. I really need a smoke though."

They hand me my pack and my lighter. They had me empty my pockets on the way in. Standard procedure, I guess.

They are going to arrest me anyway, and they say they have me on tape, so it's time to talk.

"Where's this tape? Can I see it?"

"We have to convert it. It's on a hard drive."

"How do you know it's me?"

"There was a reflection on the safe, and we could make out your face pretty clearly."

"The safe was black." And there was no reflection.

"We saw your face on the tape."

I am kind of shutting down, and I am so exhausted that I can't think. I just spill it and tell them everything. I actually think if I tell the whole story that they might have sympathy or something.

"Well, you're under arrest." Then, they read me my rights.

"What happens now?"

"Well, you're going to be processed, but you should bond out, and then they'll give you a court date. If you make full restitution, the judge should go light."

I have no idea what any of that means.

They take me to a cell and close the door.

There is a stainless-steel toilet with no lid and a metal slab with holes in it that I guess is supposed to be a bed.

It is freezing in here. It is the beginning of September, and it's around eighty degrees outside, but in here, I'd be surprised if it were forty. I guess they keep it cold so that guys on drugs detox faster. At least, that's what I'd heard.

Since it is nice outside, I'm just wearing jeans and a t-shirt. I pull my arms into my sleeves and try to get some sleep. At least it's a single cell, and there is no one with me.

It is probably around three in the afternoon.

It's just too fucking cold to sleep. What am I supposed to do now? What's next?

I stay up the whole time just thinking. I guess I slept a little in the morning, but it was maybe an hour or two.

They come in at probably eight in the morning and are yelling and banging stuff. They take my picture like you see in the movies. Then they take my fingerprints, but it is on this computerized copier-like thing with no ink. Then they pile about twenty of us into this truck.

I have no idea where I'm going.

They are taking us out of the truck after a thirty-minute ride and pushing us into another building. We go through several hallways and stairways, then we end up in this giant room with all these chain link cages. There are maybe twenty cages, and they are all holding about fifty to a hundred guys.

About twenty at a time, they are leading us through this maze of lines and various stages of the process. I guess this is what they mean by being processed. They are writing numbers and stuff on our arms at all the different stages. There are numbers all up my right arm and my left forearm, the letters M-I-N. I think it means minimum security. I am surrounded by hundreds of other guys with other things written on their arms with permanent marker. Some of them read MAX. Maximum security. There is no separation between the murders and the thieves.

I get to one stage, and they ask about my mental health. I start to tell them that I think I might suffer from depression. The guy at the table asks, "Do you want to be put in with all the crazies?"

I think not, but I want some help.

I'm not going to get any.

They form us into a line again, and we go one by one into a room. The judge is on a TV and she is asking questions. I answer everything into a microphone, then I'm asked to take a step back. This is where I am supposed to bond out.

"Fifteen thousand." She bangs the gavel, and I'm moved back to the hallway.

No bond.

Then, they take us about a hundred at a time into another hallway. We get to a point and stop. We are supposed to stand there and not move. There is a guy right in front of me, shaking and kinda flopping around. He is coming off something.

A guard comes up and kicks him in the back, hitting me along the way. The guy almost falls to the ground, but if he falls, he'll probably get hit again. He stays standing and is now still.

This is the strip search. We have to take our clothes off piece by piece and shake them out without popping them. We are supposed to be shaking out any bugs. We get to the point where everyone is completely naked, and we are supposed to stand still. We stand here for like ten minutes.

They take our clothes. We are allowed to keep our underwear and a t-shirt if the t-shirt is just plain white. A lot of guys have plain white t-shirts. They came prepared. It's freezing in here, too. My shirt is brown with a picture of Ray Charles on it, so I'm not allowed to keep it.

They move us into another room where we get uniforms. Then they break us into smaller groups, and we head down some more hallways and stairways. The groups get smaller and smaller as we go along. People are getting put into rooms, or they are taken down other hallways.

It is down to just me and one other guy, and we come to a door with a small window in it. They open the door and shove us in.

Someone yells out, "On the new." And what looks like a hundred men rush the door we've been pushed in.

This guy is looking right at me and asks, "What are you?" He could see that I don't know what he means and asks, "Who are you with?"

"Um, no one. I'm nothing."

He turns his head and yells, "Neutron." Then, I'm pushed aside and kind of taken into a group of white supremacists.

If you think you might ever end up in jail, never shave your head. A bald white guy is automatically considered a Nazi. In a way, it was fine. Maybe I would be protected.

The whole place is just this one giant room with beds and tables and a TV.

One of the skin heads shows me to a bunk. There are two lines of about fifty sets of bunk beds. I get the top one, and there is no ladder. I have to kinda pull myself up, and it's strangely high. I don't have much upper body strength.

"First you gotta shower. Everyone showers as soon as they come in."

Everyone has heard the stories of showering in jail, but I don't have a choice.

They have a huge curtain made out of sheets separating the urinals and the showers. Although there are around twenty shower heads, the rule is 'one at a time.' Good to know. I shower and put my uniform back on really quickly.

There are two phones, but it's probably two in the morning, so I'll have to wait.

I'm kind of sitting with the skin heads, and they are watching TV. It's all court shows. People's Court, Judge Mathis and a couple of others. That is all they ever watch.

One of the skin heads asks if I'm gay. I answer, "No." and try to change the subject quickly. "So, what is the routine around here?"

"It's different for everybody. You kinda just do your own thing.

We get up at eight and do two hundred push-ups and then..."

I start laughing. I can't do twenty push-ups. Two hundred has to be a joke, but he's not joking.

You could stay up all night if you wanted to and some do, but when I see everyone else going to bed, I go to my bunk and lift myself up there. There are no sheets, covers, or pillow and the mattress is crazy itchy.

I am kind of glad there are no covers. I've seen movies where they grab the covers, pull on both sides, and sort of strap you down. Then they beat the shit out of you. It's cold, but I'll survive.

I still don't get any sleep.

At around eight, they call out, "On that chow."

It is breakfast time.

We line up and are led to the kitchen to pick up our trays and then back to our individual dorm type place.

The tables fill up quickly, and I find a place by some black guys. The Nazis grab me and move me to their table.

The whole place is just yelling and screaming while we try to eat. Everyone is trading and selling their food. You couldn't smoke in jail anymore, so they give you these candies that are supposed to help with the cravings. These are valuable items.

After we empty our trays, we clean up and then everyone is free to do whatever. Some read books, others watch TV and some play cards. I get into a Spades game with a few black guys. This time, the skin heads let me play the game.

Then, I have to take a shit. When I think about it, it's probably been two days.

I go in the bathroom, but don't see a toilet, just urinals. I push the curtain aside and the toilet is in there by the showers. There is somebody showering, but I have to go really badly.

Before I can even get to the toilet, I'm being pulled from behind. It seems like twenty guys are dragging me out of the bathroom. The 'one person at a time' rule means one person past the curtain at a time. Showering or shitting... 'One at a time.'

The skin heads pull me aside.

I've been saved.

I get to the phones, and it's all collect calls from here. You just dial the number, and the system does the rest. There are only a few numbers that I know by heart. Once they are all in your phone, you forget them.

I call my dad first. The answering machine picks up, and I hear the system saying, "This is a collect call from Cook County Jail. If you accept the charges press one."

Well, I don't have to worry about saying where I am.

I don't leave a message.

I call my sister... no answer. I call another sister... no answer.

Of all my friends, Ken's number is the only one that I know by heart. It's a pretty easy one to remember. Almost like five-eight-eight-two-three-hundred.

He answers.

The system has already told him where I am, and he doesn't ask any questions.

"Look, I tried everyone in my family first, no one was home. I was supposed to bond out, but they wouldn't let me."

"How much is bail?"

"Fifteen hundred."

"I'll get there as soon as I can."

A few more hours go by, and it's, "On that chow," again.

Lunch.

A few more hours go by, and I hear my name called. I go to the door.

"Let's go."

I'm led down another set of hallways, then to a room where they have my clothes, then to another room where I'm asked to wait.

It takes six hours to get out.

Ken doesn't wait around. I'm glad; I wouldn't have wanted him to have waited that long. I remember when I was trying to bail out Billy, they treated everyone like a criminal, whether you were coming from the outside or the inside. I hate that Ken had to go through that.

Before I leave, I ask, "Where am I and how do I get back downtown?"

"Twenty-sixty, and California. The Blue Line is right up the street."

I go to the train, but I don't have any money. I tell the attendant, and he lets me through a side door. This probably happens all the time.

I'm heading home. Every time I'm away, I hope all my stuff is still there when I get back. I'm also hoping that the mail has come. I'm waiting for some birthday cards in September.

When I get home, there is no mail. All my stuff is still there, and I drop into the bed and pass out. It's been at least six days since I've slept.

When I get the mail the next day, I realize that I must have spent more than I thought on my trip. There is only about two thousand left. What did I do with it all?

I was gone a total of three days with the whole trip. The bus tickets weren't expensive, and I didn't spend that much at the strip club. Maybe the hooker took some, but that couldn't have happened; it was safely strapped to my ankles. Maybe some got lost in the mail.

Chicago mail sucks. I don't know what I did with all that money. I'm trying to retrace my steps, but a lot of the trip is just a blur.

I pay a little rent, but I'm four months behind, and I only pay two. I have to make this last. I'm not going to go without food again. I don't know when I'll find work again, and with a record now, it'll just be harder. Who knows when I'll see any more money?

All of this scares me a lot, and I have to get some help.

I've been on medication, and I've been in therapy for depression on and off since I was fifteen, but it's been a while and this all feels like something more.

I remember going to some clinic not far from here when I first moved to the city and got on some medication and did some therapy. I'll try them again.

The medication usually just makes me more nuts, but I gotta do something. My life is way out of control.

I have to wait two weeks before I can get in to see someone at the clinic.

They work on a sliding scale and go by your income. I shouldn't have to pay too much for this, but it doesn't matter. I have to do something. I'm scared for my life.

If I could go that far and do what I've done, what wouldn't I do?

During the first meeting with the doctor, she asks a lot of questions, and I answer honestly. I tell her as much as I can in an hour. Evidently, my recent actions are pretty much text book mania. She comes to the quick conclusion that I'm bi-polar and puts me on medications right away. After explaining a little about what bi-polar is, it all makes sense. The sleeplessness, the racing thoughts, the spending sprees, the promiscuity, the just plain dangerous behavior, the deep depressions... everything. It all makes perfect sense. I've probably had this my whole life.

I'll see her once a month and also see a therapist once a week. Since I'm not working, I don't have to pay anything for this.

I feel like I'm finally doing the right thing.

The first court date has me going out to Skokie. It takes me three hours to get to the court house, and I make sure that I'm at least a half an hour early. After I go in, it's two more hours before they call my case.

At this point, I'm looking to get a court appointed lawyer. I see most of the people ahead of me getting assigned to one, but when I get up there, he tells me I have to find a lawyer.

"I don't have any money for a lawyer. I'm not working."

"You got fifteen hundred for bail; you can get a lawyer."

"That's not my money. I have to pay that back."

"Take the fifteen hundred and find a lawyer."

He sends me on my way and gives me another court date.

I go to a phone book and call around to a few places, but everyone wants at least three thousand.

The next court date comes, and I go back to court and tell him that I can't afford a lawyer and that I looked and tried. He insists that I find one. He says that there are like hundreds of lawyers right here in this building and that I should be able to find one. He gives me two weeks.

I don't know where to begin, and I'm not going to start asking random people in the building if they'll represent me.

Two weeks go by, and I tell him again I can't find one. He gives me a name and tells me to call this guy. So, I do. The guy wants three thousand, but knows this judge and understands that the judge is insisting, and he'll have to do it for the fifteen hundred.

Ken is not going to get his money back.

The lawyer talks to the DA, and they decide that if I make full restitution that I will only get probation and community service. No jail time.

No jail is the best news, but where am I going to get four thousand dollars? My money is gone, and I can't ask for that much from anyone.

I have no choice. I call my dad. Again.

"Dad, I'm in trouble."

"What is it this time?"

I'm not going to waste any time, so I tell him straight out, "I robbed the place that I used to work at after they refused to pay me, and if I don't give the money back, I'm going to jail."

He's not prepared for it to be this serious and goes off: "What the hell is the matter with you? Have you lost your God damn mind? Maybe you should go into the military. Maybe they can straighten you out."

"I tried to get into the military years ago. I have asthma."

"I forgot about the asthma." His tone is way calmer and understanding now. "I don't know if I can help you here."

"Dad, I'm begging you. I can't go to jail."

"I'm not really flush right now, and I don't know where I can get the money, but... I'll get it."

"Thank you, dad." I start to cry uncontrollably, and I know he can hear me.

He just hangs up.

I'm steadily going to therapy and staying on top of my medication, but I'm still in outer space as far as my thoughts are concerned. I can't sleep unless it's been a couple of days, and I end up crashing. I can't shut off my brain.

I find a job at a bar in the Loop. It's right up the street from the stock exchange and just around the corner from the theater district. The place is busy all the time and needed a fast bartender. I'm their man.

I can really make good money here, and I need it. Mine is fast running out. I don't know why it's running out so quickly. It's not like I'm living like a king or doing anything crazy. It's just going. I don't really know where I'm spending it.

My first day on the job is on a Tuesday. I figured that a Tuesday afternoon would be kind of slow, but they are packed. Traders and anyone that works at the exchange are notorious for drinking a lot and doing a ton of cocaine. The cocaine makes it possible to drink more. Looking at half these guys, you know they are lit.

I guess I did well enough.

They call me to work the next day. A day shift shouldn't be too bad.

It's busy as hell. I'm kicking ass and making drinks nonstop. There's no end in sight. I love the rush, but this is out of control. The servers are impressed with my speed.

I barely have time to look up till around seven, and the night bartender isn't showing up. They ask me to stay. It's by far the busiest place I've ever worked, but I'm hanging in there.

At the end of the night, the owner comes in and can tell I'm exhausted. He tells me to go home, and he'll do all the cleanup. I shove my tips in my backpack and head home.

When I get home, I count a little more than four hundred dollars.

I'm gonna like this job, and I just might get caught up.

I pay another month's rent, but it's October now, and I'm still two months behind. I really don't know where my money is going.

I'm due at court again, and this time my dad has to come out to make the payment. It's a three-hour ride for me on the trains and buses, but a four-hour drive for him.

I get there early and wait for my dad. When he gets here, it's still unclear when everything is supposed to start.

We actually have a really nice talk while we are waiting. I figured he would be pissed and not really want to talk, but we talk about all kinds of stuff.

A few years ago, we had gone to a Cubs game. Back when I was dating Cindy. I had asked someone before the game how long baseball games were. I really didn't know. They told me around three to four hours. I wondered what my dad and I would talk about for four hours, but that day, there was really no break in the conversation. That Cubs game was the best day I'd ever had with my dad.

Today reminds me of that a lot. It's great to spend time with my dad, regardless of the circumstance.

The lawyer comes out to where we are waiting in the hall and tells us we are just waiting for Michael to show up and accept the money in open court.

Dad wants to get going. It's been hours already, so he gives me the money and takes off. He hands me the four thousand, and then gave me two hundred so I could get by. He knows I'm struggling through all this and genuinely wants to help.

I almost cry again, but I hold it together.

Michael never shows up.

His partner comes in after another two hours of waiting.

We make the payment in open court, and the DA explains everything. The charges will be reduced to a misdemeanor. I'll be put on a one-year probation and meet with a probation officer once a month. I'll be drug tested once a month, and I'll have to do ten days of community service. If, for any reason, I don't comply, I could do six months in jail.

I'm NOT going back to jail. The three and a half days that I was there was plenty for me. I'm NOT going back for anything.

After everything is said and done, my lawyer finally tells me that there is no tape. I had confessed, and I couldn't change that. I just don't care.

They lied. They flat out lied to my face just to get me to talk, and I fell for it. I knew there was no tape. I knew they had nothing on me.

If there is anything to be learned, it is that, any time a cop asks you if you want to talk to a lawyer... say 'YES'. Regardless of how innocent or guilty you may be. The innocent need it even more.

I was totally guilty, but they had nothing. Always get a lawyer before saying one fucking word.

I could have completely gotten away with it. I wouldn't have had to have borrowed from Ken, and I wouldn't have had to have gone to my dad. I could have gotten caught up on rent and would have been completely fine. I could have gotten away with it.

I could have... I guess I 'could have' a lot of things.

When I get home, the reality of it all hits me, and I completely break down. Bawling my eyes out and collapsing onto the bed, I'm overwhelmed by guilt and shame, and the fact that I had to get my dad involved is the worst.

My dad kind of only knows one way to say 'I love you' and that is with money. He couldn't say the words, but he would help out when he was called. He has never said the words to me, and he has never even hugged me. A handshake was as much as I'd ever gotten. Despite never showing it, I knew it, and it made me feel good to know that he'd always be there. But could I really ever ask him for anything ever again? Twice in one year. This has to be the last time. I don't want to be that kind of son.

At this point, my emotions are just going nuts.

They call me into work again the next day. It's gonna be another double shift, but this time, I know going in. I'm expecting another big day.

This day is just as busy, and I'm cranking out drinks nonstop all day long, but my head is spinning. Too much on my mind.

At around one in the morning, only an hour left, my heart starts pounding, and I start feeling like I'm going to lose it.

I tell one of the waitresses that I have to go, and she calls the owner. She was the one that had trained me behind the bar. Tonight, she's gonna have to take over because I'm about to pop.

I make it to last call, but I gotta leave. The waitress will have to close out all the tabs and do all the cleanup and breakdown. There are still around thirty tabs open. Any tips from the open tabs she can have. I'm out of here.

I start walking around downtown. I'm wandering around at two in the morning with a bag of money on my back. Just wandering.

Frantic and on the verge of complete implosion, I call Nate.

"Dude, I'm flippin' the fuck out. I just walked out of another job. I can't hold on to anything. Bartending is all I've ever known how to do, and I can't do it anymore. Maybe Dan was right, and I should get out of the business. I'm really losing it. I just want to die. I can't take it anymore." I'm crying and yelling into the phone and rambling on and on. "I just can't stop fuckin' up. I'm a God damn loser, and I always will be. Julie's gone, and I'll never see her again. Everything is gone. Everything is over."

"Dude, try to take it easy. You'll get through this."

"You know, I've been through a lot and I always say that I've been through worse and I'll get through this too, but not this time. I can't say that anymore. I haven't been through worse. This is the worst it's ever been, and I don't think I'm gonna make it. I've tried. All year, I've tried. After she left, I didn't stop. I kept trying, but what good has trying done? I'm completely fucked here. I'm done. It's over."

He really couldn't say anything to calm me down, so I tell him that I have to go, and I hang up. I try to figure out where I am. I'm lost downtown with a bag of money on my back.

I look up to see where the Sears Tower is. I can figure my way home from there. The tower is to my right, so I must be headed south. I have to turn around and find the Red Line. I have to get home.

When I get home, I actually get some sleep. I sleep for seventeen hours. It's now eight o'clock at night, and I don't know what to do. My mind is racing again, and I'm going over and over everything again.

I take a few sleeping pills and go back to bed. I've been popping sleeping pills for months now. It's really the only way I can get any sleep.

The next morning at around 10AM, I count my tips. It's enough for another month's rent, so I go to the office.

I hand her the money, and she tells me to wait. She's been looking over the books, and I've been late every month this year and even after all my little payments, I'm still four months behind.

She gives me another thirty-day notice.

Throughout my wreckage of a life right now, I continue to look for work, but my mind is completely fucked up, and I'm still freaking out.

I've pretty much given up on ever working in the business again, but what else can I do? I don't know how to do anything else. I don't know how to live any other way.

I get a part time job at Marshall Field's as a gift wrapper. I'm willing to do anything, but this is not going to last.

I go across the street from my place to the grocery store, and I get hired as a bagger.

There are three days of training, and then I'm on my own. The first day on my own is the day before Thanksgiving. You can imagine how busy a grocery store is on the day before Thanksgiving.

It's busy, and I'm just not in it. I'm not even in my own head. I can't handle it. I can't handle anything right now.

I make it to my ten-minute break, and instead of just stepping outside for a smoke, I grab my coat and walk back across the street to my place. I'm done.

I sleep for three days straight. It has finally caught up to me, and I don't have any reason to wake up anyway. There is just no reason for anything.

This is it. I've had it. I'm done.

I'm going to be evicted. I haven't eaten in three days and other than a few good meals on my trip, I haven't had a decent meal all year. I've lost Julie. I've lost six different jobs in one year. I'm completely broke. I still might wind up in jail, and I'm definitely going to wind up homeless. I'm going to be the one crying at the bus stop. This pain is just unbearable, and it all has to end.

I put on some warm clothes and leave everything behind.

I'm walking the streets. I'm not looking where I'm going, and I don't think I stopped for traffic once. Who cares if I get hit? I'm going to die anyway. I'm heading for the lake.

It's the end of November, and it's exceptionally cold this year. The lakefront is frozen over. I'll just walk out onto the ice, and it will eventually break underneath me. I can't swim and probably wouldn't survive even if I could. My body might not be found until spring (if it's found at all.)

It'll be easy.

It'll all be over fast.

I'm done.

I'm almost to Lake Shore Drive. All I have to do is go under the street, and I'll be there. It'll all be over.

I look up for a second, and I realize that I'm right by my therapist's office. I haven't gone to see him in something like a month.

Something stops me from continuing on to the lake.

I go up to his office instead.

Chapter Thirteen: Life Support

I go to the desk and check in. It's Wednesday afternoon, and it's my regular day to see my therapist. It has been at least a month since I've seen him, but I check in as if I haven't missed a day.

The look of pain and hopelessness must be showing on my face. Everyone I see looks at me with pity and concern. I'm walking dead.

I sit in the waiting room for a while, staring at the walls, and my therapist and my psychiatrist come in to get me. I've never seen them at the same time before. It's going to take a team to get me to come around. I don't care anymore.

They sit me down in one of the offices. With my therapist in the chair across from me and my psychiatrist at the desk, they start asking me questions, but I can't hear them. My mind is gone.

The next thing I know, a security guard is in the room with us. Two security guards. The four of them walk me out of the building to a car that looks like a squad car, complete with the bulletproof glass between the front and the back.

My therapist says something, and he and my psychiatrist stay on the sidewalk while the security guards close the door and drive away.

We arrive at the emergency room, and they lead me inside. I sit down at a desk and someone starts asking me questions. I'm still virtually catatonic, and I don't respond at all.

Then, I'm led to an exam room and told to wait. Wait for what, I have no idea.

A doctor comes in, gives me a once over, and then leaves. There is nothing physically wrong with me.

I'm moved into the same padded room I had been in a few years ago. I sit on the edge of the bed and stare at the wall.

A few hours go by, and someone comes to get me. Just someone in a suit and a name tag. He puts me in a wheelchair and pushes me through a bunch of hallways and two different elevators.

I'm thankful for the wheelchair. I don't have the strength to walk anywhere.

We get to a door, and he pushes a button. After a few minutes, the door opens, and he rolls me inside. It seems a little familiar, but I'm sure that I've never been here before.

I'm put into a smaller room, and they take all the things out of my pockets and set them aside. They have me strip and thoroughly search my clothes, then they give them back to me. They keep all the stuff from my pockets. I hadn't planned to hold on to anything when I'd left the apartment. I only have my cell phone which has probably been shut off by now and my wallet. I don't even have my keys with me. I knew I would never need them again.

I'm walked to a room that looks a little like a typical hospital room, but still different. They are saying something, but I still can't hear them. I think I might have heard them, but I just don't care what they're saying.

I lie down on the bed and fall asleep almost instantly. I don't really know what is going on, but I feel weirdly comfortable for some reason.

A few hours go by, and someone comes to the room and knocks.

"Dinner is here if you want to eat."

I haven't really eaten anything in about three days, so I get up and follow her through a few rooms that look like someone's family room. Then we get to another room with a bunch of tables, and there are close to twenty other people here.

I'm still just walking dead.

I find a spot and sit down and eat. I don't even know what it is or if it tastes good.

Right after, I go back to what I guess is my room and fall back to sleep.

This goes on for a few days. Sleep, eat something, then sleep some more. Occasionally, someone will come around and take me to an office and talk to me. I'm not paying any attention, and I don't think I've said a word. I just don't care.

Every day, sleep... eat... talk to someone... sleep some more.

A few more days go by, and I start to feel a little better. Physically... that is. Mentally... I'm sort of coming around, but still, nothing matters.

I start to talk back to people when they speak to me, and I catch on that when I'm led to an office that I'm supposed to talk about what's going on. I start to explain everything that has happened this year and what I was planning to do about it, but I have no emotion or expression of any kind. Just walking dead. The only difference now is that I'm at least talking.

This goes on for a while. Then, one of the people that talks to me a lot asks a question that hits me.

"What do you think happens when you die?"

I have no answer.

I don't really know if I believe in heaven or hell, but if they exist, I'm going to hell. That is clear. I start to think about what hell might be like. Then, I start to hope that nothing happens after you die. It would just be over. Everything would just be over. That's what I hope would happen, but I don't really believe it. My Catholic upbringing has had its effect. Hell is my future.

I start to think that life might suck, but death just might suck more, and death is, regardless of what I believe, forever. All eternity in hell. Burning, suffering, constant pain and agony. Right now that isn't much different than life, but maybe this is just temporary.

Maybe it is temporary, but it is bound to repeat itself, and I can't take going through this again. I've prayed that it would all be over. I've prayed to God to end it all. But, if I believe in God, then I will have to accept heaven and hell. So, I'm back to going to hell.

Maybe I'm already in hell, and sometime during all those years of trying to die, I was successful at one point, and this is it, this is hell. Pain and suffering, over and over forever. But... I'm not really suffering that much right now.

The meds are helping.

They made some medication changes as soon as I got there, and I've actually had three square meals a day. I'm sleeping every night with the help of more medication. Medication time is a big part of the routine here. Sleep, eat, meds, talk to someone, sleep some more. Every day.

Now the question: 'What happens after you die?' is circling in my head.

After maybe three weeks, I start to feel like I might want to live, but how?

No money, no ability to hold a job, no ability to maintain any relationships, and jail is still hanging over my head. All my personal belongings are gone, and there doesn't seem to be much to live for. The only difference now is that I believe that death would be worse. I don't want to die, but I don't want to live either.

I need help, and I understand that that is what all these people are trying to do, but they can try all they want; they are not going to change anything.

I meet with a social worker and a psychiatrist. I go to a variety of group therapy sessions... eat, meds, and sleep. I'm doing what I'm asked to do and following the program, but I still can't imagine a normal life ever again.

Working steadily, a wife, kids, a family, a home, a car and a life... all seems like a pipe dream, and it will never happen. A normal life will never exist for me. The life I've led up to now, I just managed to survive it all, but why, and for how long, can I go on like this? I still want it to end.

The social worker is working hard to put together some answers and solutions. She contacts my landlord and my probation officer.

She makes arrangements to have my stuff held for me in the basement of my old building, but eviction is something no one can stop.

She talks to my probation officer and explains why I haven't reported yet and gets all the details about what I'm supposed to do to get through the process.

She makes arrangements for me to live in a temporary housing program for the homeless with mental illnesses.

There have been so many times in my life that I was sure, absolutely positive, that I wasn't making any footprints in the sand.

This is definitely one of those times.

She takes the things that I'm most concerned about and provides quick, but temporary, solutions. I won't be on the street, my things won't get thrown out, and I won't have to go back to jail.

Just by turning to walk into this hospital, so much has changed, improved even, but I'm still not all there yet. I still feel pretty hopeless.

The psychiatrist that I speak to in the hospital talks to me about my future.

I don't see a future for myself. I never have.

I'd lived my whole life day to day. I'd had no hopes for the future. My only hope was to die someday, and the sooner that came, the better.

I never dreamed of what I would do when I grew up when I was a kid. There were no fantasy jobs. Some kids dreamed of being a cop or firefighter or a cowboy. There were no future dreams... never in my life.

All my life, people would ask, "Where do you see yourself in ten years?" I would laugh because I didn't know where I would be in the next ten minutes, and I never really cared.

The psychiatrist suggests that I go back to school. I've actually thought about it in the past, but I could never afford it, and now there is no way.

She explains that, given my situation, I'd be eligible for grants and would be able to go back to school for free. It would cost me nothing but time, and I have plenty of that... I guess.

The idea of going to school, and the idea of starting my life completely over seems possible for the first time. There just might be hope.

The hospital wants me to move on and get out.

There is only so much hospital time that they'll pay for.

The psychiatrist waves her fees, and that allows me to stay one more week.

I need every second of that time.

While I've been here, I've missed Thanksgiving with my family, and I'll still be here through Christmas.

My social worker had contacted my family when I got to the hospital so they wouldn't worry and so they would know what was going on. She could explain it better than I could.

I contact Nate on my own. He is the only friend that I have that would care what was going on. He tells me to get well and take care of myself. He's always been understanding, but will I ever really get well?

My sisters Shannon and Annie come for visits.

Shannon brings me some flannel pants for warmth and a travel bag to put my things in. I don't have anything, but I guess she didn't know that. I might need it later. The pants will come in handy so that I have something to change into when I do laundry instead of having to wear a hospital gown anytime I want to wash my clothes. I've been wearing the same clothes for weeks, and the first three weeks I didn't shower, so I'm getting kind of funky.

During Annie's visit, one of the other patients kind of loses it and throws something across the dining room that almost hits my brother-in-law. They take it in stride and don't really react.

The staff gathers around the patient, and one of them hits her with the harpoon. A quick shot of Haldol. Then, they take her to her room.

The level of crazy that all the other patients are in varies a lot.

The look on my sister's face is priceless. They are both shocked, but trying hard not to show it. Everything is normal. Nothing strange going on here.

My family cares, and that means a lot to me.

On Christmas day, the whole family calls me, and I do mean the 'whole' family. Shannon is on the line when I pick up the phone, then she hands the phone off to another sister. They pass the phone around to everyone at the party. About thirty people. My nieces and nephews, all my sisters and my brother, my sister-in-law and all my brothers-in-law. Everyone says, 'Merry Christmas,' and wishes me well. It's all I can do to keep from bawling.

Only a few minutes after I hang up, one of the staff brings me an envelope. It's a Christmas card addressed to the hospital. It's from my dad, and he actually signed it himself. If I ever got a card from him in the past, it was his wife that put it all together, and she would just sign for the both of them. I doubt if my dad even knew they were sent.

The card has a hundred-dollar bill in it. My dad's way of saying, 'I love you.'

I just go to my room and cry for like an hour.

My family may never really understand what I've gone through or even what I'm going through now or may continue to go through, but they love me regardless. However, they show it, it's there. It means a lot, but I feel so unworthy.

I've done nothing for them, and I've taken advantage of them at every turn. I've lived with most of them and screwed them over. I've borrowed money from several and screwed them over. I can't ask them for anything anymore. They wouldn't help if I did. I have destroyed that part of our relationships, but they still want me around at family get-togethers and always wish the best for me.

I'm alone in so many ways, but Nate and my family will always be there for, at the very least, emotional support. Emotional support is all I can ask for now.

This huge expression of unconditional love is overwhelming. I feel horrible and guilty and ashamed. I can't face them as I am. I can't face them at all any more.

I vow to stay away until I can be someone to be proud of. They all mean the world to me, but I just can't face them knowing what I've done and how I've acted and who I am. I need to be a better person. I need to be worthy of their love and support. I have to stand on my own and be my own man before I can comfortably see them again.

The holidays will be lonely, but this is time for me to rebuild, and if I get to that point where I can stand myself and the guilt has at least lessened... then maybe I can face them again. As long as I'm holding this shame and guilt, seeing them or being around them is too painful. Maybe this is selfish thinking, but I need to be selfish right now if I'm going to rebuild myself into a person that matters.

The day has come for me to leave the hospital. The housing program that I'm supposed to go to isn't ready for me yet. They make arrangements for me to stay in a shelter until a spot opens up in a few weeks.

I'm going to live in a homeless shelter for two weeks. This is what my life has come to.

I'm still a little shaky and not all there yet, but it is time to move on.

At least I'm not completely broke. I have my dad's money and that should get me through the next two weeks easily.

I follow the directions on the paperwork they give me and find the shelter. It's just a few blocks from Wrigley Field.

I have to be there by nine at night, or they won't let me in. It's only eight.

When I get there, I see all these desperate faces and around thirty men that all look very homeless. This is it. This is what's next for me.

I hadn't smoked for the five weeks I was in the hospital, so I had considered staying smoke free, but after seeing how I will have to live for the next two weeks, I have to get a pack.

I go to the nearest gas station and pick up a pack of smokes, then get in line to go into the shelter. It all seems unreal.

I recognize one of the guys. David Gleiss. He was in the hospital with me. He left a few days before I did and was only up there for a few days. He was pretty much just detoxing and didn't really have a mental illness, so he wasn't there long.

It's nice to see a familiar face, and we start talking. He's been in a few different shelters and knows the deal. I'll have a kind of guide for being homeless.

I check in at a little before nine, and they are going to serve dinner soon, so we just sit at the tables and wait. Most of the guys are pretty friendly and upbeat. This is going to be weird.

Dinner is served, and it is almost better than the hospital food.

As soon as everyone is finished eating, we all clear the tables and clean up the room. The tables need to be folded up and pushed to the side. Then, we all get our mats. They are these three-inch-thick rubber mats. These are our beds.

It's eleven o'clock when everyone finally goes to sleep.

I take my nighttime medicine and fall asleep within an hour.

At 6AM, they wake us all up. We put away our mats and set up the tables for breakfast. Ham, eggs, and grits. It's not a bad meal at all.

By 7:30, we're all kicked out and have to find something to do until nine at night when they'll let us back in again.

Some guys just ride the train all day. It's a way to keep warm and stay reasonably safe, but if you fall asleep, you are bound to get robbed. Even the homeless that have nothing weren't safe.

Some of the bolder ones would find a busy spot in the city and shake a cup. I could never do this. It wasn't that I had too much pride. I just couldn't beg... it isn't in me. Asking people close to me for help is hard enough, but complete strangers... it just isn't going to happen. I can't do it.

I think sometimes when people beg for change, the word 'change' has two meanings. They aren't always talking about money. Sometimes they want circumstances or really anything to change and for there to be some kind of hope.

Some go to the library and hang out there for a while. Another way to stay warm, but if you look homeless and smell homeless, you'll get kicked out pretty easily.

Others spend all day in coffee shops, but it's the same situation as the library.

Still, others would just find a spot and rest. They didn't care about the cold or anything else for that matter.

Since I have a little money, David and I go to McDonald's and get coffee. We stay for about three hours. Then ride the trains for a while. Then to the library to kill some more time.

The library has some public computers, so I check my email. There's still nothing from Julie. I send her one, another one, but don't expect a response. I try to explain everything that I've been through, but don't want to sound too desperate. I want there to still be hope for us to reconnect.

David and I manage to kill the day and go back to the shelter at nine.

The next day, we do our usual coffee run, then we decide to go to an AA meeting. It's part of my probation and a great way to kill time. We go to three different meetings throughout the day.

At the meetings, I meet a lot of people and talk about what I've been through. These meeting usually have a few people that can relate, at least a little. Plus, the free coffee is always a good thing.

Breakfast, breakdown, street, meetings, coffee, library, street, nine o'clock check in, dinner, then six hours of sleep... repeat.

After about ten days of this, it starts to catch up to me. My back is killing me from sleeping on the floor, and there just isn't enough to do during the day to keep busy.

On Sunday, I go to Nate's church to see him.

Before I go in, there are these two guys at the door who tell me I have to take off my hat. I have been wearing this hat every day for over a month. I've actually been wearing the same Blackhawks hat nearly every day for close to twelve years.

I go to the bathroom to try to fix myself up. When I look in the mirror... I see a homeless man.

I look and smell like a homeless man.

I can't face Nate. I'm not going to take off my hat, so I can't even go into the church if I wanted to.

It feels like I just got turned away from church.

This is a new low.

A long time ago, I said that if I ever ended up homeless that I would break the law every day. At least in jail, you get three hots and a cot.

Now that I've been in jail and homeless, homeless isn't that bad. I'll never go back to jail. The beds were a little better in jail, but I would never go back.

Not long ago, I spent a big part of my days when I worked at the bar chasing homeless away. They would beg from the customers and hassle people on the way in. They would beg everyone that walked by. It was just bad for business.

I spoke to a lot of them, and most of the time I was civil, but other times I would have to physically move them down the street. I was at constant odds with the homeless.

Maybe all this is karma.

I have four more days to get through.

The day after getting turned away from church, I wake up and can't move. My back is just one big monkey fist, and it is so tight that I can't move at all.

They are always in a pretty big rush to get people up so they can clear the floor for breakfast, but I'm not moving.

It takes David and one other guy to get me on my feet. Just moving is pure agony. They prop me up against a wall outside, and I'm in such excruciating pain, so they call an ambulance.

It's pouring rain out, and the paramedics put me on the gurney, but take a long time getting me into the ambulance. The rain beats on my face.

When we get to the hospital, they take me to a curtained off area, and I lie there for hours, and no one comes to see me. No one.

After at least three hours, I struggle my way to my feet and walk out. No one makes any effort to stop me. They don't care. I guess this is how they treat the homeless.

Walking is pure agony, but I have to get some help. I walk all the way from the North Side to the same hospital where I had stayed for the last five weeks in River North.

As soon as I get there, they can see my pain. They put me in a wheelchair and take me back to a room. They help me into the bed, and I wait thirty minutes until someone comes in and gives me a shot. I start to feel better pretty quickly.

They take me for x-rays and an MRI, but can't find anything really wrong.

It's just a massive muscle spasm.

I've thrown my back out a few times in the past. Once, I was moving a keg and twisted it. Another time, I was lifting a huge garbage can by myself. It was filled with water and food and was probably two hundred pounds.

It was always bad, but never this bad.

They let me rest for a little while, then they gave me a bottle of pain pills and sent me on my way. I feel better, but I'm still moving pretty slowly.

I get back to the shelter just before nine, and the attendant guy lets me use two mats for the night. It doesn't make much of a difference, but the pain pills allow me to sleep.

It's Friday now, and I'm done with my time in the shelter.

I follow the directions to the temporary housing program that is run by the hospital. It's in the same high rise downtown where I lived when I first moved to the city. I meet with a social worker there, and she shows me around.

I'll be in a double room with another guy, and there are about twenty-five rooms all together. They are small rooms, but it's private. There were thirty guys in the shelter, and it was just one big room.

Everyone up here is homeless and has some sort of mental illness. You don't know the extent of anyone's illness, and no one really asks. It's like in jail where no one asks why you're there, and you don't talk about it.

Everyone is pretty docile and probably heavily medicated. It has a calmer feel to it than the shelter.

The rooms have a vanity with a sink and a mirror, but the bathroom is down the hall. There is a small TV room and a dining room where some of the people play cards.

It's kind of like a weird combination of the hospital and the shelter, but it's comfortable enough. Plus, here they don't kick you out in the morning. You can stay all day, or you could come and go as you pleased, but you have to be in by ten o'clock. At ten, you take your meds, and then go to bed. Generally, after I take my meds, it doesn't take long before I have to be in bed, or I'd probably pass out on the floor.

They offer cereal and fruit in the morning, cold sandwiches in the afternoon and a hot meal for dinner. The hospital supplies the food.

The food at the shelter was actually better. Most nights in the shelter, generous people would come and make a real home cooked meal for everyone. It was the best part and maybe the only good part about the shelter.

Here, I'm really glad to have a real bed, but both places I was grateful to have a warm place to sleep. It's January in Chicago.

I make arrangements with Ken to help me get my stuff from my old place.

One of the things that I have is a mini fridge that belongs to him. So, if he wants it back, he would kind of have to help me.

Reluctantly, he helps.

Two trips in his small car and I have everything. I don't own much. I never did.

This would be the last favor I would ever ask of Ken.

I pick up the routine pretty quickly. I'm sleeping regular hours: from eleven at night till eight in the morning when they wake us up for meds. Here you can go back to sleep if you want to, but I'm gonna try to keep busy.

They set me up with a bunch of groups that I attend throughout the week. As a bit of a reward for attending the groups, we get a voucher for a free lunch at the hospital cafeteria. It's still hospital food, but it's free and better than just cold sandwiches.

I meet with my therapist once a week and my psychiatrist once a month. I meet with my probation officer once a month and start my community service a couple of times a week. The weeks stay busy.

All along, I have a social worker helping with all the red tape of getting on disability. I don't really think I'm that crazy or that I can't work ever again, but I know I can't work right now.

A letter from my psychiatrist and a breakdown of my work history is a part of the application. The breakdown of my work history includes every job I've ever had since I started with a paper route at the age of ten.

It's a list of more than a hundred jobs. No lie.

Since most of the jobs were in the restaurant business and I hadn't always claimed all of my tips, to the government, it didn't look like I'd ever made much money. So, if I'm approved, I'm told not to expect much. Anything is better than nothing, but I don't think I'll get approved at all.

I had applied for assistance years ago on my own and was denied. The social worker at that time actually told me that if I were a minority or had a drug problem, I would probably get the help, but since I was a reasonably healthy white guy, there was no way.

The social workers who are helping me now have pretty high hopes. The severity of my illness is clearer to people who do this kind of work.

Bipolar is more than just mood swings. It's crippling lows, frightening highs, numb lows, numb highs; everything is inconsistent and difficult to control. Thoughts are everywhere, and concentration and focus seem impossible. It varies in severity for everyone, but I've seen the extremes, and for me... Yes, it is a disability.

I go on with the day to day and go through the motions. Hoping for change, but not really counting on it.

Time goes by pretty quickly.

Although I hadn't really worked that much the year before, I still file taxes. I'll probably get back around thirty dollars, but anything will help. My dad's money is gone.

I found the engagement ring that Evan had given me. I decide to go ahead and pawn it. They give me about a hundred dollars. I have finally accepted that I will never see Julie again.

I have my meals taken care of, and I can walk just about anywhere I have to go. If I have to take the bus or train somewhere, they provide me with a transfer card. I don't really need much of my own money to get by. The only real expense are smokes.

I had learned to roll my own in the shelter. Rolling your own is a whole lot cheaper. You can get a bag for around two bucks, and it'll make the equivalent of about two packs. Your fingers get all yellow and you're always spitting tobacco, but they smoke like a smoke, and I still need it to get through the days.

You see a lot of homeless smoking. It makes things easier to take. It's very necessary.

I get my tax return in the mail, and it's the thirty bucks that I thought it would be. Then only about a week later, I get another tax return. It's like two thousand.

I go to the social workers to ask them if they thought it was a mistake. They tell me that my social security has come through. The checks look exactly the same.

I get a letter the next day saying that I should expect a check for two thousand, then expect six hundred dollars a month every month after that. I don't really know how anyone is supposed to live on six hundred a month, but at this point its way better than nothing.

It's only been five months since we processed the application. They had told me it could take around a year, and for some, even longer. I got lucky.

A month later, I'm accepted into a more permanent housing program. This program only has ten people in it, and I can stay here just about as long as I want. There are two people here that have lived here for around five years.

I'm still seeing my therapist and psychiatrist and continuing with my probation. I go to my groups and maintain a fairly comfortable life.

It's amazing what I now consider 'comfortable.'

Nate and I are hanging out a lot again, but I'm the one paying for dinner and the movies. Just like before, he kind of expects me to pick up the check. This has been going on for years. I thought that now that I'm basically homeless, he'd pay his way, but I don't see the point in saying anything about it... yet.

My money is really tight. Now that I'm drawing disability, I'm required to start paying rent. They set it up like a subsidy, so it's only thirty percent of my check, but it doesn't leave me with much.

Things have to change.

It's uncomfortable, but I have a long talk with Nate about money and tell him I can't hang out because I can't afford it.

He calls me a week later and asks if I want to see a movie.

"I don't have any money."

"Did I ask you if you had any money, bitch?"

He starts picking up the tab all the time, and we hang out every weekend. I feel bad not being able to pay my share, but he insists that it's no big deal. He's making good money now.

He's actually supporting his mom and his cousin and covering all the bills with no problem. He and I both have had our struggles with money, but he's really on top of it these days.

I don't know what I would have done if he hadn't been around. He's been my best friend now for close to thirteen years. I've never had any friends that long.

One night, Nate and I are hanging out and meet up at a restaurant before the movies. I get there first and put our name on the list.

When Nate arrives, I tell him, "It will be about ten to fifteen minutes."

"They put Nathaniel Williams II on a wait? That's just not acceptable. Nathaniel Williams II doesn't wait to be seated anywhere." He's just joking around but might have been half serious.

"Sorry, they don't know that you're famous. But then again... no one does."

Part of living in the program is I have to take random drug tests. It's also a part of my probation. So, they share results. It just so happens that every time they would ask me to drop, I had just gone to the bathroom and didn't have to go. I would go get them the next time I had to go, but sometimes it would be a while in between. Or, I would forget and have to do it the next day.

They tell me that if it's more than twenty-four hours between the time they ask me to drop and the time I actually do it, then it's considered dirty. I could get kicked out, and it will affect my probation, too. I didn't even think about what would happen if I were kicked out, but how would it look to my probation officer?

I stay on top of it after that. Nothing is going to take me back to jail.

Time goes by and things are fine. Two years have passed, and I have completed my probation and all the requirements. Now, I have to go all the way back to Skokie to appear in court again.

My mind starts going over everything.

If I had had a better lawyer, they would have made an issue about the fact that the cops didn't read me my rights until after the confession. I should have asked for a lawyer at the very beginning anyway. There was no tape, and there was no evidence against me. None of this had to happen.

I go over and over it in my head all the time, and I never once think about not stealing the money, just how I could have gotten away with it.

When I get to the courthouse, I wait two hours for my name to be called. The whole time they are talking amongst themselves and don't say anything to me. Then finally, the judge looks up and tells me, "That's it. You're done."

I don't wait around for any paperwork, and no one makes any attempt to have me stay for anything else, so I head home.

That's it. It's over now.

While on probation, I had walked a thin line and put up with a lot without doing or saying anything about it, but... The whole time I've lived in this program, the security staff has been up my ass. Power play. They just want to flex their so-called authority. You put people in a uniform, and they think they're big shots.

Wherever I stand outside to smoke, they are always telling me to move. "You can't stand here." Anywhere I go: "You can't stand here."

It gets really annoying.

The state passed a law that made the city smoke free. You can't smoke in public buildings anymore, and you have to be more than fifteen feet away from any entrance. That is the law, but the security wants to say that I can't smoke anywhere near the building. That is bullshit.

Throughout the rest of the building, you can smoke in your room, but since where I live is technically a hospital facility we can't smoke in our rooms. It's no big deal. I don't mind smoking outside in any weather.

When I would see the security staff light up right in front of the building, even within the fifteen feet mark, it was not acceptable. I'm far too old for 'do as I say, not as I do.'

Anyway... it was a constant fight.

I also have to go to the security desk to pick up packages.

I've been ordering a lot of CDs and get a lot of packages. My music collection has always been very important to me. As a DJ, I had a little of everything and a huge collection, but anytime I would get financially strapped, I would have to sell them. It always hurt to have to get rid of them, but the money was more important at the time.

Now, I'm covering my bills, and I'm able to get a disc or two every month to rebuild the collection. It makes me feel better.

Since I fight with the security so much over where I can stand in front of the building, they will often hold my packages or even send them back. They are screwing with me, and it's pissing me off.

They also know that the seventh floor is the 'mental floor.' They figure they can fuck with us, and no one will say anything.

One day I'm standing in my usual spot along the side of the building, significantly more that fifteen feet from any entrance. The security guard comes by, smoking a cigarette himself, and tells me that I have to move. I tell him, "No." and stand my ground.

He walks away.

Later that week, I get a thirty-day notice. The security guard had me written up, and the building management was going to override the program and have me kicked out.

It's all so stupid.

I speak to the social worker in charge of the program, and she isn't interested in backing me up on this one. I'm pissed. I'm going to be homeless again because the security staff are assholes.

Despite all my fighting, it isn't worth it, and I end up backing down. I hate backing down when I know I'm right.

As fellow Chicagoan Billy Corgan would say, "Despite all my rage, I'm still just a rat in a cage."

So... I start smoking off the property, and I'm left alone. Meanwhile, the security staff continues to smoke right in front of the building.

Bullshit, but not worth it.

Time continues to roll by.

I start thinking about what my psychiatrist in the hospital said about going back to school and decide to refocus on making things better.

My social worker gets me into this college prep course that will be free. It's run by another program that helps the homeless. It'll be great.

They cover writing essays, English, basic math, and basic computer skills. They ask us to read a classic novel and do a report on it. I'm not much of a reader, but this is going to be a big part of going back to school.

I've probably only read six books from cover to cover in my whole life.

I pick, 'To Kill a Mockingbird'. It's a great book, and my report gets an A. I actually get straight A's throughout all the courses.

After a few weeks of this, the guy running it gets a different job, and the whole program shuts down. This sucks. I was learning a lot, and I was finally feeling like I just might be able to go back to school.

You have to either be going to school, working, or doing some sort of volunteer work to stay in the housing program. This was my school. Now I have to find something else, and I'm not ready to go back to work.

I try a few different places to volunteer, but never really stick with it.

Another part of living in the program is chores. Something else I don't really stick to.

Not doing my chores, not volunteering and not going to school... I'm on the verge of getting kicked out again.

My social worker tries to get me a subsidized room in the building, but my application is turned down. My criminal record still shows up with a felony on it. It is supposed to be a misdemeanor.

I go back to my probation officer and ask about it. She has me go to the clerk's office, and they say it is on there as a misdemeanor.

Apparently, it shows up as a felony reduced to a misdemeanor, but the word 'felony' still shows up and that isn't going to change.

So, I'm turned down from living in the building, and there are really no other options for me.

I get a little better about doing my chores and continue to attempt to do volunteer work, but nothing sticks.

By this time, I've been here almost three years.

I'm going through the motions and following the program the best I can, and they lighten up a little since they see I'm trying.

Life is flying by, but I never really feel stabilized. The ups and downs of life go along with regular changes to my medications. This makes things harder. As soon as one set of medications are adjusted, they'd only work for a few months, then we'd have to start over with something else. It's been three years now, and I don't think I've ever been properly medicated. How long is this going to last?

After I started getting disability, I got sick of the roll-your-own smokes and start to make monthly trips to Indiana for real smokes, just cheaper ones.

Every time I go out there, I try to visit with Crystal or Ashley, or both, if their schedules sync up.

Crystal Davis and Ashley Dale are both part of 'The Club Deluxe', this group that I had hung out with around the time my mom died.

There were six of us. We had worked together and hung out all the time way back then: Nate, Crystal, Ashley, Jessica, Matthew, and myself. I've known them for like seventeen years now, but it has been around seven years since I've seen anyone other than Nate.

Jessica and Matthew have moved away, and I don't see or hear from them at all, but Crystal and Ashley live in Indiana, and we see each other every now and then. Any time I'm in Indiana, we try to meet up.

I see Crystal a lot more than Ashley and occasionally spend the weekend at her house. Since we spend so much time together, a few people have asked why we aren't a couple. We are just too close of friends to go down that road.

On this month's smoke run, Crystal is having a party, and I get to see Ashley, too.

It's great that after all these years we still stay in touch. Even after going years without really hanging out, we pick up right where we left off.

I don't really have that many these days, but my friends have always been very important to me.

Nate goes to Indiana to hang out with us every now and then, but he is generally really busy.

When he does come out, we all sit around and tell old stories. Having worked together and hung out so much for so long makes for a lot of stories.

One of Nate's favorites happened before we were actually friends.

I was waiting tables, and he was the host. He was seating me pretty steadily, and it was a really comfortable night.

Then, he sat me this party of nine black folks, and they were just staring daggers at me the whole time. Every time I went to the table, they would look at me like they wanted to kill me.

I treat everyone the same no matter what color they are, and I treated these guys very well, but they seemed to hate me.

It was a full year after this happened when I overheard Nate telling the story at a party: "I sat him with nothing but white folks all night long and left his party table open, waiting for the perfect group to set him up." He was telling the story and not mentioning any names. "Then the perfect group came in, and I told them that the only table available was in this guy's station, and he's probably the biggest racist that I've ever known. I warned them, but explained to them that I had no choice but to put them in his section. I promised that I would help out and make sure they were treated right.

The whole time, they just stared at this guy with this look of death and..."

"Hey, that was me. You set me up."

We all laughed about it. It had been a year, and he had kept it a secret the whole time. I had almost forgotten about it, and I wasn't even a part of the conversation. I just overheard it. He held on to it for a year. It was hilarious.

To us, it's hilarious, and even after seventeen years, he still tells it all the time. It was one of those events that made us friends in the first place.

Reconnecting with old friends and building new friendships with my nine roommates keeps me in pretty good spirits these days.

All the things I hear in AA meetings or with all my friends or in therapy or in groups... it's a lot to process. There are judges, probation officers, social workers, therapists, and doctors telling me new stuff. Most of it is good information and helpful in a lot of ways, but some reminds me of tougher times. Everything I hear is either a life lesson or complete bullshit.

My mind is like a coin separator. It takes in ideas and opinions and sorts them out according to value. However, like a coin separator, every once in a while, you'd get a button mixed in, or something that had no value. That's just life.

I used to worry all the time about how people saw me, what they thought of me and what kind of impression I was making. I was generally a loser and did a lot of wrong, and I never thought anyone had much respect for me. They had every right to take what I did and said and brush it away.

Before, other people's opinions used to shape my actions.

Now, I hope that my actions shape their opinions.

Probation is over, and I've been living in the same place for over three years. I'm getting more comfortable in my own skin, and things are going pretty well.

When I first moved into the program, I got on a few lists for permanent subsidized housing. The waiting lists for places like this are usually several years long. One of the applications finally finds its way onto someone's desk, and I get a call.

The felony still shows up on my record, and my credit is pure shit, but this place doesn't seem to mind. No other place would look away from all of that. Even if I'm not totally ready to move out, I have to jump on this deal. I would have sworn that I'd never have been able to live anywhere outside the program. This place is willing to give me a chance.

It's a small studio apartment, but I will have my own bathroom, I can smoke freely, and live without any restrictions at all. I won't have to worry about chores or any other requirements of the program, and I can stop worrying about getting kicked out.

I will finally be completely on my own again.

I'll continue to take medication and see my therapist and doctor on a regular basis, but I'm free to do whatever I want.

The problem is... what do I want to do?

Chapter Fourteen: Corporate Takeover

While living in the housing program, my social workers set me up with the disability I'm receiving and got me into subsidized housing. Just before moving out, they also set me up with food stamps to help pay for groceries. In the program, the hospital supplied food, but now I'm on my own. They also set me up with a program that gets me an unlimited free bus card.

I thank God for all the help I've received. I wouldn't have survived without it all. The social workers, therapists, doctors... everybody. They saved my life. I don't fear living on the street. I don't fear going to jail. I don't fear going hungry. I don't fear dying. I don't fear living.

My basic needs are taken care of.

But what do I do with my time?

I still go to see my therapist and doctors, but no more groups and no more meetings. I don't belong in AA.

Since I've been properly medicated, I haven't even thought about drinking or any drugs. I'm scared of how they might mix with my medication, and I'm not messing with my meds. I'm not going back to the person I used to be. I'm not, not drinking because my probation and the program dictate it; I just don't want to anymore. Or more appropriately, I don't need it anymore.

I have spent 10 years in and out of AA and studied the disease, but now that I've had time to think about it... I'm not an alcoholic. I don't have that disease. I love the meetings, but I feel like an outsider now. I don't belong there. I feel like an impostor, and it's an insult to the people who really need it for me to be there.

The groups were part of the program, but I can still go if I want. I don't want to anymore. I'm independent now, and I have learned what I needed to learn from the groups.

I have to find something to fill my time, though. Once a week with my therapist and once a month with my doctor doesn't fill my schedule enough.

Even though it's no longer a requirement, I still want to go back to school. So, I look into it, and it isn't going to be that hard-to-get in. The grants should cover one hundred percent of the cost, and that had always been my biggest concern. Without the debilitating thought of how much it would cost and never being able to afford it, it is finally possible. Changing my life is finally possible.

Now, I have to attend classes and try for decent grades. This shouldn't be too hard... right?

I haven't been in school for almost twenty years, and to say I'm out of practice is a serious understatement. I never got good grades before and probably shouldn't have graduated high school, but here I am.

Most of the other students are right out of high school, but there are still plenty who are my age or even older.

I'm ready for this step in my life, and I want it badly.

Nate hits me with some bad news. Good news for him, but bad news for me. His company was bought out, and his job is moving him to Seattle. You can't get much farther away and still be in the United States. He'll be getting a significant raise, and he is excited about the move.

I'm happy for him, but selfishly want him to still be around.

I don't get out much, but when I do, it's almost always with him. I don't know what I'll do without him around.

Any time I would move or I would be someplace else, Texas or North Carolina or anywhere, we'd always stay in touch, and this time would be no different. Seventeen years as friends isn't going to end. It was just going to be hard.

I go on with my day to day and am doing really good in school. I haven't gotten too many papers back so far, but the ones I have gotten have been all A's. Not bad for someone who has been out of it for twenty years. True enough I'm taking all remedial classes, and it shouldn't be that hard, but I'm still proud of myself.

Before starting, I had to take a placement test, and I didn't do that great. I'll have to take about three courses that aren't college level just to get caught up. I'm ready to do whatever it takes, though.

I do, however, make the mistake of taking too many classes. I remembered in high school and grade school we had like six or seven classes a day, so I thought I could handle the same now. I can't.

It starts to catch up to me quickly, and I start missing classes left and right. I'm over sleeping and not able to get all the work done. I'm getting really behind.

I eventually have to drop out.

It crushes me, and I go into a pretty deep depression.

I start missing doctor and therapy appointments and start to think that I might lose my spot in the clinic.

I go down for about three weeks.

For three weeks, I don't leave the house. I do nothing. I shut down.

When I start to come around, I go back to therapy, and everything gets back to normal in a week or two. Sometimes, I just have to ride it out. The meds don't work, and I have no control over how I feel or what I can do about it, but I remember that it's temporary, and I ride it out.

But now the dream of school is out the door.

My schedule goes from being way too busy back to just two things a week. I see my therapist on Wednesdays, and I occasionally go back to my old housing program on Fridays to watch a movie. Even though I don't live there anymore and I'm not part of their services, they let me join them for movie night.

It becomes an alumni type night where people who used to live there come back and hang out with old friends and get to know the new people. It's nice to stay in touch with these people. These nine people were a huge part of my life for three and a half years. I'm not really ready to leave them all behind. It's also nice to have something to do on the weekends. Nate and I used to go out every Friday night, but now that he's gone... well, it's nice to have something to do. And it helps remind me of where I came from and what I had to go through and what I'm still going through. It's never about the movie. It's about getting out of the house and being social.

The other five days of the week I try to keep busy: I do jigsaw puzzles, grocery shopping, laundry, keep the place clean and spend a lot of time on the computer. I'm addicted to Facebook.

Through Facebook, I'm able to get back in touch with a lot of old friends. Some are old friends whom I've wronged, and I'm able to apologize and make amends. I even get a hold of Jeri Proesel (the angriest of my ex's), and we talk a lot about everything that's happened between us. Just by sending messages back and forth and being sincere and telling the truth we get passed it all... whoever it is and however bad it may have been, I'm able to make amends through Facebook and feel a little better about myself.

There is one girl I haven't seen since I was twelve, but I hurt her badly. I don't know if it stuck with her, but it stuck with me.

She was not very popular, and kids would tease her a lot. Some of the guys thought it would be funny if I acted like I was going to take her to a dance. So, like an idiot, I played it out. I asked her to the dance, she accepted, and when she showed up, I snuck out before she even saw me. I blew her off and really never talked to her again. She bought a nice dress and showed up to the dance, and I bolted like an asshole.

Like I say, I don't know if it stuck with her, but I never forgot, so I mentioned it in a message to her on Facebook. She remembered.

We talk about it, and then I actually get on a train and go out to Indiana to apologize in person... face to face and for real.

It's a cleansing feeling I don't think I've experienced before. Hopefully the start of a new trend of being a better person.

The computer keeps me entertained, but mostly I sleep a lot.

Sleeping too much is probably the worst thing you can do if you suffer from depression. Keeping a regular schedule and staying active is really important. It's just as important as the medication and in some ways more important.

Life right now is kinda boring, but I have to wonder what's worse... sporadic success mixed with chaotic disaster... or... boring?

Boring is fine for now.

My medical doctor notices a high cholesterol count and has to put me on medication to bring it down. He tells me I'm forty pounds overweight. I need to start eating better and exercising.

I'd always been skinny. I was a senior in high school before I broke a hundred pounds. I could eat whatever I wanted and never gain a pound.

I did gain some weight when I lived with Jerry, but that just brought me up to normal. I never struggled with weight.

Now, I can tell that I'm bigger. I can see it in my face, my gut and my boobs. Yep, I got boobs now.

I once heard someone say, "I don't think of myself as getting fatter. I think of it as my bellybutton getting deeper. I keep change in there now."

Psych meds make everyone gain weight. It seems nuts that to help you not be depressed, it gives you something to be depressed about. I've put on like eighty pounds since I've been medicated. Everyone I know now is in the same boat, so I take it in stride. It is one of those things, but I do have to start taking better care of myself.

I haven't exercised since I played hockey in high school, but I have to do something. My health is at serious risk according to my doctor.

As a New Year's resolution, I start going to the exercise room in my building and using the treadmill for a half an hour every day.

It's hard for me to stick to something for even three days in a row, but I do this for over three weeks straight, and I do feel a lot better. Mentally and physically. It's also a great way to kill time.

Since I'm feeling better all-around, I decide to give school another shot.

This time, I only take three classes and take it easy. I can handle three classes.

It starts out fine, and I'm getting good grades, but after only two months into it, my back goes out.

I have to go to the emergency room again, and they put me on pain pills.

I'm laid up for three weeks and miss too many classes.

I have to drop out. Again.

That's it. I have given up on school and don't have enough to fill my week without it. I have to do something.

Every step forward takes me a few steps back. I get a little better, then I hit a wall. The doc changes the meds, and it take like six weeks to see it take effect and decide if it's working. Then even if it does work, it usually stops working after a few months.

I don't have to worry about going hungry or having a roof over my head, but I'm still not stable. I can't maintain my moods to take on anything significant. School proved that. I have to do something.

I decide to leave the hospital and clinic that saved my life and got me all the help and support I have now. They've done all they can, and I have to move on and try something new - a new perspective on my situation and maybe better luck finding the right meds and more consistency with a good therapist.

I get into a clinic that isn't far from my place and get started right away. A few minor med changes and a fresh start with a new doc and a new therapist.

I feel good about this.

Break the patterns. Break the routines. Break the habits and everything that has been keeping me stagnant and complacent.

I feel good about this.

Another Christmas has passed, and I realize it's been years since I've seen or talked to my family. I may not be the perfect man yet, but I'm better. I don't know if I'm proud of who I am or what I'm doing, but if I wait till, I'm great... I'll never see them again.

I send out friend requests to all my family members who are on Facebook.

They all accept.

It's a start.

In the beginning of March, it hits me that my dad is turning eighty at the end of the month. Through Facebook, I contact my family to see if we can put something together for him. I have no car, no place and no money really, so there isn't much I can do about it, but if I get my sisters on board, we can make something happen.

Since that day in the courthouse, I promised to never ask him for anything anymore, but I've also been trying to make a point of calling him for reasons other than: 'hey, dad I'm in trouble' kinda calls. I've been calling him on his birthday, Father's Day, and Christmas for the last couple years. For his eightieth, I figure he deserves something more than a call.

My sister, Annie, gets it all together, but half the family either can't make it or doesn't want to go. Not everyone wants to see him.

I get on a train out of the city and meet up with my sister in Indiana. We drive another hour to where my dad lives and have a nice little get together. A few of my sisters and I show up, and we have cupcakes and sing Happy Birthday. It's nice. Nothing special, but I don't remember celebrating my dad's birthday at all before now. Once in eighty years doesn't seem like enough.

Oh well. It's about trying to do better Now.

Meanwhile, Nate has been doing great in Seattle. His job is rolling along just fine and he starts to go around to churches all over the country to preach. On top of that, he is going to small business conferences and giving talks.

I can't believe it. In all these years, I've rarely seen this seriously ambitious side of him. I kinda have to see it to believe it. He's having an event here in Chicago, so I go to see him.

Seeing him in action… well, I'm thoroughly impressed.

He's succinct and direct. His points are strong, and he has a way of hammering them home that rocks. People watch and listen in awe. He is great.

After the event, we go out to dinner, and he tells me about everything that has been going on. He is on fire, and nothing is going to stop him from probably becoming famous. He is selling himself and his ideas, and he is one of the best salesmen I've ever seen.

I tell him something I heard on 'ER': "Your talent is God's gift to you. What you do with it is your gift back to God."

It always floors him when I hit him with God stuff. He's the preacher. I'm the heathen… not really anymore.

He inspires me. I'm going to try and go back to work.

I don't really know how it works, but I think I can make, maybe, up to nine hundred a month and not lose my disability. That's my biggest fear about going back to work. I might be working just long enough to lose my disability, then lose the job and wind up homeless again. I don't want to take that risk.

Now, I'm set up pretty well, and although life isn't exactly exciting, I'm doing pretty good.

Nine hundred total per month means a part time job. The question of what to do is back, and now it seems worse.

All I know is the restaurant business. As much as the business was killing me... what else can I do? I don't know how to do anything else, and the job market is ridiculously fucked up right now. People with multiple degrees and tons of training can't find work. How am I supposed to?

My resume is really out of date, and how am I going to explain the last five years of being unemployed?

I decide that I'll tell people that I won the lottery, and I took a brief retirement, but the money is running out, so that's why I'm looking for work now.

I put The Cork and Tap on the resume and describe seven years on and off working with them. I write down all the positions I've held, which is every position there is, and all the locations where I'd worked. Despite how I left Gurnee, it is the most impressive part of my resume.

I also list the six years with The House, but I hope that they won't call for a reference. 'I employed him because I felt sorry for him,' isn't going to help me.

Then, I list nine years of construction work with my dad to show some diversity in my work history. I type a short paragraph outlining fifteen years' experience in the business and the fact that I've held every position possible. My training in this field is pretty impressive.

I can't count on any references. They'll be really out of date or kind of negative. And the five years unemployed will be a difficult sell, but what do I have to lose? If I don't find work, I can pretty much live out my life on disability, but I'm too young to think about that.

I put out around fifty resumes and applications. It's the end of April, and business is starting to pick up, and most places are fully staffed, but I'm hoping for the best.

I've been at my new place for a year and a half at this point, and I'm getting really comfortable here. I know the neighborhood. The buses and trains are convenient, and there are lots of places to eat. I like it here, and things are basically good.

I did, however, just get a notice slid under my door saying that the real estate company that owns the building is being bought out.

How will this affect my subsidy? Will I still be able to afford to live here? If not, is it possible to reenter the program? What am I going to do?

Before I get too worked up about it, I go to the office to ask them about it. They tell me that the new management will be here on Monday, and I should talk to them.

Monday comes and goes, and I forget about it. Then, I get another notice under my door.

The subsidy is going to change, but when they revamp everything, my rent will actually go down by about forty bucks a month.

Forty bucks is a lot of money when you're living on the shoestring budget that I live on. I might be able to start saving and start paying back everyone I owe.

It will probably take years to save enough to pay back Ken, but whatever it takes and no matter how long it takes, I will pay him back. It will never save our relationship, but I'll sleep a little better.

It's now May, and I get a letter in the mail that looks like a typical bump-letter that will tell me why I didn't get some job. I've gotten about twenty of them so far, but this one is different. This one is actually setting up an interview. I never get letters for this. It's usually a phone call.

The letter gives me a time, a name, and an address. I'm supposed to meet with James Adalbert, Tuesday, the twelfth at 9AM, at an address I recognize.

It's The House.

When I was in the housing program downtown, I was only a few blocks away from The House, but I never even walked by it. I went out of my way to put that place out of my life.

Now, I have to go back.

Who is James Adalbert?

It turns out that he owns fifteen Cork and Taps in the Chicagoland area and has always wanted a place in the city. He bought The House.

The Cork and Tap is a neighborhood place and doesn't really fit in a major city. There are no locations in any other big city. It just doesn't work like that.

This will be an interesting interview.

When I get there, the place is under construction, and there's scaffolding all over the front of the building, but it doesn't look like anyone is working.

I walk in the door, and there is one guy here. It must be James.

"Jeff? Come on in and take a seat."

"Thank you."

He sets me up with a glass of water, and we start talking.

"So, you've worked for The Cork and Tap for a long time. How did you like it?"

"It was great. It was comfortable, because it was always run well, and they had a habit of hiring a great staff."

"You were a manager with them?"

"I held every position there was. I managed for a little while, but to be honest, it wasn't for that long. I did run the training team and trained people in the front of the house and the back of the house."

"Good. You have kitchen experience. How long did you work here at The House?"

"On and off for six years."

"Did you manage here?"

"Not really. There weren't really any mangers. There were two owners: one that was here all the time, and the other guy was kind of hands off. Then, whoever was bartending played the part of manager. I did do a lot of the inventory and ordering."

"You bartended here, too?"

"Yea."

"So, you were a manager... technically."

"I guess so."

"I don't see anything on here about work for the last five years. What have you been doing?"

"It's kinda embarrassing, but I won the lottery and was living off of that, but it's fast running out."

"That's amazing. How much did you win?"

I hadn't planned for that question, "After taxes, it was around a hundred and fifty thousand."

"I guess you can live for five years pretty easily on a that."

Little did he know I have been living on around nine thousand a year for the last five years.

"You think you're ready to go back to work?"

The truth is I don't think so. It has been a long time, and it was really rough before.

I have to say something and make it sound good.

"Absolutely. I miss it. I've always loved this business. There's just this rush, and it drives me."

"How do you think a Cork and Tap will do in this neighborhood?"

"If you can redevelop the same regulars that held The House together, you'll do really, really well."

"You think that's possible?"

"If there is any chance of hiring the same crew so there will be familiar faces, I think it will work out fine."

"The place has been closed for six months. I'd like to think that all the old employees have found other jobs by now, but if they apply, we'll jump all over it. Are you in touch with any of them?"

"No. Unfortunately, we fell out of touch years ago."

"What changes should we make here?"

"You have to put in a kitchen to maintain the license, and I see you're in the middle of that, but I really wouldn't change much. The regulars have always felt at home here, and if it changes too much, they might not come back. You offer the perfect menu for this place, and the way you run your stores will work out well here. That would probably be the biggest change. Being more organized and having a solid and established system in place."

"Well, I wanted to hire you as soon as I read your resume. You have exactly the work history that we are looking for. Both front of the house and back of the house experience, and you already know this place. We want to offer you forty to start, and you would be the general manager. I think for the rest of the management staff, we are going to use the chef and some of the bartenders. I talked to Steven about how he did things and that seemed to work out really well.

We are looking to open around the Fourth of July, but we want you to start right away. We need you to start hiring right away and to put together a training system. We'd also like for you to kind of oversee the construction. With your background, you might have a better idea of what they are doing around here, but mostly, we just need someone to show their face so the guys don't slack off. The hiring and getting to know the vendors are the most important part. The ads are already in the papers and some applications have already come in. It will be your job to go through them. You seem to know what a good staff is supposed to look like, and you might know a lot of the applicants after working and living in the city for twelve years. So, what do you think?"

"I think that would be great. I can't wait to get moving on all of it."

I'm actually really concerned about whether or not I can handle all of this, but it is really exactly what I was looking for.

"Do you have any questions?"

"Really just one: Why did Steven sell?"

"We made him an offer he couldn't refuse."

"What?"

"We offered him probably double what the place is actually worth. I've wanted a place in the city for a long time, and this location is perfect. There is no other place like us anywhere in the area, and I think we'll do really well here."

"Were you able to hold on to the four o'clock license?"

"We worked hard on that one, but we just couldn't make it happen."

"Good, those hours are rough."

"Speaking of hours... we don't want you working every day. Hire people you trust, and we'll develop a few that can close and open once in a while. Why don't you come in tomorrow, and I'll introduce you to Aaron, the chef and my partner."

"What time?"

"How about noon? We'll have lunch somewhere, but we'll meet here."

"Sounds good." I shake his hand, and I can't tell whose smile is bigger: his or mine.

I can't believe it. I'm going back to work. I'll lose my disability for sure, and I'll lose all of my benefits, but I feel like I can keep this together. My rent will go up, too. Market rate is six hundred, but I should be able to cover that. As long as I stay on my medications and keep all of my appointments with my therapist and doctors, I really think I can make this all work.

I'm ready, and it's certainly time.

A new life and a new start are what it really is, and I'm ready.

It won't be the same old place. They are going to make plenty of changes, and it will have a completely different staff and a completely different way of doing things. A solid training program, set and organized inventory systems, and an established order... it will work.

I go in the next day and James introduces me to Aaron Lockerbie. He moved here to make this all happen, but James lives in the suburbs and will come and go. Aaron as a partner will have more authority than I will, but that actually takes a lot of pressure off me.

He'll hire the kitchen staff and run me through the back of the house training, so I will be able to fill in or help out when needed. He already has about seven guys in mind.

We have lunch, and they talk and talk about the place. They are crazy excited about everything that is happening and seem just as excited to have me on board. I share their excitement, but there is still a big part of me that wonders if I can really do it.

I pop my head in Monday through Friday and look over applications while the construction is getting done. It's a pretty big job. They are digging up the back patio and adding on to the basement to make room for the walk-in freezer and a small prep area. They are also adding on to the back of the building to make the kitchen. They're making the bathrooms bigger, and the kitchen will fill the rest of the space. The kitchen is kind of small, but it is set up really well. Built for speed.

Per my suggestion, they don't change the front of the house at all. The bar looks exactly the same.

After a few weeks, the scaffolding in front of the building comes down, and they hang the new Cork and Tap sign.

We are ready to start hiring.

It's early June.

I've looked at about two hundred applications, but we only need about nineteen front of the house employees. Six bartenders, seven servers, two door men, and four bussers who will double as bar-backs.

I start interviewing and tell everyone that we'll be starting in a few weeks.

I set up meetings with all the vendors, and I recognize some of them, although none of them remember me. We don't really have any idea what kind of volume we will do in the beginning, so I order kind of light. We will still stock twenty-five drafts and around eighty different beers. Micro-brews and hard to find stuff... popular stuff.

The front of the house is clean, and we conduct all the interviews in the bar so they can see what kind of place it will be. The menu is set with mostly the same items that all the suburban locations carry. Simple stuff that tastes great and can be prepared quickly. Also, we can sell them for cheap. It's better than your typical bar food, but we still want it to be inexpensive.

We are able to hire a great group of people. I can't wait to get them all together and see how they will work as a team. They are all very experienced and know the city well. They are friendly and have upbeat personalities. They will be just the right group to start building a set of strong regulars, and we have high hopes of drawing back most of The House's old regulars from the neighborhood.

I can't get a hold of any of the old staff, but I don't really try that hard. I send a few messages via Facebook. As far as a familiar face, I will have to try and fill that part.

On Father's Day, I call my dad to wish him a happy Father's Day, and to see how things are with him and yea, to tell him about the job. I'm fishing for a little 'proud of you, son,' but not counting on it.

Since it's been a while since I've called him for money or some kind of desperate situation, he's happy to hear from me, and we talk for a while.

Then, he kinda lightheartedly and casually mentions that he has prostate cancer and has been getting treatment for it for the last six months. That means he had it when we had the birthday party for him, but he didn't say anything.

He tells me the treatment has been tolerable, and he hasn't had any of the typical side effects. He tells me he's fine and figures it'll be a few more months of treatment, then everything will be back to normal.

He had skin cancer a while back, and after a little treatment, he was fine so this time should be OK... I guess.

He doesn't seem impressed by my going back to work, but that's OK.

The construction at the bar finishes two days before training is supposed to start. We do two weeks of training and get everyone very familiar with the menu and the computer system. This is what I'm good at: training and developing a new staff. I'm right in my element, and I'm right back in it as if I hadn't missed a day. I'm in it, and I feel better than ever.

All along, we have our eye out for standouts that we can count on to open and close every once in a while. Otherwise, Aaron will open and I will close five days a week, and James will cover two days a week for a little while.

The bar is stocked, the staff is ready, and the place looks great.

We're ready to open Monday, right on the Fourth of July.

Chapter Fifteen: Gray Hair or No Hair

I get Steven's number from James and decide to call him.

"Hey, Steven. How have you been?"

"Not bad. Sailing all the time and loving life. How about you? How's the bar?"

"I'm doing OK. The bar has been great. Almost two years now, and it's still going strong. We were even able to get back some of your regulars. They miss you."

"Well, tell them I said 'hey'. Why are you calling?" We haven't talked in years.

"Two things: I'm still getting a lot of your mail, and there are two that look like wedding invitations. Also, I was wondering if you're still in touch with Ken."

"I'll update the post office tomorrow, and I'll pick up the invitations Friday. I've been expecting them. You know one of them is Alex. Sorry about not changing my address. I just never got around to it because I didn't really care anymore. It's usually just magazines or stuff for the bar, so I don't really miss it. Why do you want to get a hold of Ken? You know he's not your biggest fan."

"I owe him a ton of money, but I've finally been able to save, and I want to pay him back. It's been so long that maybe he's forgotten or just given up on me, but I never forgot, and I need to get this check to him."

"I can give you his address, but I don't think I should give you, his number. He really doesn't want to hear from you. He remembers and will never forget. You screwed him pretty good. What do you owe him, like seven grand?"

"Yea, give or take. I got a check for eight, and I really want him to have it. I don't expect it to fix our friendship; I just need him to have it."

"That's good that you don't expect to fix your friendship because you won't. He pretty much hates you."

"I don't blame him."

He gives me Ken's address, but stresses that I shouldn't try to visit, just send the check. We have a little small talk, and I tell him how the bar is running. He had built a great business, and we are just trying to keep it going. I thought I'd pay him a compliment, but after he had said, 'he felt sorry for me'... well, that still stings after all these years.

He's the only one I could go to for info on Ken. I'd lost touch with everyone else over the years. While on disability, I had learned how to live cheaply, and I haven't changed much. So, saving the money has taken two years, but I got it. Finally.

"Do you have any info on Jason? I'm getting mail for him too."

"Yea, I can give you, his number. You know he got married a year ago now. Hey, it was cool talking to ya, but I gotta run. I'll see ya Friday."

That's it.

I think he still feels sorry for me. He didn't seem proud or happy that the bar was running great or that I was doing a lot of what he used to do to keep it going. He had taught me a lot, and I wanted him to know that, but he didn't care.

He came by Friday morning, but I work Friday nights.

Aaron gave him his mail.

At Thanksgiving, the phone rings in the middle of dinner. My whole family is here, so who could it be? Annie takes the call and within seconds she's crying.

Dad had a heart attack.

After Annie calms down, we find out that he's more or less OK, but still in the hospital. We go along with the party like normal, but I was thinking about my dad the whole time. The party wraps up, and Annie lets me stay over so I don't have to go back to the city tonight.

We are going to the hospital tomorrow.

It's another hour drive to see my dad, and when we get there, he's alone and sleeping. He kinda looks like hell, but who doesn't when they're in the hospital?

"Oh, ya gotta be kiddin' me." He's really surprised and maybe not so happy to see us.

We make calm and basic small talk while Annie tries to find out exactly what's happening.

It turns out the prostate cancer is back, and this time, has metastasized to his back and lungs. The current treatment has made him weak and that's what caused the heart attack. The heart attack was a mild one, but they've got him here just to be careful, and he'll probably be released tomorrow.

He asks where his wife is and says kinda halfheartedly that she should be here for suicide watch. He's fed up with all the doctors and treatments and just wants it to end, but the fact that he used the word 'suicide' bothers me a lot.

My sister's trying to get me to leave it alone, but I ask anyway. "Dad, why would you be thinking that?"

"What's the point? I'm gonna die anyway, and the treatments, and the doctors, and the hospitals and life in general are all pointless."

"Well, you gotta just do what you can with whatever time you've got." I want to say more, but who am I to be the one to tell anyone that life is always worth living? I've been suicidal, but I've never been terminal, and I've never been in my eighties.

He doesn't have any more to say anyway.

A nurse comes in to do some test, and I take her aside and tell her he used the word suicide. I know they have to take it seriously.

She asks him, and he admits to it, but nothing more is said. The nurse's tests are done and she leaves, but I follow her out into the hall to the desk where all the other nurses are. In front of everyone at the desk, I ask, "Are you going to put him on a hold?"

"It's not our call."

"At least get a psych consult and do something."

"We will."

They don't.

We get ready to leave, and my sister gives our dad a big hug and says, "I love you," and he says it back. My nephew gives him a hug, and so does my nephew's fiancée.

I'm next, so I go in for the hug, and my dad puts out his hand. I shake his hand and tell him to take care of himself, and then we all leave.

He is discharged the next day.

Two weeks after leaving the hospital and stopping all treatment and medications, my dad dies, just like he wanted to. At home, alone with his wife, clearheaded, with no medication or suffering. He died on his terms.

But I still hate him for not fighting.

I never got the chance to really know my dad, and he never really knew me. I made good on my promise to never ask him for anything again and to call without being desperate or needing something. I guess the last few years of his life, I did my best, but I'll never get over the handshake.

I've forgiven him for not giving it more of a fight, but it's the handshake that I'm still hung up on.

My sister, whom he was closest to, gets a hug and an 'I love you.' My nephew gets a hug. Even my nephew's fiancée, whom he barely knew, got a hug. I got a handshake. The last time I would see him alive, and I get a handshake like a stranger. And that's how I've always felt to him. Like a stranger.

Time passes, and I kinda float through the days. I'm turning forty in two weeks, and I'm feeling pretty old.

Jason is married, and Alex is getting married this summer. Dell and Amanda have been married this whole time, and the last time I saw Dell, he told me that Amanda was pregnant. Crystal has gotten married again and has four kids. Ashley has been married for years now, and her daughter is getting ready to graduate high school.

Everyone is getting married and having kids. I feel like I'm really falling behind.

I check my bank account online, and the day after his birthday, Ken processes the check I mailed to him.

I'm in kind of a funk right now, but I'm not letting work suffer. It's the one constant and I've been working the same job for over two years now. That's a new record. I've also lived in the same place for almost four years. That is definitely a record. I'm doing pretty well these days, and I can't afford to let myself go down.

My doctor has tweaked my medication again, and Nate is coming to town for my birthday.

Things should be looking up.

I have to get myself to come around.

As soon as Nate hits O'Hare, he calls me.

"Hey, I got big news. I'll see you in about an hour."

I think I know what the news is.

He comes into the bar with a giant grin on his face and gives me this huge hug.

"Man, it's great to see you. The place looks great. So, guess what?

I'm getting married."

"Of course, you are."

"Huh?"

"I mean, congratulations. That's fantastic."

I give him a big hug and take him to the bar to get a drink.

"I want you to be the best man. We're going to have it next summer here in Chicago. I'm moving back here. My company is growing, and I need to be more centrally located. I'm doing another conference next weekend, so I'm gonna be in town for two weeks this time."

"That's awesome. By the way, what's her name? Where did you meet? What's she like? Is she here with you?"

"She's perfect. We met in church. She's actually from around here. Grew up in the suburbs. Her family is still out here. She showed up to one of my talks at a Bible study. She's actually checking into the hotel right now. She'll be here in about thirty."

"Great. I'll treat you guys to lunch, and we can get caught up."

When his fiancée arrives, we talk for hours. She is perfect. She is a female version of Nate. I always used to joke that if Nate were a girl, I'd marry him. This is the female Nate. They are so alike that it blows my mind. Their love is radiating from them, and I can't believe it. I couldn't be happier for them. This is fantastic.

Right after we finish lunch, Dedra, his fiancée, says that she is tired and goes back to the hotel to get some rest. It has been a long day.

Nate and I continue talking just like old times. There are a few regulars around, and he tells them the story about how he set me up. The whole 'table he said that I was a racist' story. Then, he tells the story about when we first started to be friends. Now, more than twenty years later, it's still great to hear.

He had come into the restaurant we were both working at on his day off and handed me what looked like a beer in a paper bag. I said, "Thanks, but I'm not going to drink at work."

"No, it's my barbeque sauce." He had made it from scratch.

I took it to the kitchen, and me and the cooks made up some chicken and tried it. It was probably the best barbeque sauce I'd ever had. Sweet, but with a really nice bite to it. The perfect balance.

He likes to say that I hated him or at least resented the fact that he had so much restaurant experience, which was partially true. Except that I didn't hate him, but that is the way he tells the story.

We quickly found that we had a lot in common, and we had a lot of fun together at work. We became fast friends, and now we have been friends for more than twenty years. It had all started with barbeque sauce.

We've lived all over the country and spent years apart, but we've always stayed in touch and we could always count on each other.

Now that he's moving back here, I feel complete again, but I'm still in a bit of a funk.

I go to see my therapist on our usual day, and it's silent for the first five minutes or so. He's waiting for me to collect my head.

I don't want to say anything, and then I just take off. I tell him that I'm happy that the job is going well, and I'm happy that Nate is back, but I can't help but think that if I'd chosen a different path... well, if I'd done that, I wouldn't even know Nate.

When I graduated high school and dropped out of college, I had to get a job. I'd been working with my dad for years at that point, but I chose to see if I could do something else.

My sister got me into the restaurant she worked at, and at that first interview when the manager asked, 'Why do you want to do this for a living?' I should have said, 'I don't.'

I don't, but what else am I gonna do?

If I had stayed working with my dad, I could have built a solid and great relationship with him. We could have gotten to know each other. He would have taught me everything I needed to know about the construction business and everything he does.

I probably would have ended up running Echterling Builders on my own. I would have been successful and stable. I probably would have had my own home, a wife, kids... the whole nine.

My dad would have retired happy and been proud of me, and I'd have a completely different life...but

But who's to say that I wouldn't have felt trapped in that life? Who's to say I wouldn't have had the same kind of breakdown? Who's to say I wouldn't have lost it all no matter what path I chose?

But I guess I'll never know; will I?

"No, you won't because you didn't choose that path. That's not the life you've lived. That's not who you are. So, what do you do now?"

"Great question. What do I do now?"

"You do what you've always done. You keep going. You live your life and you keep going. Winston Churchill said, 'If you're going through hell... Keep going.' You can't change the past. You can't know the future, but if you do what's right, right now, your future will be what it is supposed to be."

It usually takes a while before I can process what I've said and what my therapist has said, but I guess the answer is... Keep going.

Nate comes to see me again and starts right in.

"So, what's up? You still single?"

"Yea."

"It's been nine years since Julie. You gotta be over her by now."

"I knew deep down that when I saw her off at the airport that would be the last time, I would ever see her. The last time I would hold her, and the last time I would kiss her. I knew she was gone forever. I haven't so much as dated anyone since. Not because she was the one and anyone else would always be a distant second at best, but because when she left, she took everything that I was with her, and I've been nothing ever since."

"Maybe she took the old you with her, but the man you are today is a much better man. You got four years at the same apartment. Minus the four months you spent in North Carolina you got like fifteen years in the same city. And now two years at the same job. You've been stable for at least five years now, and things are going good for you. You're a new man, a better man, so let her have the old you and move on. It's time. You've always held the key to the cage you're in, but do you have the strength to use it, and the courage to see the outside?"

"You're probably right. I'm just kind of in a funk right now."

"Get yourself some twenty-two-year-old girl and have a midlife crisis. You gotta get laid if it's been nine years. That's just nuts."

He's probably right across the board, and I start to climb out of my funk, but it is more than just thinking of Julie again.

Julie was one part of one wall of the cage I had built for myself a long, long time ago.

One wall – my terrible relationships... Another wall – my moving around and keeping a place to live... Another wall – my family, and the guilt and shame that keeps me from them... Another wall – my past... Another wall – my friendships... And the biggest part of the cage is my work history or mostly this business.

I'm held in one place, in one state of mind, all due to this business, because I can't imagine doing anything else. I'm trapped in a life that I hate and love and keeps me alive while killing me. The only thing that has been consistent in my life is the instability and chaos of this business, and this life I'm stuck in.

But maybe Nate is right, and the man who died when Julie left, the person I was who left with her... maybe that life, those patterns and that cage is gone, too... maybe.

Anyway, with Nate in town, it is going to be a great month, and I've got a lot to look forward to. Looking backward never goes well.

The day of my birthday, Nate and Dedra take me to dinner at The Chop House. It's not far from the hotel where they are staying. Nate knows all the best places in the city and still has connections, but Dedra wants to stay close to the hotel. She gets frequent headaches and has to rest a lot.

We have these amazing giant steaks.

We've always loved steak but could never afford the really good ones, so we went to chain or family restaurants.

Once, Nate had a broken arm, and we had gone to an Outback Steakhouse.

Since his left hand, his primary hand, was in a cast, he asked the waitress if they could cut up his steak for him.

I just laughed. No one was going to do that.

But they did. The twenty-four-ounce steak came to the table all cut up into bite sized pieces. I couldn't believe it. Sometimes people do go out of their way to take care of the guests.

After dinner, we go to The Cork and Tap and have drinks. Nate and I are drinking Cokes, and Dedra has a glass of wine. Our wine selection is pretty good, and I'm able to recommend one of the best whites for her.

I don't think the staff knows that it's my birthday. We didn't celebrate the last one. In fact, I haven't really celebrated a birthday in years.

Lee and Jose, the bartenders, bring out two big cakes, and the whole bar sings Happy Birthday. There's enough cake for the whole place. There are close to sixty people there on a Thursday night at ten o'clock, and they are all our best regulars. Every one of them comes up to me throughout the night to wish me a happy birthday.

I feel pretty loved.

I take the weekend off, and Friday I go to Nate's conference.

He has really perfected his art. It is amazing.

He's now preaching and speaking full-time and holds the sales job for kicks.

I go out to Indiana Saturday morning and buy smokes. I haven't paid full Chicago prices for cigarettes in a very long time.

While I'm out here, Crystal throws me a party and the whole 'Club Deluxe' is there.

Jessica and Matthew have flown in for the weekend just for the reunion. All six of us reunite after twenty years. I knew she was throwing me a party, but the reunion is a big surprise.

Nate had bought the plane tickets and made sure everyone would be here.

Nate and Dedra go back to Seattle, but will officially move back to Chicago in three weeks.

The following summer, their wedding is beautiful, and there are close to four hundred people there. Her family, friends from all over the country, his whole family, all his friends and people he knows through his business and church... everyone he knows is there. Ever since I met him, he always seemed to know everyone, and it's like he's friends with everyone. Everybody just loves this guy.

Unlike Nate, I have never spoken in front of that many people before, but my best man speech goes over fine. I can blame the sweat on the weather.

I start to think that now that he is married, I won't see him that much, but he comes around all the time. It's just like old times. Movies and dinner at least once a week, and he pops in a couple of times a week just to say 'hey.'

A while later, I start noticing this new regular. She comes in just about every night. She works at a nearby restaurant and always comes in with friends. The whole group are strong regulars by this point. She is a wonderful girl. At twenty-seven, she is pretty young for me, but it doesn't stop us from flirting all the time.

Jennifer Anderson. She has a law degree, but hasn't taken the bar yet. She is having too much fun in this business right now. She figures that somewhere in her thirties, she'll start slowing down, and then she'll take the bar.

She is brilliant and so much fun to talk to. Long curly dark hair, beautiful green eyes and so upbeat and happy all the time. It's impossible to not feel the same when you are around her.

She's asked me out on more than one occasion, mostly to join her and her friend at some other bars, but a few times, she asked me to join her for dinner or a movie. Real date stuff.

I always turn her down. There is the age difference, and I'm still not really ready.

I haven't dated at all in the last ten years or so, mostly because when I was on disability, I didn't really have anything to bring to the table. There wasn't enough money to buy dinner or take anyone out. Money doesn't always matter, but I wanted to at least be able to cover my share. I was no leech, and I never felt right when girls would pay for everything. I saw it as too much to ask or expect. I have to have something to bring to the table.

Not to mention I'm an emotional mess.

I've been working again for years at this point, and things are good financially, but I don't know if I'm ready to get my heart broken again. To even consider dating anyone, I have to know them really well first.

Some time goes by, and Jennifer loses her job at her restaurant over some bullshit.

I can totally relate, so I hire her for the bar.

Over the last few years, we've changed our staff a lot. We realize that we don't really need that many employees to get by, so we pretty much cut the staff in half. Plus, there is always a lot of turnover in this business.

There are six people that have been with us from the very beginning, and they've earned a great deal of trust. They close and open for us and do a lot of extra around the bar. They are the reason our regulars stay with us. Their personalities are perfect, and their skills are right on.

Jennifer will fit in right away.

She works the floor as well as the bar and is very skilled. She can talk to anyone about anything and never ceases to impress. She makes people feel at home, and everybody is her friend. She is the perfect employee, and she has a real love for the work.

We talk a lot and really get to know each other well. She continues to try and get me to hang out with her outside of work, but I'm still turning her down.

There's still the age difference that really doesn't bother me that much, but now she's an employee.

Dating employees is usually a really big 'no-no,' but in this business, it happens all the time, and as long as it doesn't interfere with work, it's perfectly acceptable. In fact, James and Aaron themselves suggested that I go for it with her.

"She's perfect for you."

"I don't know. I'm just an old fart now. I'm completely out of shape at around thirty pounds overweight, and my hair is almost completely gray. For the first time in my life, I actually look much older than I am."

"No one cares if you are bald, gray, or purple. By the way, never shave your head again. Nate tells us you used to do it all the time, and you looked like a serial killer. I can just imagine. It's obvious that she likes you, and she's a great girl. What's the problem?"

"I'm just not in the right place to date right now."

"You gotta get over that in a hurry. It's time. It's way past time."

I'm still not ready.

I'm in the basement, in my office, when Jennifer comes down with the mail.

There is another obvious wedding invitation addressed to Jason and his wife.

The name on the return address reads, 'Julie Hartzell and Josh Patterson.'

"Fuck."

"What is it? You, OK?"

"She stayed in touch with him all these years. Over ten years, they've stayed in touch. Over ten years, and he never mentioned to me once that Julie's OK, and she's doing well. All this time, I didn't know if she was dead or alive, and he had been in touch with her this whole time."

"Who?"

"It doesn't matter."

"Is that the Julie you sometimes talk about, the one you were engaged to?"

"Yea, that's the one."

"That's gotta suck."

"I don't care that she's getting married." And I really don't. "Good for her. I'm just pissed that he never said anything to me. He has to know that I would want to hear that she was OK. He knows how to find me. He knows how to get a hold of me."

I wrap up all of Jason's mail and send it to him with a note explaining that anything else I get, I'm going to throw away. I want so badly to throw this one away, but who am I to stop him from going to her wedding. I don't know either one of them anymore, and I don't care. I just don't need to be reminded.

I didn't need Jennifer to see my reaction to the invitation. I certainly hope she doesn't think that I'm still hung up on Julie. I am completely passed all that. Nate is right. I'm a new person and a better person. Even if I do see Julie again, by now we would have nothing in common, and there would be nothing between us.

The past is the past for a reason, and despite what a lot of people say, it doesn't have to be repeated. I've moved on.

The next day, I'm talking to Jennifer, and she invites me out for drinks with the guys.

This time I go along, but I spend most of my time playing darts with Lee and Jose.

They are great guys, and I feel like they respect me as a boss and look at me as a friend.

I'm friends with all my employees. I know that I've earned their respect, but it's important to me that they like me as more than just a boss.

Steven showed me that. He's still friends with all of his old employees and still hangs out with them. They are out of my life now, but I have new friends.

I'm thinking of all the friends I've had that have made an impact on me.

I'm also thinking of all the people at the old housing program, the hospital, all the doctors and therapists along the way.

I'm thinking about my family, and I see the importance of keeping them close.

My mom and my dad... All the people that played a big part in making me who I am.

Not just the people who helped me, but the people who hurt me, as well as the people whom I've hurt... everybody. They all did their part making me who I am today.

And for the first time in my life... I like this guy.

Chapter Sixteen: Old Questions, Old Answers, New Light

Things are getting a little weird. Whenever things are going well, there was inevitably a crash coming right around the corner.

It has been years since my last significant low, and I don't even remember the last real crash. Things are good. In the past, every time things were going along pretty well, the floor would eventually come up and hit me in the face. Then, I'd dig a deeper hole and just wallow in it. With every good, there's the bad, and with every bad, there's good. I guess that's life.

My life has been a pretty serious roller coaster, but things have leveled off.

Finally.

Ten years in the same tiny apartment, nineteen years in the same city, almost seven years at the same job... all due to thirteen years of medication and therapy.

I think about that summer all the time. About... how I could have gotten away with it... how I should have asked for a lawyer... how I could have done things differently.

Then, I think that if none of that had happened... I wouldn't be here today.

I never would have gotten the help I needed, and I would never be this stable now.

My mom used to always say that everything happens for a reason, and I've learned over the years that real faith means not always having to know what those reasons are.

I'm a better person now. Not in spite of everything that I've been through, but because of everything I've been through.

It took years, but the med combination is right, work life is stable, my living situation is stable, I have a stronger relationship with family, and my friends are close.

Life is good, and I have to stop letting good things scare me.

It's a Monday, and I'm calling in all my orders.

James is here. He hasn't been here in a long time. I'm hoping nothing is wrong.

"You got a minute."

"Yea, sure."

"I've been talking to Aaron, and we feel that it's time for you to get a raise. How's forty-five sound?"

In today's world, forty-five isn't a huge amount of money for all I do, but I've started a 401k and have a great health insurance plan through this job. I also make a little extra cash whenever I bartend. Another five grand a year would be nice, though.

"Great."

"We also wanted to ask to see if you wanted to start buying in. It would be a percentage of your checks each week that we would hold onto and would build up to your becoming a partner. I guess it would seem like you're not getting a raise at all because all of that extra money would be going towards buying in, but after a few years, you'll start profit sharing."

"That sounds fantastic."

"We didn't really know if you wanted to commit yourself here for that long, but we would really like for you to stick around."

"Thank you. I would be willing to work out the rest of my life here. You guys have been great to me."

"You never know when the time will come where you just can't take it anymore and when you are as hands-on as you are, it might come up on you quick. We want to give you a strong enough incentive to stay as long as you can possibly bear it."

"I'm in."

"There's one other thing. Are you still in that tiny studio apartment?"

"Yea, it's little, but it's all I really need."

"You know we got the place on the third floor, and it's been vacant this whole time. No one seems to want to live above a bar. We can cut you a fair price on it."

"Even a one bedroom in this neighborhood would probably be two grand a month."

"What are you paying now?"

"Seven hundred." It had gone up a little over the years, but not much.

"Then, that's your price. The only thing is you have to promise to not be here every day. Living right upstairs, it's too easy to come in all the time. You have to agree to stay completely out of the place at least one full day a week."

"I can do that."

"I'm not kidding. If we see you here every day and you never take a day off... you're fired."

I know he isn't joking.

If I'm living right upstairs, it might be too easy for people to be calling me in all the time. However, things run really smoothly and I haven't gotten a call on an off day in years. They can handle things and won't be calling me down every day.

I like hanging out here, and it will be hard to not be here every day, but I have to agree that I should take at least twenty-four hours a week that is completely out of this place.

I have plenty of things to do nowadays, so it really shouldn't be hard to stay away.

I can do this.

Since they bought the place and remodeled, the apartment on the third floor has been vacant. The basement is the office, storage, and the coolers. The main floor is the bar and kitchen. The second floor is storage, and the third floor will now be my apartment.

I don't mind living above a bar. I can't hear anything through the floors because they put in soundboards in both ceilings, but I do hear the street.

I love the busy street sounds. The sirens, the yelling, the traffic, the constant noise. There is energy to it all. I love it. I've always loved it. I can't sleep when it's too quiet.

There are three big things that I love about living in the city:

One - I don't need a car. The public transportation system is one of the best in the world. I haven't owned a car in more than twenty years.

Two - The live music. There is always a show I can catch, and I love the little clubs that only seat like a hundred or two.

Third - The noise, the energy, the excitement.

I haven't walked the streets in a very long time, and I'm not out for danger anymore. I've out grown all that shit. Just walking to the store or going out to eat or the movies... anywhere... there is an energy that drives me. I love it.

My lease is up on the first of July which is still a month away, but I start moving my stuff in right away.

I have to get all new furniture, but I've been saving really well over the last few years, and I can afford it.

I have to furnish a one bedroom, and all I have at this point is a desk, a TV stand and a bed. And the bed still belongs to my real estate company. They supplied it when I moved in, back when I was still on disability and couldn't afford to buy one myself.

I order pretty much everything online, and it comes in two weeks, piece by piece. It is nice to be able to see it all through and still be right at work. It's like watching any other order come in. It's just going upstairs.

The strange thought which comes to mind is, what if I bring someone home? The whole bar will see, but... that is not really an issue.

This is going to be great.

By the second week of June, I'm all moved in and set up. I haven't been this comfortable in... well, I've never been this comfortable.

Now that she is officially in her thirties, last week Jennifer took the bar exam.

On her third attempt, she passes.

I put together a huge party for her here at the bar. She is so happy she can't stop smiling and laughing.

"So, I guess this means you're going to leave us."

"Not for a while, and I'll always come around. I love this place, and you guys are the best. I'm not going anywhere, really."

"How long do you think you'll still be working here?"

"It depends on how long it takes for me to get a job. Why? Are you in a hurry to see me go?"

"Absolutely not. I know that your life is about to change in a big way, and I'm hoping you get it all as quickly as possible. You've worked hard for this, and it's time it all comes together for you."

"Thanks, Jeff."

She looks at me with those glowing eyes all filled with tears, but still they shine. Red eyes or green, she is beautiful.

Jennifer has inspired me, and now that I'm going to work my way into being a partner, I feel like I should get back to furthering my education.

I go to Harold Washington to look into classes. I'll take all the prerequisites and a few business classes. Maybe this time, I'll make it through.

One or two classes and only a day or two a week. I'm working too much to do anymore, but I do feel like I should at least try. It doesn't matter how long it takes. I'm in no hurry these days.

I'm much more confident that this time I'll make it work. I have things together right now and the time is right.

Even with all the hours I'm working, I still get in at least seven hours of sleep every day. I don't stay up all night, and I don't go days without sleeping. I get up with an alarm and get my day started. I'm waking up these days and not just coming to.

This apartment, this city, this job, and all my friends... I've never felt more at home.

My caffeine intake is at a respectable level, and I don't overdo it anymore. A good sleep routine is too important to mess with.

The year is pretty full with baseball season and hockey season. There is no shortage of games to watch at the bar and never a shortage of what to talk about. The crazier and the more ridiculous the story is, the better.

I don't feel like a vampire anymore. The hours are still rough, but I'm not preying on the weak anymore. I also don't feel like I'm the weak one anymore.

I think of Victor and Ryan and all those who didn't make it, and for the first time in my life, I'm not wishing that it had been me. I'm glad I'm still alive, and life has been good. Even the hard times have just made me stronger.

I still love a good hot-dog and a pint of ice cream here and there, but I don't have to live on it.

I'm not playing a part anymore. I'm actually who I am. I know who I am now, and I like the guy.

I know I'm not alone, and I make sure that my family and friends know just how much I appreciate them.

The pieces of my life have come together, and I've never felt so complete.

I'm confident of my future, my future with this job, this city, this life. I believe in the future now, and I want to make it great. I'll take the lows, always knowing that there is a high right around the corner.

Today, I'm sitting at my desk and going over the sales for the last few weeks.

Business has been really good.

I notice out of the corner of my eye that Tom seems to be wandering around the basement.

Tom has been with us for two years now. He had gone to Bartending School, and I usually never hire anyone from one of those schools. Yea, you learn how to make a ton of drinks, but the real skill of bartending can't be taught. Either you have it, or you don't.

I hired him because he's ambitious and has an incredibly friendly personality. He can talk on any subject, which is important. He is just a good kid all around.

Today, he is standing around and staring at the walls.

Then, he wanders into my office.

"Jeff, am I lost?"

"It depends on where you want to be. If you want to be in my office, then you're not lost."

"That's not what I mean. I mean in life."

"Why are you asking me?"

"I respect your opinion."

"Well, I guess the answer is the same. It depends on where you want to be. If you're there or working on getting there... then you're not lost. In your case, you're going to school, you're working full time, you've got a lot of friends, everyone here loves you, you've got a nice place, and your future looks pretty good."

"I don't know if I'm really doing what I'm meant to be doing."

"The old saying is that even if you're on the right track, you'll still get hit by the train if you just sit there. You're not just sitting there. Like I said. It depends on where you want to be. You live your life. Your life. No one else's. I've had my ups and downs, to say the least. I've made mistakes, took some wrong turns, hurt people, and I got hurt myself. But all in all, I've lived my life. My life. No one else's. I take all the blame and all the credit in the good and in the bad. I felt lost most of my life, but I never was. Everything you do, right or wrong, takes you to where you're meant to be."

He kind of smiles, but still has a confused look on his face as he goes back upstairs.

I've never been asked advice on life. I'm asked questions all the time, but it's stuff I know, like stuff about the business.

Asking me about life is like asking an Eskimo about beaches and surfing.

I'm starting to find the answers for myself, but if the physician can't heal himself... well... I just don't know.

Nate calls me that morning and makes sure that I'm still on for tonight. He and Dedra are taking me to dinner, and then we are going to see a movie.

"Hey. Would it be all right if I brought someone?"

"You got a date? Who?"

"I don't really know yet, but I'm gonna give it a try. Just in case though, would it be all right?"

"Yea, of course. Man, it's about time."

"See you tonight around eight?"

"Sounds good."

Just after we hang up, Jennifer comes down with the mail.

"Hey, Jen. I'm going to see a movie tonight. You want to join me?"

"Jeff, are you asking me out?" She has this funny grin on her face.

"Not necessarily. I want to see this movie, and I thought that it would be better if you were there."

"Right. I'd love to go. I get off at six."

"I know. I scheduled you that way."

"So, you were pretty confident that I would say yes, huh?"

"I don't know if I'd say confident, just hopeful."

She smiles, hands me the mail, and turns to go back upstairs. Just before she hits the bottom step, she turns to say, "Hey, Jeff."

"What's up?"

"Happy birthday."

That one year, that one horrible year, I'll never forget. It was probably the most difficult time in my life, but I survived it, and it led me to get the help that I needed and made me the man I am today. I don't regret anything that happened that year.

I'll never forget all the people that got me back on my feet. The therapists, the psychiatrists, the doctors, the social workers, the friends, and my family. Their work and their strength will never be forgotten, and I will always do my best to stay in touch and make sure they know just how much I appreciate everything they've done for me.

This job is the concrete that holds me together now. My life revolves around this place, but I wouldn't have it any other way.

No matter how old I get or how badly I age, today I know who I am. and as long as I keep that, I'll be fine.

The nightmares and the constant worry about where I'm going, where I am, what I'm doing, when are things going to blow up, how badly am I going to get hurt this time, where am I going to live, how am I going to eat... everything that has been a constant question in my head over the years: is all at peace now.

I've found my smile, and I wear it all the time, but the Blackhawks hat has been hung up for years now.

There's peace now, but there is still work to be done.

It's Wednesday, June twentieth, and today's my forty-fifth birthday. I've got one interview this afternoon, then I'm done for the day.

The guy just turned twenty-one a week ago, and he's friends with Jose. He wants to be a bartender but is more than willing to start at the door. He's willing to start anywhere. He really wants to work here. He's heard a lot of stories from Jose.

Jose has been selling this guy for weeks. Unless he's a complete dope in the interview, I'm going to hire him. We need another doorman, and Jose's recommendation carries a lot of weight.

As soon as I get upstairs, I see the guy. He's wearing a suit. That's hilarious.

"Kevin? Come on over and have a seat. You want something to drink?"

"Water is fine." I've had potential hires ask for a beer. Those interviews are usually short.

I get him his water, and I grab my coffee. We shake hands, and he's sweating. It's June, and he's wearing a suit, so that's reason enough to sweat, but I can tell the kid is nervous.

I throw him a few softball questions, asking about how he knows Jose and whether or not he played any sports in school. Then, I have to get a few basic ones out of the way.

"So, you've never worked in this business before?"

"No, I've been working at Sports Authority, mostly selling shoes."

"This is sales, so you do have experience." It looks like the guy is going to faint.

I can tell he wants this badly. "Take a drink and relax. I just have one more question:

Why do you want to do this for a living?"

www.ingramcontent.com/pod-product-compliance
Ingram Content Group UK Ltd.
Pitfield, Milton Keynes, MK11 3LW, UK
UKHW041632190726
13854UKWH00006B/2448